0046329

DATE DUE

OCT 8 19	
JUL 23 1998	

BRODART, INC.   Cat. No. 23-2

PENGUIN BOOKS

SPLENDOURS OF THE RAJ

Philip Davies read history at Queens' College, Cambridge, before taking a postgraduate diploma in town planning. He worked first in the GLC Historic Buildings Division and is now a principal historic buildings adviser to the Westminster City Council. He visited India several times when researching *Splendours of the Raj*, financed in part by grants from the British Academy.

Philip Davies

SPLENDOURS OF THE RAJ

British Architecture in India, 1660–1947

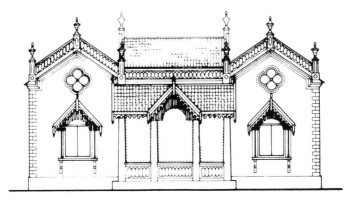

Penguin Books

Penguin Books Ltd, Harmondsworth, Middlesex, England
Viking Penguin Inc., 40 West 23rd Street, New York, New York 10010, U.S.A.
Penguin Books Australia Ltd, Ringwood, Victoria, Australia
Penguin Books Canada Limited, 2801 John Street, Markham, Ontario, Canada, L3R 1B4
Penguin Books (N.Z.) Ltd, 182–190 Wairau Road, Auckland 10, New Zealand

First published by John Murray 1985
Published in Penguin Books 1987

Made and printed in Great Britain by
Butler & Tanner Ltd, Frome and London
Typeset in Monophoto Apollo

CONTENTS

The city is not ruinous, although
Great ruins of an unremembered past,
With others of a few short years ago
More sad, are found within its precincts vast.

from *The City of Dreadful Night*
JAMES THOMSON

Out of her ruins is her honour made
Into a glory not of ships or trade:
And those who fought for her and those who died
Are stronger than the crumbling of her stone.

EVOE (E.V. KNOX) of *Punch* 1941

We build 'em nice barracks – they swear they are bad
That our Colonels are Methodist, married or mad,
Insultin' Her Majesty's Royal Engineer,
With the rank and pay of a Sapper!

'Sappers' RUDYARD KIPLING

ACKNOWLEDGEMENTS

Since I began to research this book unprecedented attention has been focused on the British Raj, not all of it objective or dispassionate. As it recedes into history the need to conserve the buildings and memorials of the period becomes more compelling, for they bear witness to an extraordinary historical episode and provide a unique insight into a way of life which has vanished. It is my sincere hope that others will recognise the value and importance of this fascinating shared heritage, and that effective measures will be taken to ensure its long-term conservation.

Some have recognised its worth already. My particular thanks are extended to Gavin Stamp, who has pioneered research into this neglected field, for his advice and help, and also to Jan Morris, for releasing her manuscript of *Stones of Empire* to me long before publication. Whilst we may differ in our conclusions, our affection for the subject is a shared one. Special thanks are also due to Liisa Davies who typed the manuscript and offered constructive criticism. Many individuals have offered helpful advice, support or assistance, or have provided me with photographs, material or useful leads, principally: Mildred Archer; Lady Betjeman; William Bingley; Gerald Cobb; Susanna Powers; Jane Davies; Professor Paul Davies; Giles Eyre; Roger Hudson; Donald Insall; Dieter Klein; Pippa Mason; S Muthiah; Foy Nissen; Bruce Norman; Janet Pott; John Martin Robinson; John Sambrook; Amit Sen; Clive Smith; Elizabeth Staley; Angus Stirling; D E W Shaw; the late Professor Eric Stokes; Gail Weber and Theon Wilkinson.

Special thanks are also due to the British Association for Cemeteries in South Asia, the British Council, *Country Life*, Eyre & Hobhouse, the Hongkong and Shanghai Bank, and the *Illustrated London News;* also the staff of the following libraries or institutions: BBC Hulton Picture Library, British Architectural Library/RIBA, British Library (India Office Records and Prints and Drawings Collection); Courtauld Institute of Art, Illustrated London News Library, National Army Museum, National Portrait Gallery, Trustees of the Victoria Memorial Library (Calcutta) and Westminster City Council Libraries.

The support and assistance of the British Academy is gratefully acknowledged, without which, this book would not have been possible.

PHOTOGRAPHS

All the photographs were taken by the author or are from the author's own private collection of illustrations except the following:
British Architectural Library/RIBA: 84, 153, 185; British Association for Cemeteries in South Asia: 19, 61 (right), 62 (courtesy of Lady Betjeman); BBC Hulton Picture Library: 109; British Library (India Office Records): 17, 25 (top), 44, 48, 90, 91, 119, 122 (top), 135, 145, 202 and 204; *The Builder*: 158, 169, 170 (top), 174; *Building News*: 165, 189, 190 (bottom; *Bombay Builder*: 168 (bottom); Eyre & Hobhouse: 32 (top), 40, 57 (top), 66; Courtauld Institute of Art (Witt Library): 88; Centre for South Asian Studies, Cambridge: 223; Hongkong and Shanghai Bank: 95 (top), 99 (top); *Illustrated London News*: 10, 16, 69, 137; Cassells Publishers (successors to) 55, 68, 82; Lady Betjeman: 229, 237 (top); Gerald Cobb: 28, 41, 51, 53 (bottom), 57 (centre); 64, 71 (top), 73 (top), 78, 101 (top), 116, 152, 156, 159, 161, 162, 170 (bottom), 176 (left), 177, 197, 208, 247; Quentin Hughes: 25 (bottom), 50; Donald Insall: 39, 45, 104, 195; John Nankivell: 30; Foy Nissen: 157 (top); John Sambrook: drawings on title page and 110; Elizabeth Staley (courtesy of Janet Pott) 108 (top right, centre and bottom).

To Liisa and Anya

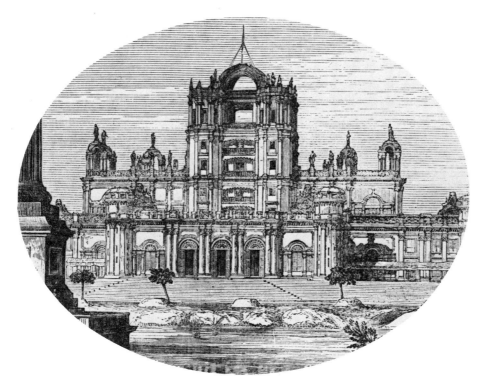

Constantia, Lucknow

IMPERIAL MYTHS

They that dig foundations deep,
Fit for realms to rise upon,
Little honour do they reap
Of their generation,
Any more than mountains gain
Stature till we reach the plain.*

Historical objectivity is an elusive commodity. Post-imperial assumptions and prejudices have hindered the search for truth about the British Empire. For some its dissolution is the logical culmination of generations of effort; for many it has been equated with emasculation and a loss of British greatness. But for most the British Empire seems like some sort of dated music-hall joke, in which stereotyped Englishmen engage in embarrassing banter about fuzzy-wuzzies and trouble in the Khyber. To those who fought on the North-West Frontier, and their latter-day successors, the Khyber Pass is about as funny as the Berlin Wall, but in Britain the fictional images of Empire have long since superseded the cold truths of global *realpolitik*, and it is hard to see how a sense of historical balance can ever be fully achieved.

Other deeper cultural assumptions exacerbate the search for objectivity. The British have always had a sense of social and cultural superiority towards their colonies: the Mother of the Empire smiling benignly but condescendingly on her callow and gauche offspring, even such huge and gifted children as the United States. Underneath lie still deeper racial undertones which reflect older, atavistic instincts. Overlying both of these are more potent, post-imperial attitudes, coloured by false Marxist rhetoric, which have promoted the popular belief that the Empire was inherently wicked and malevolent, an insidious stage in the evolution of capitalist society arising from the need to invest surplus wealth overseas.

One of the most pervasive myths is that of imperial unity. It was a dream which obsessed many, but in truth the Empire was never more than a diverse collection of territories acquired for a multitude of different reasons and often against the better judgement of Whitehall. Climatic, political, economic, racial and regional differences fostered heterogeneity. In the gaudy tapestry of Empire some territories hung by slender threads, a few, in time, were severed altogether, whilst others like the great white dominions were woven close to the fabric of British national life. The search for a true imperial identity through the

*The sources of this and other quotations are listed on page 258.

medium of architecture and the fine arts never became a dominant concern, but it continued for generations.

The imperial impulse was chivalric yet bullying, self-seeking yet magnanimous, sometimes astonishingly insensitive, yet generally just and high-minded. These contrary but pervasive elements were expressed in the architecture of the Empire, and they achieved their most eloquent expression in the buildings of British India. India was an epitome of the Empire itself, where a multitude of different races, religions, languages and cultures mostly co-existed but sometimes murdered each other in erratic outbursts of communal violence. If imperial unity could be achieved in brick and stone here, then it might be attained globally.

In the historiography of the Empire architecture has remained a footnote. This can be attributed to withdrawal symptoms and to the complex prejudices of modern British society, but it has as much to do with the rigid anglocentric and modernist approach of architectural historians. In the past sixty years the ideals of the Modern Movement have been dominant, but the rise of a new generation of 'postmodernist' architects and architectural historians has now liberated the subject from this intellectual straitjacket. The rehabilitation of Lutyens, and the awareness of a continuing classical and vernacular tradition have meant a reappraisal of long-held prejudices. The historical method of avant-garde modernists relied for its credibility on disregarding whole areas of architectural endeavour. The architecture of the Empire was dismissed as second-rate, still-born, decadent and irrelevant. The fact that some of the great cities of India and therefore the world were the products of imperialism was ignored. Even that free-thinking champion of New Delhi, Robert Byron, could allow himself to refer to Bombay as 'an architectural Sodom'. Full-blown modernists regarded New Delhi as the institutional expression of an hierarchical society that was colonial and thoroughly evil, unrelated to the real needs of modern India, even though paradoxically it provided a focus for rising nationalism. When the modernists were given their head in the euphoric climate of post-Independence India, their contribution to India's 'real needs' was Le Corbusier's Chandigarh, a dismal piece of paternalistic architecture poorly related to the climate.

Contrary to popular belief, there was never a definitive Imperial style, but the search for one occupied the British for the duration of their stay in India. In the early years under the East India Company collective and individual aspirations fundamentally were commercial and this was reflected in the buildings. These were erected by amateur architects, dilettanti, or more usually, by military engineers using available pattern-books for prototypes, and they deployed considerable skill and ingenuity in their design. The work of British military engineers is one of the most enduring legacies of empire, and they were expected to undertake a wide variety of civil and military tasks. In the early years they were in great demand. In 1763 the Court of Directors of the Company wrote to Calcutta: 'We should very gladly comply with your request for sending you young Persons to be brought up as Assistants in the Engineering Branch, but as we find it extremely difficult to procure such, you will do well to employ any who have a talent that way amongst the Cadets or others.'

From 1794 there was a surveying school in Madras. After 1809 Addiscombe College, and later the Royal Engineers' Institution at Chatham, provided a degree of professional education, but self-instruction was the most common form of practical knowledge using published reference books and architectural treatises. The works of Gibbs, Chambers, Stuart and Revett, and the Adam Brothers were available in Calcutta and Madras, together with French and Italian books. Others besides military engineers consulted them. Interested amateurs such as C. K. Robison, J. P. Parker, James Prinsep and Claude Martin were all self-taught enthusiasts with considerable personal skills.

In the late 18th century there was a major change in British perceptions. Only twenty years separate Writers' Buildings and Government House, Calcutta, yet one is a simple stucco barrack block relieved only by an Ionic centrepiece, and the other a magnificent Georgian palace of considerable sophistication. British aspirations had become overtly imperial and were expressed accordingly. Architecture was vested with immense symbolic significance. It could be used as an instrument of policy as well as an expression of paramountcy: at the Residency at Hyderabad grandiloquence was used as a substitute for actual military power. Architecture was cheaper than sepoys, particularly when the local Nizam paid for it. It was acknowledged at the time that in India power was judged by its outward expression and there were many who felt that the parsimonious attitude of the East India Company diminished both its political stature and commercial prospects.

The transformation of Calcutta and Madras from commercial trading enclaves into elegant imperial cities coincided with this changing view of British activity in India. Trade remained important, but the conscious reflection of the civilised values of ancient Greece and Rome in the buildings of the period demonstrates a growing awareness of this wider political and social role. It was believed that the greatness of a civilisation was expressed in its architecture. The legacy of Greece and Rome, the civilising influence of their cities, and the creation of a classical language of architecture of supreme simplicity and eloquence, set a precedent which the British strove to emulate. India could be transformed into a self-improving, civilised western nation, providing English education, justice and moral values prevailed. It was this interventionist, self-righteous idealism that fostered some of the greatest social and political reforms, but it also aroused the deeply conservative basis of Indian society in a primitive and violent reaction which burst out in the Great Mutiny of 1857. In its aftermath the Bengal, Madras and Bombay Engineers were amalgamated with the Royal Engineers in 1862 and, owing to the great expansion in civil engineering work, the Public Works Department (PWD) began to recruit largely civil engineers.

With the introduction of the Gothic Revival in India and its

13

widespread adoption in the years after the Mutiny a new series of architectural experiments began; to adapt the forms and styles of mediaeval Europe to the functional and climatic conditions of 19th-century India. In her recent book *Stones of Empire* Jan Morris alleged that 'actually Gothic was far less suitable to the environment than the classical styles.' This is quite untrue. In 1862 James Fergusson, the architectural expert on India, wrote: 'If used with freedom and taste, no style might be better adapted for Indian use than Gothic', and many agreed with him. Based on arcuated principles of construction, often it was far more flexible and capable of adaptation to local conditions than classical architecture. The most widely-used and adaptable form of Gothic was Venetian, a style which had its origins in the Levant, and which lent itself ideally to hot tropical locations. Indeed Gilbert Scott's design for the Convocation Hall and Library of Bombay University revels in the freedom given to design in an authentic Italian Gothic style unhindered by those concessions to the climate which were necessary in England. The result is one of his finest, but least known works with open spiral staircases, arcaded galleries and a careful balance of indoor and outdoor space; a building perfectly related to the climate: cool, efficient and highly functional.

For all its evocative and elegiac overtones of a lost civilisation *Stones of Empire* unfortunately does little to dispel many long-held myths about imperial architecture. The architectural history of British India is the story of constant experimentation with different styles of building and these experiments reflected the moral and ethical values of the period. The process began with the efforts of military engineers and amateur architects to adapt the classical language of architecture to a tropical context, adjusting proportions, intercolumniation and forms to local needs and circumstances. Great resource was displayed in the adaptation of the classical portico to climatic and functional requirements. Certainly mistakes were made and much of what was built was not strictly according to the rules of architectural grammar. The fudged abacus on the Calcutta Mint by Forbes is a good example, whilst contrary to Jan Morris's assertion that 'Sam Russell never put a foot wrong when he designed the Hyderabad Residency', its proportions do not bear scrutiny and it is riddled with architectural solecisms. However, much the same sort of criticism can be levelled against contemporary works in England. Houses on some of the great London estates such as Belgravia and Regent's Park, show much the same disregard for correct architectural grammar. Repeated experiments with different classical styles – Palladian, Neo-classical, Greek and Roman – and the serial construction of Anglo-Indian houses and public buildings over decades fostered greater sophistication and eloquence, even if structural failure remained a recurrent problem.

Similarly with the Gothic style, in Bombay in particular: the instruction of a native workforce in the skills of stone carving, and the availability of fine local building stones transformed the quality of architecture there. By the 1870s the architecture of Bombay was regarded generally as far superior to that of Calcutta. This was not only due to the excellence of the local materials, but also because the

Bombay Public Works Department employed professional officers educated and trained in civil architecture, whilst in Calcutta the amateur military engineer prevailed. The Bombay professionals seem to have maintained a closer interest in the latest Gothic styles than their Calcutta counterparts, and this probably accounts for their rapid mastery of the complex structural principles of Gothic architecture, which often failed when used elsewhere. The collapse of the gun carriage works at Allahabad in 1871 was a spectacular example, but the structural inadequacy of many arched buildings was a popular lament at the time.

In Bombay techniques and skills were learnt quickly. The Afghan Memorial Church of 1847 at Colaba was the great Gothic prototype in India, but it was marred by lack of local expertise in stone carving. In 1863 a scheme of Colonel St Clair Wilkins was regarded as 'out of the question' owing to the introduction of carved ornamental details and foliated capitals, but within two years the influence of John Lockwood Kipling and the Bombay School of Art transformed the position and whole new avenues of Indo-Gothic architecture were explored. These reached their culmination in the Gothic and the Indo-Saracenic buildings of the 80s and 90s, which display an extraordinary level of professional skill and represent a very sophisticated form of Victorian eclecticism. They are monumental statements of Victorian imperial and civic pride, in what for many was a genuine Indian Imperial style. Others considered the process of hybridisation to be a retrograde step, not just architecturally but politically. An article in *The Builder* of 1912 stated:

> The confusion consequent on the attempt to combine the characteristics of a modern European and Indian building in one and the same structure, to erect for the native that which by tradition he alone is capable of erecting for himself, is to invite not only the scorn of the Imperialist, but also the ridicule of those whose own noble architecture has been so grossly caricatured. As a compliment in political diplomacy it is shallow, and from every point of view a grave error.

As a reaction against such criticism some, such as Sir Samuel Swinton Jacob, attempted a far more scholarly approach based on precise antiquarian observation of Indian precedents, and in turn, this fostered greater interest in the conservation of ancient monuments and temples.

It is at New Delhi that the architectural experiments of the previous generations find their resolution in a wholly original style of architecture that is neither Indian nor European, but a complete fusion of the two traditions. The work of Lutyens and his acolytes, Henry Medd and Arthur Shoosmith, achieves the highest levels of sophistication, a genuine mutated style born of Anglo-Indian parenthood. To Jan Morris, 'once the Empire lost its assurance, it lost its virtue and so did its constructions.' To allege that 'British India bowed itself out in an unmemorable blandness of the neo-classical' and that it 'went out gently, even apologetically at the end' just cannot be sustained. The

15

monumental conception and scale of New Delhi is the crowning achievement of British architecture in India, and it is the supreme irony that it found greatest eloquence at the very moment that the imperial impulse was faltering. To Gavin Stamp, 'New Delhi is one of the greatest things the British have ever done and it seems little short of a miracle that an architect of towering genius was able to realise almost all of his conception.' To Robert Byron writing in *Country Life* in 1931 Lutyens 'accomplished a fusion of East and West and created a novel work of art. He took the best of both traditions, and made of them "a double magnificence".'

This extraordinary diversity of opinion reflects the difficulty of analysing objectively the architectural history of British India, for in Britain the subject is still fraught with prejudice, preconception and complex emotional responses. Ironically in India this is far less so. Sufficient time has elapsed for the buildings in this book to be taken seriously as works of architecture in their own right, as the particular expressions of a society which now may have vanished, but one which created the framework of the modern Indian state. The buildings are a heritage shared by two countries and it is a heritage which needs to be acknowledged and assessed as objectively as any other.

The Sassoon Institute, Bombay: commissioned by a Baghdadi Jew in Venetian Gothic.

16

CHAPTER 1

TWO TOMBS

India always has exerted a strong allure for Europe. Alexander the Great reached the borders of India, leaving cultural and social traces in the Hunza Valley, on the far north-western fringes of the country, and the Romans certainly knew it, trading direct in jewels, ivory, perfumes and spices. Therefore when Vasco da Gama landed on the site of the Roman settlement at Calicut in 1498, it was not so much the discovery of a new alien culture, as the resumption of a pattern of social and economic intercourse which had been enjoyed by the Ancient World, but which had been severed by the fall of Rome and the rise of Islam. By the mid-16th century at least three Portuguese settlements – Daman, Diu and Bassein – were heavily protected along European lines with polygonal walls, embrasures and lunettes in the manner of Renaissance fortifications. The three town plans share a similarity of layout with grid-iron street patterns around a central fort or redoubt. At Daman the walls embraced all the principal buildings including the factory. By 1680 Bassein had many notable buildings, including a cathedral, five convents, thirteen churches and an asylum for orphans erected over a subterranean network of bomb-proof tunnels and caverns. Although the Portuguese impact on India was immediate, it was never extensive because in 1612 the English displaced the Portuguese as the naval auxiliaries of the Moghul Empire.

The first English factory at Surat founded in 1613, was a simple but robust building based on local vernacular architecture. The terraces referred to by John Fryer may be seen clearly. Note the weather vane in the form of an East Indiaman.

The English were late comers to India. On 31st December 1600 Elizabeth I granted the East India Company its charter 'as well for the honour of this our realm of England as for the increase of our navigation and advancement of trade'. Inspired by the same commercial dreams as the Dutch, they arrived in their wake and attempted to break the Dutch monopoly of the East Indies. At the Massacre of Amboyna in 1623 the Dutch seized the English factory and executed the occupants. Under-capitalised and rebuffed by their rivals, the English company turned its attentions to the less attractive consolation of India.

English influence spread steadily at the expense of their European rivals. The first English factory was established at Surat in 1613. Others followed rapidly at Broach, Agra, Ahmadabad, and at Armagaum on the Coromandel coast. These early factories were isolated introverted enclaves rigidly governed by a President and with a lifestyle more like the routine of an Oxford or Cambridge college than anything their Oriental milieu might lead one to expect.

John Fryer visited the factory at Surat in 1674–75 and left this description:

> The House the English live in at Surat is partly the King's Gift, partly hired; Built of stone and excellent timber with good Carving without Representations; very strong, for that each Floor is Half a Yard thick at least, of the best plastered Cement, which is very weighty. It is contrived after the Moor's Buildings with upper and lower Galleries or Terras-walks. The President has spacious Lodgings, noble Rooms for Counsel and Entertainment, pleasant Tanks, Yards and an Hummum to wash in; but no Gardens in the city.

Architecturally the factory sounds much like the old traditional buildings of Gujarat with few European influences. The President cultivated extravagant Oriental ceremonial being 'carried in a Palki, emblazoned with the royal escutcheon and lined with red silks'. The factory at Agra was 'In the heart of the city where we live after this country in manner of meat, drink and apparel . . . for the most part after the Custom of this place, sitting on the ground at our meat or discourse. The rooms in general covered with carpets with great round high cushions to lean on.'

The first fortifications erected by the English were at Armagaum on the east coast. In 1628–29 the settlement was described as being defended by 'twelve pieces of cannon mounted around the factory and by a guard of twenty-three factors and soldiers'. The defences were more a protection against the marauding Dutch than from any local threat: 'the Dutch will never leave us in quiet; till they have by one means or other rooted us out.' Improved security also promoted local trade.

By 1647 there were twenty-three English factories, some shared with Dutch or French traders, but life expectancy was low. In 1668 the Company acquired Bombay. It had formed part of the marriage dowry of Catherine of Braganza to Charles II, and it was notorious for its bad

The curious Oxinden mausoleum at Surat crowned by an open-cross cupola denoting a Christian tomb. The graves in the foreground are of other English factors.

climate. Of eight hundred white inhabitants, only one hundred survived the seasonal rains of 1692. The two months which followed the monsoon, September and October, were usually fatal. Conditions were not improved by the insalubrious practice of putting dry fish around the roots of trees as a manure. A visitor noted 'in the Mornings there is generally seen a thick Fog among those Trees that affects both the Brains and Lungs of Europeans and breeds Consumptions, Fevers and Fluxes.'

It is no surprise to discover that one of the earliest surviving English monuments in India is the huge stone tomb of the Oxinden family at Surat. Sir George Oxinden was the Governor of Bombay when it was transferred to the Company in 1668. The family mausoleum, one of the largest in India, is a two-storeyed Oriental kiosk forty feet high and twenty-five feet wide with massive columns carrying two cupolas, which rise one above the other. Around the interior are galleries reached by flights of steps; on the lower level lies Christopher and on the upper George – 'Anglorum in India, Persia, Arabia, Praeses'. Architecturally it is a hybrid affair, but with a pronounced Indian character. Not for another century were purer forms of classical funerary architecture used.

The east coast enjoyed a much healthier reputation and in the early years it became the centre of English influence. A fine new station was

19

established at Madraspatam in 1639 by Francis Day, one of the consuls at Armagaum. He enthused: 'If you suffer this opportunity to pass over you shall perhaps in vain afterwards pursue the same when it is fled and gone.' Without waiting for clearance by the Court of Directors in London, work began on a new fort and factory on 1st March 1640. The factory was 'a plain box-like edifice, three storeys high without verandah or external ornament'. A parapet encircled the flat roof which was crowned by a quaint dome. The ground floor was given over to warehouses and above was the Consultation Room or Council Chamber. The agent's quarters were on the top floor and other facilities included a communal dining room and lodgings for merchants, writers and apprentices. The factory was placed diagonally in a paved courtyard and enclosed by battlemented walls. The fortifications were completed by 1653 and boasted eight guns. The foundation of Fort St George, as it was known, was influenced by considerations of economy and utility and the earliest structure built by Cogan and Day was little more than a common square measuring one hundred yards by eighty yards adjoining the Cooum river, yet for the next 130 years it remained the nerve-centre of English power in the East.

It was from Madras that early ventures were made to the north and Bengal. A tentative presence had been maintained at Hooghly at the mouth of the Ganges, but this was not consolidated until, on the strength of a few half-hearted promises, Job Charnock decided to try again. He landed at Sutanuti on 24th April 1690. The return was a bold venture. The Nawab had not given his authority and trade required an Imperial *firman* from the Great Moghul in Delhi. The Emperor, provoked already by the seizure of Imperial ships by the English, had besieged Bombay in 1689. If the timing was hardly auspicious, neither was the site: an unhealthy stretch of marshy ground close to the Hindu temple at Kalighat. Captain Alexander Hamilton travelled between the Cape and India regularly from 1688 to 1723. He described the site on which Charnock was to lay the foundations of Calcutta:

> He could not have chosen a more unhealthful place on all the River; for three miles to the North Eastern is a salt-water lake that overflows in September and October, and then prodigious numbers of fish resort thither, but in November and December, when the floods are dissipated, these fishes are left dry, and with their putrefaction affect the air with thick stinking vapours, which the North-East Winds bring with them to Fort William, that they cause a yearly Mortality.

The earliest settlement was a miserable affair of 'cutcha' buildings made from local mud and thatch. The President of Fort St George was concerned enough at the perilous nature of the foothold to write to the Court of Directors: 'They live in a wild unsettled condition at Chuttanuttee, neither fortified houses nor godowns, only tents, huts and boats.'

It is a testimony to Charnock's character that he persisted in his determination to re-establish an English presence in Bengal. His motive, like that of the Company, was trade not dominion, and his choice of site was shrewd. Legend has it that he chose the site because of the presence of a huge baobab tree beneath which he found a welcome respite from the intolerable heat. That the tree existed is beyond dispute, for ninety years later Warren Hastings attempted to prevent it being felled. But it is more realistic to assume that as an experienced merchant, with an eye for potential prospects, Charnock had noted that the east bank of the river had a better anchorage, and that the surrounding villages were developing cotton marts in their own right. In fact two English merchants had migrated to the east bank already, having recognised its better potential.

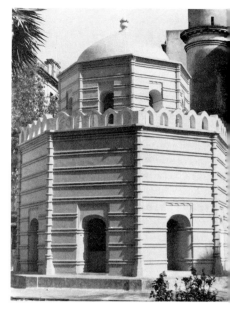

The distinctive Oriental tomb of Job Charnock, founder of Calcutta, in St John's Churchyard there.

Charnock is a fascinating character. He was the son of a London solicitor and was born in the parish of St Katherine, Creechurch around 1630. He arrived in Bengal in 1656 and by 1664 had risen to be chief at the factory in Patna. By 1675 he was Fifth in the Council at Madras, having served at several ports, and when he returned to Sutanuti in 1690 he was Agent of the company in Bengal. Stubborn, determined and ruthless, he refused to admit defeat. Today his name is gilded with romance. It is reputed that one evening as he passed the burning ghat on the river frontage at Hooghly he saw that the pyre was ready to receive a young widow who was preparing herself for suttee. She was fifteen years old, tall, fair-skinned and exceptionally beautiful. Charnock instructed his guards to rescue her and they married. The incident is commemorated in the poetic epitaph of Joseph Townsend, the 'Pilot of the Ganges', whose tomb lies close to that of his friend Charnock:

> Cries Charnock 'scatter the faggots! Double that
>   Brahmin in two!
> The tall pale widow is mine Joe – the little brown
>   girl's for you.'

It was an unlikely liaison — he a fifty-year-old rough merchant adventurer and she a dutiful Brahmin widow, but 'they lived lovingly many years and had several children', Mary, Elizabeth and Katherine, whose baptisms are recorded in the parish annals of St Mary's, Madras, for 18th August 1689. When she died in Calcutta Charnock kept her memory alive by sacrificing a cock over her tomb on each anniversary in a bizarre misinterpretation of Bihari ritual. Charnock died thirty months after his return to Bengal in 1692, and his son-in-law, Charles Eyre, first President of Fort William, built a massive and curious mausoleum in his honour. It survives in a corner of St John's Churchyard, Calcutta, and it is of outstanding historical significance, for concentrated in and around that one mausoleum survive some of the earliest traces of English life in India. Unfortunately it is threatened with oblivion. Proposals are in hand to develop the churchyard.

Architecturally the mausoleum is Oriental in conception, an octagonal pavilion surmounted by a serrated parapet and a ponderous kiosk, which in turn is crowned with a shallow cupola and funeral urn. The faces are cut into horizontal stone ribs which give the appearance of

21

iron strapwork, but the whole edifice is constructed of hard Pallavaram gneiss from quarries near Madras, and called 'charnockite', ever since. Now whitewashed, each face of the tomb is pierced by a low pointed arch, three of which are closed by four raised tombstones. The monument is surrounded by thirty gravestones relocated here at the time of the erection of the church in 1787. In 1983 more were concentrated here including Admiral Watson's pedimented sepulchre crowned by a spectacular obelisk. A number of the tombs are enriched with baroque devices such as coats of arms and skull and crossbones, but it is the four raised stones closing the arches which are of interest.

Originally Charnock's stone lay flat over the grave, which he was supposed to share with his wife. When repairs were carried out to the mausoleum in 1892 the opportunity was taken to inspect the foundations. No vault was found, but the grave and some bones were revealed, suggesting that the two do lie here together, united in death.

The third slab in the row is to Surgeon William Hamilton who died at Fort William in 1717, and it was to his medical expertise that the Company owed its successful subsequent expansion. Hamilton cured the Moghul Emperor Farrukhsiyar of what was described at the time as 'a malignant distemper and swelling of the groin' (a euphemism for rampant venereal disease), and in return the Company received permission to trade freely in Bengal at a fixed rate of 3,000 rupees a year plus the right to purchase and collect revenue from thirty-eight villages. Unfortunately the Moghul Empire itself could not be cured so easily and during the first half of the 18th century it was in terminal decline.

By the 1760s the British found themselves masters of Bengal and the Carnatic. Their small coastal settlements at Madras and Calcutta were poised to expand from defensive enclaves into vibrant cities where mercantile and later, imperial values were expressed in the elegant architectural forms of the 18th century.

CHAPTER 2

MADRAS :
VISIONS OF ANTIQUITY

The approach to Madras always impressed European arrivals. The journey along the Coromandel coast contrasted markedly with the privations of the ocean voyage around the Cape – distant views of palm-fringed beaches, rolling surf, tropical blue skies and fresh land breezes. In the early years Madras was the centre of English activity. In sharp comparison to both Bombay and Calcutta it was a healthy settlement with pleasant surrounding countryside which offered opportunities for country retreat during the hot weather.

Charles Lockyer arrived in 1710 and left an effusive description of the character and appearance of Madras at this time:

> The prospect it gives is most delightful; nor appears it less magnificent by Land; the great variety of fine Buildings that gracefully overlook its Walls, affording an inexpressible Satisfaction to a curious Eye ... The streets are straight and wide, pav'd with Brick on each Side, but the Middle is deep sand for carts to pass in; Where are no Houses are Causeways with trees on each side to supply the Defect ... There are five Gates – the Sea, St Thomas, Water, Choultry and Middle Gate ... The Publick Buildings are the Town Hall, St Mary's Church, The College, New House and Hospital, with the Governor's Lodgings in the inner Fort ... The inhabitants enjoy perfect health ...

Madras was not a natural harbour. Until the late 19th century ships anchored in the roads half a mile off the Fort. Disembarkation was a risky business with passengers and freight being unloaded into *Masula* boats. These distinctive local craft were made of mango wood, caulked with straw and sewn together with coconut fibre. The boats pulled alongside and then returned through the surf to strike the beach as close to the Fort as possible. It must have been an unnerving and dangerous experience. A swell of twenty-five feet or more was common. Ladies were tied into chairs and lowered into the boats from the ship's yard arm. In 1836 one visitor recalled: 'We landed in a great boat with twelve boatmen, all singing a queer kind of howl, and with very small matters of clothes on, but their black skins prevent them from looking so very uncomfortable as Europeans would in the same minus state.' In 1746, 1782 and 1811 frightful hurricanes occurred which devastated shipping anchored in the roads causing great loss of life. One of the reasons for the later success of Calcutta and Bombay was that both offered natural harbours. It was a problem which vexed most administrations. Warren Hastings noted that 'the surf at Margate was as great as Madras and the Margate pier might well be adopted for this city.' Not until 1858 when an iron pier was erected to the designs of Frederick Johnson was disembarkation improved, and only in 1879, when two breakwaters were formed to the north and south of the Custom House, was reasonable provision made.

Early European settlement was concentrated in the Fort which came to be called Christian or White Town, in contrast to Black Town which lay outside. This was not a segregation based on concepts of racial superiority, but for reasons of defence and one which had been an inherent feature of foreign coastal settlements in India since Roman times. Interestingly even within the Fort there was a distinct separation between the military garrison, which was quartered beneath the walls, and the civil establishment which resided in the factory. In later years this separation was commonplace throughout India. Civil and military lines were nearly always discrete areas within the European cantonments.

The story of Fort St George in the late 17th and early 18th centuries is one of continuous expansion. By 1659 White Town was enclosed and fortified, and by 1682 a masonry wall had replaced the mud ramparts around Black Town. Fryer describes White Town in 1673 as 'sweet and clean', the houses two storeys in height with 'beautiful porticoes and terraced walks with shade trees planted before the doors'. In sharp contrast Black Town was filthy and an order was issued that 'any person killing hogs in the street may have them for their pains.' However, considering that similar edicts were common in London at this time, White Town must have been exceptionally salubrious. Social contact between the two towns was extensive. Often the white community was reproached for frequenting the taverns of Black Town. Men drank hard and gambling with cards and dice was popular. The Agent and Council had no qualms about inter-marriage and actually recommended that liaisons between English soldiers and local women should be encouraged to promote social and political harmony. Praises and gifts were given at the baptism of children of mixed marriages.

Within the space of sixty years Cogan and Day's early fort had grown into a major city of over 300,000 people, compared with a population of 674,000 in London in 1700. The arrangement of White Town, and the large area of Black Town outside the main walls, was distinctive with a planned grid-iron pattern of streets, which marks a substantial departure from the organic growth which characterised contemporaneous native towns. It is the earliest example of English town planning on a large scale in India.

Within the Fort a number of early buildings remain. St Mary's Church is of exceptional interest as it is the earliest surviving English building of any coherence in India. Vestiges of earlier fabric survive elsewhere, but St Mary's is also the oldest building associated with the Anglican Church in the East. Its inception was due to the zeal of the Governor, Streynsham Master, who set up a fund for the building of a church. Whether he was inspired by the church-building activities of Wren and the reconstruction of London after the Great Fire is unclear, but over thirty years later he was also responsible for the founding of St

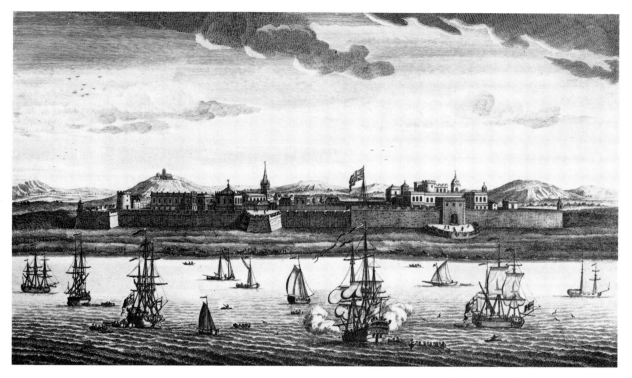

Fort St George by Jan van Ryne in 1754, depicting public buildings including St Mary's Church.

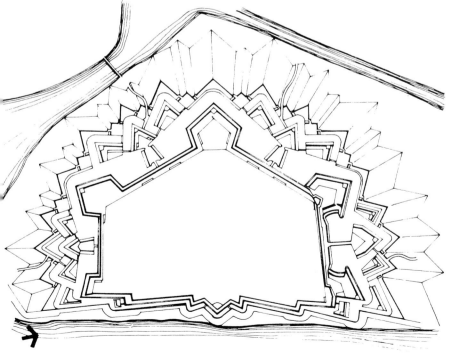

Plan of Fort St George, as remodelled by Colonel Patrick Ross in the 1770s, showing the inner bastions and outer redans.

25

St Mary's Church, Fort St George: the earliest complete English building surviving in India and the oldest Anglican church in the East. Consecrated in 1680, the distinctive obelisk spire was added in 1795 after the original was destroyed by French artillery in 1759.

George's, Queen Square in London. It is more likely that the existing Capuchin Church of St Andrew, built by the Portuguese merchants, who outnumbered the English at this time, was a challenge to Anglican self-respect and the moral authority of the Company. The Company was not interested in unprofitable expenditure and thus a private appeal was launched. Thirty-eight donors subscribed over 805 pagodas (£362). Excavations began on Lady Day 1678, hence the dedication to St Mary.

The church is eighty feet long and fifty-six feet broad. It took two and a half years to build. The architect was probably William Dixon, the Master Gunner of Fort St George at that time. It has been attributed to his successor Edward Fowle, but evidence suggests that he did not arrive in Madras until 1684. The plan is simple: three aisles with semi-circular roofs built entirely of solid masonry, two feet in thickness to withstand bombing, siege and cyclone. The outside walls are four feet thick and carried on a firm laterite foundation. No wood was used in the structure to prevent failure through the depredations of white ants. The church was consecrated in 1680, and the tower was completed in 1701. A steeple was added in 1710. The tower and belfry were detached from the body of the church until 1760 when a link was made.

The building bears witness to the vicissitudes of fortune which Madras endured during the war with the French in the mid-18th century. In 1746 when the French took the Fort, it served as a water store. After restoration to the English under the Treaty of Aix-La-Chapelle of 1748 it resumed as a place of worship, but during Lally's siege ten years later the steeple served as a look-out post and cotton bales were stored in the nave. This attracted the unwelcome attentions of the French artillery and it sustained such damage that the original steeple and tower had to be demolished. As late as 1782 when war with Hyder Ali threatened the security of Madras, it was used as a granary. The distinctive fluted obelisk spire was added in 1795 to the design of Colonel Gent, after proposals for its joint use as lighthouse were rejected on the grounds of ecclesiastical integrity.

St Mary's is of outstanding importance in the history of the British Empire, and it is a repository of evocative monuments of uncommon interest. The churchyard contains a wealth of early tombstones, many of which were moved here in 1760 after the huge mausolea in the old English cemetery had offered valuable cover for French snipers during the siege a year earlier. The churchyard is enclosed by simple 19th-century iron railings, but the graves bear the elaborate Baroque devices of the later 17th century executed in granite from the nearby Pallavaram quarries.

The interior of the church is whitewashed. Raised rose ornaments stand out in white relief on the grey vaulted ceiling. Near the entrance is the small black Pallavaram granite font in which Job Charnock's daughters were baptised in 1689, although the elaborate wooden cover is Victorian. In a recess on the end wall is the Governor's gallery which is approached by means of the external staircases which were added in 1760 to link the detached belfry to the body of the church. The gallery is enclosed by an original teak screen carved by local native craftsmen depicting elephants, parrots and the faces of bewigged men. The altarpiece is a painting of the Lord's Supper by a pupil of Raphael, who himself is reputed to have painted the chalice. It was taken from the French as part of the British spoils after the capture of Pondicherry in 1761. It was on this spot that Robert Clive married Margaret Maskelyne on 18th February 1753.

One of the most important historical associations of the church is with Elihu Yale. Born in Boston, Massachusetts in 1648 he had returned to England as a boy and arrived at Madras in 1672. By judicious dealings he made a fortune from private trading ventures and he was one of the original benefactors of the church, giving 15 pagodas. By

The formidable bastions of Fort St George with the river Cooum beyond. The spire of St Mary's Church in the middle distance and the flagstaff on the foreshore are notable landmarks.

1687 he was Governor, and when eventually he returned to London it was as a wealthy parvenu. His financial assistance was requested by the collegiate school at Saybrook in America and his gift of forty volumes raised sufficient capital to fund the foundation of a new university which was named after its benefactor. 'He was very popular with the Europeans and Indians, kept up his dignity and maintained a brave front towards the Indian powers.' His marriage to Catherine Hynmers was the first in the church and his son's pyramidal tomb lies isolated but intact in the courtyard of the nearby Indo-Saracenic Law Courts.

India has a fine heritage of funerary sculpture, and the best examples belong to the late 18th century when English sculpture reached new heights of composition and form. The revival of active piety combined with the popular vogue for austere elegance and sentimental simplicity to supersede the allegorical depiction of death and mortality associated with the funerary imagery of the Baroque and Rococo. Most sculptors, including John Flaxman and John Bacon, resorted to a few standard designs which were readily adapted to suit most situations, and which could be varied in price depending on the quality of the marble used or the degree of detail required. Common repetitive themes recur throughout India and England – the pedimented tablet surmounted by an urn flanked by the Christian virtues in high relief; the pedimented stele with draped figures in low relief mourning beside a broken pedestal or urn representing 'Resignation', or draped female figures contemplating the Bible or the heavens. Although these common

28

themes are repeated, the monuments, crisply executed in neo-classical, Greek or even whimsical Gothic styles, express a sincerity of feeling and elegiac charm, which recalls personal grief in a far more poignant fashion than the cloying sentimentality of many later Victorian tombs.

St Mary's has a large number of notable monuments including examples by Flaxman, Bacon and Chantrey. Here lies Sir Thomas Munro, probably the ablest of all English administrators in India, who died of cholera at Patticondah on 6th July 1827. He was a liberal-minded man with a passionate belief in the concept of trusteeship and eventual self-government for India – 'With what grace can we talk of paternal government if we exclude the natives from every important office?' His memory is respected in India today and a monumental equestrian statue by Chantrey is one of the few which have been retained within the City since Independence, a testimony to his own ideals and to the sensible attitude adopted by the State government to its Imperial past.

Other notable monuments are to Admiral Sir Samuel Hood, Lord Hobart and Sir John Burgoyne, but the most remarkable of all is an enormous marble tomb by John Bacon Jr for Frederick Christian Swartz. He was an outstanding missionary, and the only European to be trusted by Hyder Ali of Mysore – 'Send me the missionary whose character I hear so much from everyone. Him I will receive and trust.'

Of the secular buildings in the Fort, the oldest is the Secretariat which incorporates the nucleus of the second Fort house erected in 1694. The original dimensions of the building were preserved until 1825 when wings were added and the interior was converted into government offices, but the earlier form can still be discerned internally.

The office of the Accountant-General lies to the south of St Mary's Church and was used as the Government House until 1799. Originally the property belonged to an Armenian, but it was purchased by the Company in 1749 as a residence for the Deputy Governor. The building was extended in 1762, and again in 1778–80, and much of the fabric dates from this period. Clive knew it well and leased the building for a period. The reception hall is the largest internal space, but it was never entirely satisfactory.

Adjacent to the Accountant-General's office stands the Grand Arsenal, a long parallelogram. It was built in 1772 to the designs of Colonel Patrick Ross of the Madras Engineers, who was in charge of construction at the Fort during this period. His predecessor as Chief Engineer, Colonel Call, had been responsible for rebuilding large areas of the fort, after it had been reduced to a sad wreck during Lally's siege of 1758–59. The design of the Arsenal is curious with inverted arches forming a bomb-proof first storey. The courtyard is overlooked by an imposing portico surmounted by two large lions in *alto rilievo* carrying the Company's coat of arms, whilst the roof bristles with weapons, helmets and armour modelled in plaster. Its florid architectural style is redolent of the hybrid Indo-European palaces of Oudh. A plaque claims to mark the house where Clive pressed a pistol to his head and attempted suicide in his early days as a despairing 'writer' or company

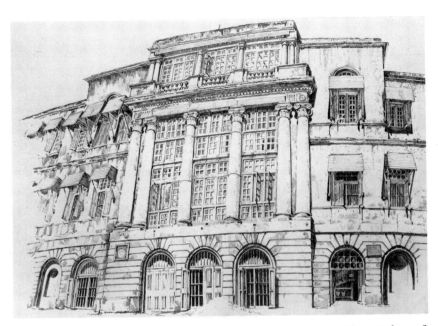

Robert Clive's house, Fort St George, now used by the Indian Navy, and embedded in later extensions. A recent drawing by John Nankivell.

clerk. Nearby stands the house once occupied by the Duke of Wellington.

The architectural focus of the entire complex is Fort Square. In 1735 Governor Pitt constructed a handsome colonnade linking the square with the Sea Gate. This was roofed over and lined with thirty-two pillars of black Pallavaram gneiss ranged in four rows. When the French captured Madras in 1746, the columns were removed as booty to Pondicherry, where they remained until 1761 when the British stormed the place and restored the columns to Pitt's arcade. Later it became the Exchange and was walled in, but in 1910 when the new Council chamber was built in classical style, the exterior was embellished with twenty of the best-preserved columns, and they stand to this day, an architectural idiosyncrasy vested with something of the totemic power of the bronze horses of St Mark's, Venice.

All the buildings in the Fort area were faced in Madras *chunam*, a form of stucco made from burnt sea shells which could be polished to a dazzling white sheen. The architectural impact of a city thus arrayed, offset by strong tropical sunlight and deep blue skies, mesmerised even the most philistine visitor. William Hodges arriving in 1781 commented:

> The stile of the buildings is in general handsome. They consist of long colonades, with open porticoes, and flat roofs and offer the eye an appearance similar to what we may conceive of a Grecian city in the age of Alexander. The clear, blue and cloudless sky, the polished white buildings, the bright sandy beach and the dark green sea present a combination totally new to the eye of an Englishman.

The transformation of Madras from an Oriental milieu into a classical vision was no fortuitous transposition of contemporary European taste, but a conscious attempt to identify the expanding British Empire in India with the civilising influence and moral values associated with classical architecture. One of the more obvious demonstrations was the provision of statuary to prominent public figures. On the northern side of Fort Square there is a large canopied pavilion which is now deprived of a centrepiece. This elegant Ionic rotunda contained a statue of Cornwallis, and was raised by public subscription to commemorate his defeat of Tipu, the Tiger of Mysore, at the siege of Seringapatam in 1799. Brass cannon enriched with tiger emblems once surrounded the memorial. The statue survives in the Connemara Library. Although it has been attributed to Chantrey, in fact it is by Thomas Banks. When Banks was preparing the model he was visited by a fellow sculptor who expressed astonishment that he had thought fit to commemorate Cornwallis's outward cast of one eye in such startling detail. Banks retorted:

If the cast had been inward it would, I conceive, have conveyed the impression of a contracted character, and I would have corrected it, but as the eyes looking to the right and left at the same moment would impart the idea of an enlarged and comprehensive mind, I have thought it due to the illustrious Governor-General to convey to posterity this natural indication of mental greatness.

The famous black Doric columns of Pallavaram gneiss once linked Pitt's colonnade with the Sea Gate. In 1910 they were incorporated into the new Council Chamber.

First Line Beach, Madras. Typical of the handsome classical buildings which visitors compared to some vision of the Ancient World.

In 1798 the second Lord Clive, eldest son of Robert Clive, became Governor of Madras. When he arrived he found the accommodation at his disposal quite insufficient for a person of his standing, particularly when compared with the grand palace of the Nawab of Arcot. The existing Company facilities were split between the old Admiralty building in the Fort, the Garden House at Triplicane and the. Public Assembly Rooms. He demonstrated that the rationalisation of Company accommodation would pay for the cost of the improvements, but the Court of Directors in London, who eschewed any suggestion of

This fine Ionic rotunda in Fort Square was raised in 1799 to celebrate Cornwallis's victory over Tipu Sultan. The original statue of Cornwallis is now in the Connemara Library, Madras.

Government House, Madras designed by John Goldingham in 1800. Classical architecture adapted to local needs with irregular intercolumniation and deep verandahs.

conspicuous expenditure on military or political aggrandisement, replied tersely: 'It is our positive order that no new and expensive buildings shall be commenced or grounds purchased for the creation of such buildings thereon without our previous sanction obtained upon the plan and estimate, as well as upon the expediency of the works.' The Court of Directors had good reason to be apprehensive. In the space of the next five years two of the most splendid public buildings ever erected by the British in India were to be raised by two separate Governors – one in Madras and one in Calcutta.

Clive appointed a civil engineer to reorganise the Engineers' Department at Madras which had come in for harsh criticism over the collapse of several arched buildings. He chose John Goldingham for the post, a Danish mathematician who had come to work in the private observatory in 1786. The Company took over the observatory and rebuilt it in 1794 and Goldingham became astronomer and marine surveyor. This accomplished scientist was also an enthusiastic architect of exceptional skill. Clive trusted him implicitly and allowed him a fifteen per cent commission on all works. In 1800 Goldingham was instructed to prepare a scheme of repairs for the old Fort House and for extensions to the Garden House at Triplicane.

The existing Garden House had been purchased from a Portuguese merchant, Luis de Madeiros in 1753. It was a typical example of a type for which the city was famous. During the French wars it had been occupied and damaged, then repaired and improved, but Goldingham remodelled it on a far grander scale. The ground floor was given over to

33

a hall and offices. On the first floor he formed a great drawing room and dining room approached by a grand double staircase with wrought-iron balustrading. One wing was given over to offices and the other to Clive's natural history collections. Goldingham's designs have a two-storey central range set forward from the wings embellished with a pedimented centrepiece of substantial projection. Both storeys have deep set colonnades to afford protection from the sun and the house is orientated towards the sea to obtain fresh breezes from the Bay of Bengal.

Architecturally the house retains its original character as a country residence, and the extensive verandahs which enclose three sides of the building demonstrate the manner in which the classical language of architecture was adapted to suit the local conditions and climate. The intercolumnar spaces vary considerably and the impact of the colonnaded verandahs is so dominant that the façade of the actual house is deeply recessed in shadow, providing much-needed shade at the expense of architectural balance.

Criticism of colonial architecture as crude, illiterate or imbalanced was once common, and it accounts for the widely-held view that the British left a legacy of architectural mediocrity. It is unfair, as it disregards the ingenious adaptations to local conditions expressed in many buildings. Moreover many classical buildings were erected in England at this time, which showed a similar lack of scholarly accuracy. Nash's terraces in Regent's Park take considerable liberties, but are widely admired.

The most extraordinary feature of the new complex of buildings was a monumental basilica designed as a completely separate Banqueting Hall. It was an entirely new structure intended for official entertainment by the Governor on a scale which hitherto had not been attempted in Madras. What is more important is that it was a symbol of the changing spirit of the age – a powerful architectural statement that British interests were no longer mercantile but Imperial. It comprises a huge temple separated from the main house. Set on a rusticated podium with a balustraded terrace to three sides of the main hall, the building is embellished with Tuscan-Doric three-quarter columns which rise through two storeys to carry an entablature with a frieze of urns and shields. Although this is a solecism, it is derived from William Chambers's *Treatise on Civil Architecture* and the lack of scholarly veracity did not worry Goldingham. The end bays on each frontage have niches at the lower level, whilst each alternate door opening is enriched with a pediment. The ends of the building are terminated with huge pediments, which once were adorned with trophies commemorating the triumph of British arms – the siege of Seringapatam over the principal northern entrance, and similar devices commemorating the Battle of Plassey over the southern entrance. The flight of steps sweeping up to the northern entrance were flanked by sphinxes, which were lost when the building was remodelled in 1875.

Today the martial trophies have been removed and replaced by the arms of the Indian Republic. The fine paintings of prominent British military figures which once hung in the main hall have been dispersed.

This collection, including pictures of Wellesley, Munro, Eyre Coote and Cornwallis, complemented the martial qualities of the building and deliberately created a formidable symbol of British ascendancy. It received fierce criticism from the Court of Directors in London, which objected to the military symbolism and continued to regard English interests in India purely in terms of the balance sheet. In 1803 the Directors wrote: 'It by no means appears to us essential to the well-being of our Government in India that the pomp, magnificence and ostentation of the Native Governments should be adopted by the former; the expense to which such a system would naturally lead must prove highly injurious to our commercial interests.' Bishop Heber regarded the whole flamboyant edifice as in vile taste, but the enraptured *Madras Government Gazette* considered it to be 'the most magnificent, beautiful specimen of architecture which the science and taste of Europe ever exhibited in India'.

The interior of the hall survives unaltered and it is an impressive space providing a magnificent setting for formal public functions. It is one large hall with side galleries lit by the attic windows, the light from which throws the ornamental moulded ceiling and cornice into sharp relief. The lower tier of columns supporting the galleries has a composite order, the upper Corinthian, and when the hall was inaugurated with a grand ball on 7th October 1802 it must have been a splendid sight. The social establishment of the entire city turned out.

Subsequently several additions were made to the building which have marred the original effect. Steps were added to the south entrance

Goldingham's Banqueting Hall evokes Imperial and martial values and consciously reflects the ideals of the Ancient World.

35

in 1875 and in 1892 it was re-roofed, but the most damaging alteration came in 1895 when the terrace was enclosed by an arcaded verandah, which truncated the façades and severely undermined the architectural effect. Today the building is renamed Rajaji Hall and it houses offices for the Tamil Nadu State Raffle – 'Fortuna Imperatrix Mundi'.

Presented with a *fait accompli*, the Court of Directors could do little. Government House was completed and occupied, but Clive paid the price of his extravagance. He was recalled to England in August 1803. The costs had been enormous – 106,000 pagodas for Government House and 74,000 pagodas for the Banqueting Hall – but the result was a magnificent complex of Georgian buildings,which were well adapted to the climate, catching the balmy breeze of the Coromandel coast, and which imparted dignity and standing to the administration.

Goldingham's plans for the government buildings were part of a wider scheme for the park in which they were situated. Fountains, basins, a mound, sunken garden and separate farmyard were all part of the overall conception, designed to recreate in India the Arcadian setting of an English country house in its own estate. A design was prepared for a bridge over the river Cooum and for a monumental bridge gate, but neither were implemented. Later two pretty classical entrance lodges leading to the main road were provided but they did not form part of the original conception.

Today the park and buildings form an oasis of calm and peace in the centre of the city which has long since engulfed the surrounding area. Others soon followed the precedent set by the Governor and built their own garden houses. Unfortunately few typical garden houses remain in their original settings. Most of those in Triplicane have been demolished or submerged in later development. One notable exception lingers on – the Madras Club – once known as the 'Ace of Clubs' and justly renowned as the finest in India. The Prince of Wales stayed here on his visit in 1875.

The Club was founded in 1831 because Madras lacked a proper focus for informal social activities. The project was undertaken privately and supported by the Governor, Stephen Lushington. Over 30,000 rupees were raised to purchase the house and grounds of a certain Mr Webster. This was a typical garden house, 'a substantial upstair building facing nearly north and in a substantial compound'. It had no outbuildings and the interior was divided into numerous small ground-floor apartments with two fine upper rooms on the first floor.

One of the earliest additions was the erection of an octagonal 'divan' some distance from the south front of the house in 1832. It was paved with Italian marble and used as a smoking room. It survives surrounded by later extensions and it retains much of its original charm and character. Ten years later much more extensive alterations were carried out which changed the form of the original house. A new smoking room was thrown forward from the centre to form the main feature of the principal west front. Over the next thirty years circumjacent buildings were acquired and included within the compound. Tennis courts, swimming baths and hot and cold steam baths were provided, conferring a reputation for luxury and relaxation which was unrivalled

Banqueting Hall: the Victorian arcaded verandah is a later addition truncating the original facades.

The derelict portals of the old Madras Club. The imposing central portico was added in 1865 demonstrating the durability of Palladian architecture well into the 19th century. The ground floor is a porte-cochère.

The octagonal divan added to the south front of the Madras Club in 1832 is still paved with Italian marble. The swastika ornament on the balustrade is a common symbol denoting well-being.

throughout India. Further extensive changes took place to the Club in 1865. It was intended to create a grand central staircase, but this had to be abandoned. The original portico was demolished to make way for a reading room across the entire upper floor and a deep verandah was erected on three sides, the north face being embellished with a pedimented classical façade which formed the distinctive main entrance facing the compound. One of the less successful innovations was the introduction of a fountain in the main hall; it proved so attractive to frogs and other non-members that it was removed some years later to the south garden.

By 1900 the pressing demand for short-term residential accommodation for officers and officials had been met by numerous extensions. Long two-storey ranges of officers' quarters were added in a traditional classical style, but the new card room built in 1882 represented a radical departure. A Gothic timber pavilion with stained glass windows perched above one of the rear wings, it was designed by Robert Fellowes Chisholm, the architect responsible for giving Madras so many of its splendid Indo-Saracenic and Gothic buildings.

For many years a shortage of ice was a major inconvenience, and enormous amounts of saltpetre were used for cooling, but in 1840 the Tudor Ice Co was formed and the Club took shares. In 1842 a curious circular building was erected on the foreshore to store huge blocks of ice imported from America. Later, with the advent of local ice factories, the building was converted, ironically, into a home for Brahmin widows, providing a highly symbolic refuge from the flames of the funeral pyre. Crowned by a slender pineapple, it is a local landmark.

Further north amongst the Indo-Saracenic domes of the Law Courts lies a graceful fluted Doric column of Pallavaram gneiss, once the old lighthouse. It was designed by Captain J. E. Smith of the Madras Engineers and opened on New Year's Day 1844. Over 120 feet high, it

The former Ice House is now a refuge for Brahmin widows.

was crowned by a polygonal lantern with the latest parabolic reflectors visible for fifteen miles, but this was removed when the new lighthouse opened in the highest minaret of the High Court, and only the column remains.

The nearby Adyar Club (now known as the Madras Club) was founded in 1891 in a fine early 19th-century house once owned by Mr George Moubray, but it represents an unusual departure from the usual local 'flat-tops', as the garden frontage facing the river is crowned by an octagonal cupola. The original design, now embedded in a later extension, comprised the central octagon with its cupola, approached by a pillared portico and two lower flanking wings. The Octagon Room survives with an arcaded perimeter surmounted by segmental-headed windows, and the walls are adorned with *trompe l'oeil* paintwork, which is now deteriorating rapidly in the salt-laden atmosphere.

Although relatively few example of Madras 'flat-tops' or garden houses survive today, a clear impression of their appearance can be obtained from contemporary drawings and pictures. An outstanding series of illustrations were made by John Gantz (1772–1853) and his son, Justinian (1802–1862), and these convey vividly their urbane elegance.

Gantz was an Austrian who worked for the East India Co as a draughtsman, architect, lithographer and topographical artist. He worked for some years with Lieutenant Thomas Fraser of the Madras Engineers and it was through him that he acquired a working knowledge of architecture and building. His son Justinian also practised as an architect. Their work is clearly influenced by contemporary pattern books such as *The Works in Architecture of Robert and James Adam* and more than one building shows a sympathy for Adamesque details. Their illustrations were fully worked up designs showing garden houses in idealised rural settings complete

The Adyar Club with its octagonal cupola. Justinian Gantz depicted a similar building type in a watercolour of 1832.

with Indian figures, but the architectural forms and detailing are typical. The houses have deep verandahs to provide shade and are adapted from Palladian prototypes. Pedimented centrepieces and semicircular bays to the garden frontages are common themes imparting a degree of grandeur and presence, as well as a welcome respite from the unremitting sun. The harsh rays reflected from the dazzling white Madras chunam created deep shadow and an impact similar to that of their classical antecedents in Ancient Greece and Rome. Architecturally the grammar was modified to suit the tropical location with column spacings altered from the classical discipline and infilled with ornamental wooden screens or cane 'tatties'. Venetian shutters were fixed to the windows and the characteristic 'flat-top' roof provided solace on hot nights when owners could retreat there to take advantage of the evening breezes off the sea. In general the main living quarters were at first-floor level with the servants or smaller rooms at ground-floor level, whilst the grander houses boasted large projecting *portes-cochères* and elephant porches capable of accommodating local grandees in a style to which they were accustomed.

Lady Gwillim, wife of the Chief Justice of Madras, arrived in 1802 and described her house and others in detailed letters to her mother and sister in England:

> The houses of all Europeans are nearly equal as to goodness and size ... They are all like Pictures of Italian Palaces with flat roofs or balustrades ... The walls, columns and balustrades are all polished. The walls of rooms are sometimes painted as stucco rooms in England of pale green blue ... Some people colour the chunam for the outside of the house of a light grey in imitation of the grey granite of the country leaving the columns, pilasters, white. The floors are also of this chunam coloured according to the fancy of the owner and here it so exactly resembles marble pavements that I should not have known if our house has black squares and white ones for the sitting rooms ... Some have Dove and Black squares ... We have folding doors in all the rooms which are half way green painted Venetians, the windows are all Venetians and no glass, but we can thus exclude the light yet have air from room to room.

A typical Madras 'flat-top' of the type illustrated by John and Justinian Gantz and described by Lady Gwillim.

The Church was tied up inextricably with the expanding power of the East India Company, and in Madras two churches became prominent new local landmarks. St Mary's in the Fort had long been part of the skyline of the city when viewed from the sea, but between 1816 and 1819 St George's Cathedral and St Andrew's Kirk were built.

The prototype for both, and also for many of the lesser edifices erected throughout India and the Empire, was St Martin's-in-the-Fields, London by James Gibbs. Its plan, elevations and distinctive tiered spire recur from Canada to Australia and from South Africa to India. Ironically its Baroque style persisted long after it had been overtaken by neo-classicism, and the Greek and Gothic revivals. As late as 1867 the Dutch Reform Church at Cradock in South Africa was designed on this prototype. Its success is not difficult to explain. Symbolically it lay at the heart of the Empire and after St Paul's, it was the grandest church in London. More importantly its details were reproduced in Gibbs's *Book of Architecture* in 1728, and therefore its plan, form and dimensions, together with alternative options were readily accessible to remote colonial engineers in need of inspiration and guidance. Functionally it is an excellent prototype with a long nave of three bays and a simple chancel at the east end. The pedimented portico, long pilastered sides with galleries and side aisles, and the plain apse with its Venetian window all convey an image of splendour and of the classical values. Architectural purists objected to the colossal tower and spire, which appeared to be unsupported, and to its vertical emphasis which detracted from the balance of the basilica beneath, but the building made up in sheer impact and presence for what it lacked in good manners.

The plan of St George's Cathedral was prepared by Captain James

An early photograph of St George's Cathedral completed in 1816. An eloquent essay in Baroque architecture.

This Ionic porch on the flank of St George's is detailed impeccably in dazzling white chunam.

Caldwell (1770–1863), but his assistant Thomas Fiott de Havilland (1775–1866) was responsible for the working designs and construction of the church. De Havilland was largely responsible for both major churches in Madras. He was born in Guernsey, the eldest son of the Bailiff Sir Peter de Havilland. Educated at Queen Elizabeth College, Guernsey, he served widely in India, and, like Caldwell, he lived to a ripe old age, returning home to enjoy his retirement. Set in a spacious compound, St George's steeple is a precise copy from Gibbs's *Book of Architecture* and his variant designs for a circular church. The flanks are embellished with Ionic porches and aedicules and the west front has a large projecting portico. The whole edifice is faced in dazzling white polished chunam – a pure white Christian monument in a heathen land. It was consecrated by Bishop Heber on 16th January 1816. Soon it became a favourite haunt of the English community. The interior is also white and conveys an impression of light and space. A double row of eighteen tall smooth Ionic columns carry an arched ceiling which is beautifully decorated in raised plasterwork. The aisles are lined with semi-circular headed stained glass windows above panelled and louvred doors which allow a free flow of air. The chancel is apsidal with a marble altarpiece of St George crowning a broken pediment. The pews have carved Gothic details to the end panels but the backs and seats are finished in light canework, a concession to the climate which is common in South India. A number of fine marble monuments line the walls including a statue of 'Faith' by Flaxman commemorating John Mousley, Archdeacon of Madras, and Chantrey's excellent monument to Bishop Heber, the second Bishop of Calcutta, and author of the hymn 'From Greenland's Icy Mountains', who drowned in a swimming pool at Trichinopoly in 1826.

To the north-east of the Church is the cemetery, approached through a pretty pavilion crowned by an octagonal cupola. The first interment was that of Elizabeth de Havilland, the architect's wife, on 14th March 1818. 'She stands first in the awful book and gives a date to the register' reads the epitaph on her sepulchre of local black granite. The cemetery is enclosed by a railing made of eleven hundred musket barrels, pikes, and halberd heads, and over one thousand and fifty pistols and bayonets. Interestingly later extended sections reproduce the same details. It is alleged that these were brought from Seringapatam after the defeat of Tipu Sultan in 1799, as a number of pieces are engraved V. Dubois, and Tipu's arsenal was run by the French, but it is more likely they were surplus war material put to good use.

At St George's de Havilland demonstrated his talent as an excellent practical architect, but at St Andrew's Kirk he developed the vocabulary of James Gibbs into a distinctive individual statement. It is the finest 19th-century church in India, standing in a large open compound overlooked from various parts of the city. The Scottish Presbyterian Church in India had requested Kirks in each Presidency. The Elders of the Kirk were eager for a quick start and wanted a circular plan form. The original plans were prepared by Lieutenant Grant, the temporary Superintending Engineer, and as he was keen to commence before he was superseded, he borrowed Gibbs's plan for a circular

church proposed for St Martin's-in-the-Fields. In spite of pressure to start, the design was criticised by Colonel Caldwell on the grounds of its unsuitability to the climate, and he modified it, retaining the circular form, but preparing an entirely new plan for its design and construction. De Havilland superintended the work of erection and dealt with the detailed constructional problems, including the sinking of pottery wells in the soft ground to carry the foundations. As at St Mary's no timber was used in the construction to prevent attacks by white ants.

Externally St Andrew's is distinguished by a steeple closely modelled on St Martin's, but twelve feet higher. The main entrance faces west and is approached through a deep porch carried on a double colonnade of twelve massive fluted Ionic columns which give an impression of great strength and power. It is surmounted by a pediment inscribed with 'Jehovah' in Hebrew and the name and date of the church in the frieze. The façade on the chancel side is most unusual with a pediment flanked by two enormous British lions and a frieze inscribed with the motto of the East India Company – 'Auspicio Regis et Senatus Angliae'.

Internally the body of the church is a circle 81 ft 6 ins in diameter with a rectangular compartment to the east and west. The circular part is crowned by a shallow dome with an annular arch around it over the aisles. The entire dome is painted sky blue and decorated with gold

The steeples and spires of St George's Cathedral (left) *and St Andrew's Kirk* (right), *bear witness to the influence of James Gibbs and St Martins-in-the-Fields.*

The nobly-proportioned interior of St Andrew's, illustrated by Justinian Gantz, showing the ambitious circular plan.

stars. The entablature and frieze are of stone with a brick cornice above, on which rests the dome. The dome's equilibrium is preserved by the lateral pressure of the annular arch around it resting on the walls of the building. Four columns are granite, the remainder local ironstone.

The complex construction of the dome must be attributed to de Havilland, as he had experimented with huge brick spans for many years. As early as 1801 he had built a huge free-standing brick arch spanning 112 feet in the garden of his bungalow at Seringapatam to prove that it was feasible, and later he used these techniques in the ballroom extension at Government House, Mysore. The arch remained until 1937 when it crumbled through neglect and from the unwelcome attentions of curious visitors, but vestiges remain. St Andrew's is perfectly adapted to the climate with cane pews, and a cool chequer-board black and white marble floor. Like St George's, the side walls are pierced with semi-circular openings infilled with louvred doors beneath stained glass fanlights. When the doors are open glimpses of the palms and tropical vegetation in the compound outside provide an exotic counterpoint to the cool European architectural forms within.

St Andrew's and St George's are important not just as architectural monuments, but because they demonstrate the growing sense of awareness amongst the British of their political power in India. Opened in 1821 St Andrew's exudes self-confidence and presence, and the incorporation of political symbolism into the external ornament is a new departure, underscoring British political and religious hegemony.

By the mid-19th century Madras had become a backwater – attention had shifted to the capital at Calcutta – but it remained an active and prosperous city rooted firmly in the classical tradition of architecture. Two prominent public buildings were erected at this time and both retain the classical vocabulary.

Pachaiyappa's College is a famous Madras institution. The school was founded on the posthumous generosity of Pachaiyappa Mudhiar, an interpreter in the East India Company's service. The present building was erected between 1846 and 1850 and was opened by Sir Henry Pottinger, the governor of Madras, as a lasting memorial to its religious and educational benefactor. Architecturally it is chastely detailed with an Ionic portico crowned by a pediment based on the Athenian Temple of Theseus. The whole edifice is raised high on a plainly detailed stucco plinth which is now submerged by the booths and shops of the bazaar area. Today it looks extraordinary, a pale Greek temple hovering over the chaotic squalor of the market beneath, the pursuit of education raised high above the pursuit of wealth, adding an accidental dimension to the architectural juxtaposition of two cultures.

The Memorial Hall was erected shortly after the Indian Mutiny as a thanks-offering for deliverance from the traumatic events of that time. Funds were raised by subscription and plans were prepared by Captain Winscom to accommodate over six hundred people plus offices for the Bible Society, Religious Tract Society and Vernacular Education Society. Consultations were carried out with a local builder, Mr Ostherder, for an estimate and in common with local practice costs were based on a sworn oath rather than contract. Work was delayed by unsettled weather and costs rose so rapidly that the plans were modified by Colonel Horsley, omitting the offices, but retaining the style, dimensions and material – local chunam on a brick core. It is a calm, dignified building, as befits a memorial of deliverance. It is cruciform in plan, raised on a low podium with a pedimented Ionic portico inscribed '1857' and with a verse from the 15th Psalm: 'The

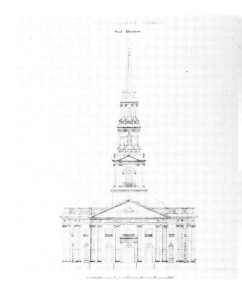

St Andrew's Kirk: The west elevation drawn by the architect Thomas Fiott de Havilland. It is the finest 19th-century church in India.

St Andrew's Kirk showing the annular arch supporting the dome. The carved Corinthian capitals are exceptionally sophisticated.

Pachaiyappa's College, 1846–1850, based on the Athenian Temple of Theseus.

Lord hath been mindful of us. He will bless us'. To those who built it, this was not a pious hope for the future but a very real conviction of continuing Divine intercession on their behalf.

The classical architectural heritage of Madras is as much an expression of late 18th- and early 19th-century English values as London's squares or the crescents and terraces of Bath, but because it lies stranded by the receding tide of Empire it has had scant attention and even less protection from demolition and decay. The once numerous Madras 'flat-tops' are becoming rarer and rarer. Even the Madras Club, the epitome of gracious European living, lies empty and derelict, the residential wings given over to mouldering files of abandoned papers. The fine octagonal divan provides shelter for a destitute family, whilst Chisholm's Gothic card room has thrown in its hand. However, extraordinarily, it seems that the building will survive. Now it is owned by Indian Express Newspapers and work is in hand to repair the main building for use as a theatre and offices for the company, an encouraging sign that it is possible to find new uses for old buildings in the most unpromising situations. For generations now Madras has had an atmosphere of splendid decay, but somehow it has survived with its integrity intact, basking in the refulgent glow of its magnificent past.

> Clive kissed me on the mouth and eyes and brow,
>   Wonderful kisses, so that I became
> Crowned above Queens – a withered beldame now,
>   Brooding on ancient fame.

46

CHAPTER 3

CALCUTTA: POWER ON SILT

'Round their little fort and close to it, by degrees they built themselves very neat, useful, if not elegant houses, a church, a court house and laid out walks, planted trees and made their own little district neat, clean and convenient.' This eye-witness account of early 18th-century Calcutta indicates how only twenty years after Job Charnock's death, the town had become a thriving European enclave. Even at this time European houses were set in their own garden compounds, but expansion was haphazard and unco-ordinated. Hamilton wrote in 1710: 'The town was built without order, as the builders thought most convenient for their own affairs, everyone taking in what ground best pleased them for gardening, so that in most houses you must pass through a garden into a house, the English building near the river side and the natives within land.'

The houses of the period are described as being without flues, Venetians, glass windows or punkahs, but with panelled doors and frames with a network of cane at the windows. Often these were quite crude structures usually with thatched roofs, but some resembled detached English town houses with rectangular window openings and balustraded roofs, completely unadapted to the climate. All the principal buildings were concentrated within the walls of Fort William – the Governor's House, barracks, factors' houses, writers' quarters, warehouses and workshops, but the church, hospital and numerous houses stood outside the ramparts, which enclosed a small area – 710 feet long by 340 wide at the north end widening to 485 feet at the south end. The Fort is described by Hamilton as 'an irregular Tetraon of brick and mortar called Puckah, which is a composition of Brick-dust, lime, Molasses and cut Hemp and is as hard as and tougher than firm Stone or Brick . . . About fifty yards from Fort William stands the Church built by the pious Charity of Merchants residing there.'

With the exception of St Anne's Church with its tall steeple, the only building of architectural distinction was the Governor's House, considered by Hamilton to be 'the most regular Piece of architecture that I ever saw in India'. It is depicted in contemporary illustrations as a symmetrical building raised on a podium above the level of the Fort walls, a central pilastered range with end wings and a monumental entrance gate facing the river. To the front of the Fort lay the Great Tank, a huge reservoir of water fed by natural springs, which survives as a central feature in the present town plan of Calcutta. At this time it was highly valued as an essential public amenity. The banks were laid out with orange groves and pleasant gravelled footpaths, and the area enclosed by iron railings.

The original Fort William in 1754 by Jan Van Ryne. The Baroque houses on the left of the picture show few concessions to the climate and could almost be in London.

Socially life for the Europeans had become more pleasant, in spite of the devastating mortality rate. The closed routine of the early factories had relaxed slightly and become less formal and introverted. Senior officials were allowed to bring out their wives, whilst many of the less exalted married into the large Armenian community who by 1724 had their own church, St Nazareth. Hamilton considered the life very pleasant: 'most gentlemen and ladies in Bengal live both splendidly and pleasantly, the forenoons being dedicated to business, and after dinner to rest, and in the evening to recreate themselves in chaises or palankins in the fields, or to gardens, or by water in their budgeroes.'

It was a period of relatively quiet consolidation and expansion when gold was plenty and labour cheap. Most Europeans worked hard to acquire wealth, tempted to risk their lives in the insalubrious climate of Bengal to obtain a level of financial security and status which was beyond their reach in England. The risks were very high indeed for Calcutta was nothing more than an undrained marsh surrounded by steaming jungle. Hamilton mentions that: 'One year I was there, and there were reckoned in August about 1200 English, and before the beginning of January there were 460 burials registered in the clerk's books of mortality.' Until 1800 the European inhabitants met on the 15th November each year to congratulate each other on having survived.

Disease and sickness were not the only disincentives to the would-be Nabob. The climate severely debilitated the European constitution. Sudden storms of terrifying violence were common, particularly

48

towards the close of the south-west monsoon. On 30th September 1737 a cyclone of immense force devastated the town. Over 300,000 people were killed in Bengal and 200 houses were destroyed in Calcutta alone. The steeple of St Anne's Church was demolished. One report alleges that it was swallowed into the ground whole without breaking, but this is unlikely as the main body of the church survived. Nevertheless the level of the river rose forty feet and barques of over sixty tons were hurled two leagues inland over the tops of high trees.

A storm of such ferocity was exceptional, even by Indian standards. A grisly postscript was reported in the *Gentleman's Magazine*, the following year. A French merchant ship was beached and wrecked by the storm and efforts were made to salvage the goods. Two men were despatched successively into the hold, each to disappear without trace. At length one more hardy than the rest ventured forth. He too disappeared. Eventually their apprehensive companions sent for torches to light the flooded hold, to be confronted by a huge alligator patiently expecting more prey. The story concludes 'it was with difficulty they killed it, when they found the three men in the creature's belly.'

By the 1740s Moghul power was waning fast. Although the Nawabs of Bengal paid allegiance to Delhi, they grew increasingly despotic as Imperial control diminished to nominal suzerainty. In 1742 Maratha horsemen invaded Bengal and Orissa sweeping all before them. Although the Nawab, Alivardi Khan, came to terms and paid tribute to remain unmolested, the speed of the advance to within a few miles of Calcutta not only demonstrated the political vacuum which the Moghuls were leaving, but also the vulnerability of the town to attack. The principal result of this scare was the construction of a three-mile ditch around Calcutta, embracing most of the European houses. Many had been constructed outside the walls of the Fort with a complete disregard for defence. The ditch was worthless as a defensive line and although there were ambitious proposals to erect an eighteen-feet high wall to the inner side with gates, lamps and drawbridges to the principal roads, nothing was done. Such complacency in the face of a volatile political situation was dangerous and provocative.

In 1756 Alivardi died. He was succeeded by his twenty-year-old son, Suraj-ud-Daulah (Lamp of the State) who was spoilt, impetuous, obstinate and profligate. He loathed the English, coveted their wealth, and as soon as an opportunity presented itself he attacked Calcutta with an army of 50,000. The Fort was untenable and it fell on 20th June 1756. One hundred and forty-six prisoners were taken, but only twenty-three survived the following night in the Black Hole.

The news took seven weeks to reach Madras, where it might have been accepted as a limited reverse, but for the fortuitous presence of Clive and Admiral Watson in command of a force of 1,500 Indians and over 900 Europeans intended for use against the French. It was diverted north immediately. Calcutta was recaptured on 2nd January 1757 and Clive went on to defeat Suraj-ud-Daulah at Plassey on 23rd June. A nominee, Mir Jafar, was put in his place with the intention of creating a controlled state in the manner in which the French under de Bussy dominated Hyderabad. Clive far exceeded his limited aims. By accident rather than design the Company found itself the master of Bengal with its merchants having a free rein throughout the province. Corruption and venality became endemic. Company servants neglected their duties and concentrated on amassing huge personal fortunes. Abuses were so commonplace that in 1773 Parliament was forced to intervene. The Company's charter was renewed with qualifications, which stipulated that the Governor of Calcutta, assisted by a Council, should be Governor-General supreme over all India.

With the resumption of British control a major change occurred in the form and pattern of European settlement, which was to transform Calcutta into a 'city of palaces', the second city of the Empire. Old Fort William was patched up and used as a customs house for a short period, but a gigantic new fort was planned to the designs of Captain John Brohier, an artillery officer transferred from Madras to Bengal in June 1757 and promoted to Chief Engineer at Calcutta. The designs are based on a modification of Vauban's 17th-century concepts of fortification with certain improvements taken from the work of Cormontaingne. Unfortunately he was a disreputable character. In 1760 he was arrested for fraud in connection with the building works at Fort William, but he absconded to Ceylon where he settled. Nevertheless the work continued under his successors, including the renowned Archibald Campbell, for thirteen years until it was completed in 1773 at a staggering cost of £2 million.

Unlike Fort St George in Madras, where the principal buildings were concentrated within the ramparts, at Fort William the public buildings

Plan of the new Fort William designed by Captain John Brohier. The complex symmetry is based on Vauban's concepts of fortification.

50

remained outside the walls. This was an important change. The static form of development based on defensive enclaves, which characterised early European settlements, gave way to a more dynamic form of dispersed settlement, one more conducive to unrestricted growth and expansion. This was a reflection of growing power and security, and of increasing wealth. Significantly the new Fort altered the entire plan of Calcutta, for to obtain an unrestricted field of fire a huge open space was cleared – the Maidan – which not only rendered the Fort unassailable but also created an enormous vista around which a magnificent collection of public buildings arose. The golden age of Calcutta had begun.

Calcutta seems to have presented a picture of almost continuous building activity at this time. Mrs Kindersley, a typical Englishwoman, arrived in 1767, and the transition from settlement to city was all too evident: 'After Madras, it does not appear much worthy describing . . . People keep constantly building . . . the appearance of the best houses is spoiled by the little straw huts . . . which are built up by the servants for themselves to sleep in: so that all the English part of the town is a confusion of very superb and very shoddy houses.'

The town was increasing in size daily impelled by a steady influx of European merchants and traders. Houses became extremely scarce and the demand for imported European comforts was insatiable. Mrs Kindersley noted that 'furniture is so exorbitantly dear, and so very difficult to procure, that one seldom sees a room where all the chairs and couches are of one part.'

With the completion of the Maidan in 1780 an opportunity was provided for the rising merchant classes to express their new-found wealth in a more visible form. The old bamboo-roofed bungalows and vernacular buildings were swept away and replaced by grander houses

Fort William in the 1860s, with an impressive array of artillery in the foreground. The bastions built by Brohier and his successors can be seen between the barracks and St Peter's Church. It was the most important symbol of British military power in Asia.

51

which blatantly reflected the aspirations and status of their European owners. This open display of wealth contrasted with Indian social values which were expressed in a totally different physical form, and so naturally led to a very different town plan. Wealthy Indian merchants concealed their properties in a maze of mean huts and dwellings. Generally their access was tortuous through alleys and courts which could be barricaded in times of riot or civil emergency. Their houses were inward looking, often arranged around central quadrangles which provided cool, shade and quiet repose even in the heart of the teeming bazaars.

The public expression of wealth by English Nabobs and merchants also contrasted with contemporary English precedents. In London town houses of the period were fairly small in size with simple external designs which relied for impact on their grouping into terraces, squares or crescents. In India Georgian town houses resemble scaled down versions of English country houses and Palladian mansions rather than the narrow London town house.

These fine Indian mansions mark the first stage in the adaptation of European forms of architecture to an Indian context. Most follow a similar pattern, a well-proportioned block of two or three storeys set in its own garden compound with the inner rooms protected by a deep verandah or portico. The siting of individual buildings in their own compounds or garden areas was as much a reflection of good planning, to promote a cool flow of air and to reduce the risk of disease, as from any desire for exaggerated individual splendour. It dictated a dispersed form of settlement with considerable distances between houses, so movement between them was either by carriages or palanquins, which afforded protection from the heat. The entrance porticos of the houses were transformed into *portes-cochères*, where carriages could wait protected from the fierce heat of the sun. Occasionally these are of enormous proportions and designed to accommodate the elephants of visiting dignitaries arriving by 'howdah' – portes-pachyderms might be more apt.

The facing materials for the houses was always the same – a brick core covered with Madras chunam, but in the harsher climate of Bengal it rapidly deteriorated and required constant re-polishing or re-painting, creating a vision more redolent of the peeling terraces of St Petersburg than the monumental masonry of Greece and Rome. The use of a material that could not stand the strain of the climate or endure over time, unlike the marmoreal permanence of Greece and Rome, disturbed many contemporary observers. However grand or heroic the conception, the effect was diminished if the façade was peeling and the brick core showed the sham beneath the structure. Bishop Heber noted: 'There is indeed nothing more striking than the apparent instability of the splendour of this great town; houses, Churches, and public buildings are all of plaistered brick; and a portico worthy of a Grecian temple is often disfigured by the falling of the stucco, and the bad rotten bricks peeping through.' In many ways the symbolism was apt for these were grand houses where the public façade was all important, built for parvenus – merchants who had acquired a veneer

Each European house was set in its own garden compound. Monumental entrance screens and other devices proclaimed the status of the occupant.

This rare early photograph of a fine Greek Calcutta mansion conveys vividly the character of the 'City of Palaces'. Note the elaborate gate piers with ball finials and the damp-stained chunam.

of upper class values and status but lacked the aristocratic substance beneath.

The spaciously planned districts of Calcutta – Chowringhee, Alipur, Garden Reach and the central Maidan itself – indicate the recognition which was afforded to the cooling effect of the wind off the river and the absolute necessity of obtaining shade from vegetation. However, in the Esplanade and Chowringhee the crowding was such that a continuous street frontage of boundary walls and gates arose complementing the classical architecture of the houses. Gate piers were rusticated, pilastered or treated with niches, pediments and ball finials. The overall effect is depicted in a variety of fine illustrations from the period, such as those of James Fraser and the Daniells. Generally verandahs were embellished with devices which provided shade but allowed a cool passage of air. Screens of wooden ribs, bamboo tatties or plaited grass were hung between the columns of the verandah and kept moist. These screens are important indigenous features which became an individual art form in themselves, recurrent ornamental elements in Anglo-Indian architecture.

Today many of the town houses of Calcutta have been submerged into the bazaars of the expanding city, but a few typical examples remain within their compounds. The Royal Calcutta Turf Club in Middleton Road, Chowringhee is a well-preserved type. Once it was the home of the Apcar family, shipping magnates, and the house was erected in about 1820. The south front has a fine pedimented verandah

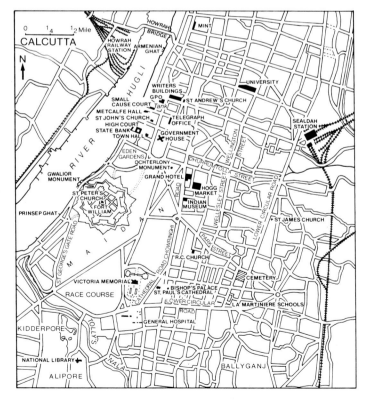

carried on coupled Doric columns, and the north front, a long projecting *porte-cochère* which protects visitors from sun and rain. Internally the entrance hall extends through two storeys, but the treatment of the staircase with warm brown panelling and teak columns is an unexpected variation from the ubiquitous use of plasterwork. Simple timber chimneypieces add to the homely relaxed atmosphere, but they seem to have been ornamental and could rarely have been of use in Bengal. Close to the Calcutta Turf Club, in Middleton Row stands the Loretto Convent, another well-preserved example of the 18th-century Calcutta house. It was once the home of Henry Vansittart, Governor of Bengal between 1760 and 1764, and also of the eminent Sir Elijah Impey, first Chief Justice of the Supreme Court from 1774 to 1782. The Bishop's Palace with its hexastyle portico dates from the early 19th century, but it is representative both in form and style of the prevailing classical ethos of the period.

At this time Chowringhee still retained something of the atmosphere of a suburb. To Emily Eden it resembled Regent's Park with individual stucco villas set in verdant garden compounds. The resemblance to a London suburb was more than just a passing fancy. Bishop Heber described his arrival at twilight: 'From Kidderpoor we passed by a mean wooden bridge over a muddy creek, which brought us to an extensive open plain like a race course, at the extremity of which we saw Calcutta, its white houses glittering through the twilight ... with an effect not unlike that of Connaught Place and its neighbourhood, as seen from a distance across Hyde Park.'

Perhaps the most evocative survival from the period is Warren Hastings' house at Alipur, once on the southern outskirts of the city. It was built around 1777 and was described as a 'perfect bijou'. Originally it was a simple, two-storeyed white cube with living quarters on the ground floor. In the particulars of sale in 1785 it is described as 'an upper roomed house ... consisting of a hall and rooms on each floor, a handsome stone staircase and a back staircase all highly finished with Madras chunam and the very best materials'. The effect of the polished

Warren Hastings's much-loved house at Alipur built in 1777. The original house is the two-storeyed centrepiece. The cavernous hoods and open shutters on the west face are common later features.

(Top) *Writers' Buildings built by Thomas Lyon in 1780, illustrated by the Daniells in 1797. This vast austere building demonstrates the mercantile preoccupations of the East India Company at this time. Holwell's monument to the Black Hole stands in the foreground.* (Middle) *With the growth of Imperial self-awareness attempts were made to embellish the original facade with pedimented porticos in the mid-19th century.* (Bottom) *In 1880 the entire block was refaced to reflect Victorian Imperial and civic pride.*

Belvedere. The famous duel between Warren Hastings and Philip Francis took place on August 17th 1780 just outside the western entrance.

chunam was blinding. Later it was extended and wings were added. Hastings loved the house and spent many happy hours there recovering from the vitriolic attacks made on him by his Council, and when he returned to England the gardens of his house at Daylesford were laid out after the fashion of his garden at Alipur. It is reputed that the house is haunted by Hastings. As late as 1947 Lady Braid-Taylor was subjected to a fearful outbreak of ghostly phenomena which centred on one particular room and which have been witnessed by most incumbents of the house. Today it is a women's college. Nearby lies Belvedere which was the scene of Hastings' famous duel with Philip Francis. Like Hastings House, the original portion is the centre section, but it has been greatly extended. Once the property of the Lieutenant Governors of Bengal, it was used by numerous Viceroys on visits to Calcutta from New Delhi, before being given over to the National Library.

In 1780 an enormous building was erected to the designs of Thomas Lyon to house the junior clerks of the East India Company. Lyon had sailed for India in 1763 to instruct the native workforce at Fort William in carpentry. His companion, Mr Fortnam, was a civil architect. Whether or not he or Fortnam was responsible for the new building is impossible to say. Illustrations of the period depict a very long plain building resembling a barracks with little architectural ornament to suggest that it was the main centre of English mercantile endeavour in India. The windows are repetitive and the entire façade is relieved only by a projecting central range enriched with Ionic pilasters and a balustraded parapet. It is an uninspiring building, but important as one of the few large ranges of classical buildings erected in India which reflect the character and form of the Georgian terraces of London built at this time by the Adam brothers, although in appearance and impact it is more redolent of a stripped version of one of Nash's terraces of the 1820s in Regent's Park. The central portion was used as classrooms for the College of Fort William where new arrivals were taught to become

writers in the Company service. Dominating the north side of the main square in Calcutta, the building was never successful as an architectural centrepiece and later it was embellished with low pediments. In 1880 the entire building was refronted using terracotta dressings with a Corinthian façade and a dummy portico and pediment, for use as the Bengal Secretariat.

Early illustrations also depict Holwell's memorial to the Black Hole, which at this time stood at the western end of Writers' Buildings. This took the form of an octagonal obelisk set on a low pedestal with four of the faces enriched with pediments and urns. Its precise date of erection is uncertain, but it was there in 1764 inscribed with the names of the dead, even though four were omitted in error. It was known popularly as 'The Monument'. In 1782 it was struck by lightning, and although repaired its brick and plaster structure fell into disrepair. In 1810 it was again struck by lightning and by 1812 the inscribed panels were illegible. Eventually in 1821 it was demolished, and although most residents welcomed the removal of a memorial to such an unhappy event, at least one indignant correspondent compared its destruction to the removal of the Elgin Marbles. A replica of the monument in Sicilian marble was reinstated by Lord Curzon in 1902. This too has disappeared from the original site to a quiet corner of St John's Churchyard, Calcutta, in a determined effort by the Indian authorities to erase the memory; and the popular Indian view remains that the massacre never took place at all.

One of the major changes in the form and appearance of late 18th-century Calcutta was the erection of St John's Church in 1787, the Cathedral church until the completion of St Paul's in 1847. It is a fascinating building of very considerable interest, portrayed by the Daniells only a year after its consecration.

The foundations were laid in 1784 at the crossing of Hastings Street and Council House Street in the heart of the town on the site of the old magazine yard. The money was raised by subscription as the Company was renowned for its parsimonious attitude. Sir John Shore noted: 'A pagan gave the ground; all characters subscribed: Lotteries, confiscations, donations received contrary to law were employed in completing it. The Company contributed but little: no great proof they think the morals of their servants connected with religion.'

The site was 'L' shaped as a burial ground restricted the west end, and the church owes its peculiar plan form to this constraint. The main approach could not be laid over the burial ground, so the entrance was placed behind the altar with a small vestibule providing access to galleries above. It was an unprecedented arrangement.

The architect was Lieutenant James Agg, Bengal Engineers, described by William Hickey, the diarist, as 'a modest and ingenious man with superior manners', the son of a Gloucestershire stonemason. He arrived with Hickey in November 1777 and worked as an assistant to the Chief Engineer, Colonel Henry Watson. It is alleged that the plan of St John's is based on St Stephen's Walbrook, but this is erroneous. Early suggestions were for a Greek cruciform plan similar to St Stephen's, but the design was rejected and instead, Agg reached for inspiration from Gibbs's common prototype, St-Martin's-in-the-Fields. The plan is similar, a three-bay nave and galleries, but the juxtaposition is entirely different. A Doric order was used throughout rather than Corinthian as the detailing was easier to carve locally from Chunar stone. Sadly the church was not built as Agg intended. The most distinctive feature of the church is the steeple and spire, which are a modification of St Martin's. The fourth tier was omitted completely to reduce not just the cost, but also the weight of the stone steeple on the marshy ground beneath. The end result is extraordinary. The steeple appears dumpy and compressed and even to the untutored eye it smacks of the amateur enthusiast rather than the gifted professional. Notwithstanding these unhappy adaptations to local conditions, the church was widely admired. Agg made a fortune and returned to England, but the church was altered again at least twice, in 1797 and 1811. The main entrance was moved to the west end under the spire and the original vestibule was abolished. A carriage porch was added to the west end, a ramp to the east end, and deep colonnaded verandahs were placed on the north and south sides to reduce glare and heat after

St John's Church designed by James Agg in 1787 showing the dumpy stone steeple and spire, the entire fourth tier having been omitted. Verandahs were added in 1797 after ladies complained of glare and heat.

The Rohilla Monument in St John's Church burial ground. The frieze is enriched with triglyphs, bucrania, and shields.

ladies complained of the power of the sun. Further mutilations were perpetrated, perhaps the worst being the addition of Corinthian capitals to the Doric columns in the nave in 1811 and the removal of the galleries in 1901.

The artist Zoffany provided a painting of the Last Supper as a new altarpiece for the church. It aroused an enormous controversy as the figures depicted were all portraits of well-known Calcutta residents, and there has been much speculation since as to who is who. The walls are lined with a number of fine marble monuments, but the most interesting lie in the burial ground outside. Here rests Job Charnock the founder of Calcutta, beneath his octagonal tomb, and also Curzon's replica of Holwell's monument. Erected in 1817 to commemorate those killed in the Rohilla War of 1794, the Rohilla Monument is a domed cenotaph carried on twelve Doric columns with a frieze enriched with triglyphs, and shields. A fine neo-classical pavilion over fifty feet high, it is closely based on Sir William Chambers's Temple of Æolus at Kew, but with the same martial qualities as the Cornwallis rotunda in Madras. There is a lovely white chunam shrine to Begum Johnson, the grandmother of the Earl of Liverpool, who died in 1812 at the age of 87, outliving her four husbands. She was the matriarch of Calcutta society when she died, with a clear memory of the earliest days of the English. Her conversation 'abounded in anecdote and fascinated all who paid homage to her.' Her tomb is truly delightful – an open pavilion pierced by Venetian arches. When she died the old burial ground was reopened especially for her, and the Governor-General led the funeral procession in his state coach.

Throughout the late 18th and early 19th century most European burials took place in South Park Street Cemetery in Chowringhee and today it looks much the same as when Maria Graham visited it in 1812: 'Many acres covered so thick with columns, urns and obelisks that there scarcely seems to be room for another and the greater number buried here are under five and twenty years of age!' It is a haunting place, like some Imperial city of the dead, and even in death the ostentatious display of power and wealth persists. In spite of all the surface grandeur, life for Europeans was precarious and always shadowed by the prospect of sudden death. Life for many was just two monsoons, and the constant repetitive misery of losing friends and loved ones etched itself deep into the Imperial consciousness. One of the most striking impressions is the high mortality amongst children and women, many of whom married at the age of fifteen or sixteen, only to die of disease or in childbirth before their seventeenth birthday. Sir William Hunter wrote: 'The price of British rule in India has always been paid with the lives of little children.'

To Sophia Goldbourne, who arrived in 1785, the Land of Regrets was aptly named. She wrote home of Park Street: 'Alas, Arabella, the Bengal burying grounds bear a melancholy testimony to the truth of my observations on the short date of existence in this climate. Obelisks and pagodas are erected at great expense; and the whole spot is surrounded by as well-turned a walk as those you traverse in Kensington Gardens.' An anonymous poem of 1811 was more direct:

The pedimented tomb of John Garstin,
architect of Calcutta Town Hall and
the Gola in Patna.

For not in quiet English fields
Are these, our brothers, lain to rest,
Where we might deck their broken shields
With all the flowers the dead love best.

For some are by the Delhi walls,
And many in the Afghan land,
And many where the Ganges falls
Through seven mouths of shifting sand.

Park Street Cemetery resembles an Imperial city of the dead,
an extraordinary repository of funerary sculpture based on
English neo-classical works.

> I hate the grounds with pyramids oppressed,
> Where ashes moulder in sepulchral rest,
> Where long effusions of the labouring pen
> Weep o'er the virtues of the best of men.

Architecturally the cemetery is a fascinating repository of neo-classical funerary sculpture in the form of pyramids, pavilions and temples without parallel in England. Many echo the designs of William Chambers and the Adam brothers and are richly imbued with the classical symbols of death – the fragmented obelisk, the urn, the pyramid and on one decayed slab, Thanatos, the genius of Death with his inverted torch depicting the flame of life snuffed out.

The sheer scale of the tombs is impressive. There is a huge pyramid standing on a low pedimented podium – the final resting place of Elizabeth Barwell, a society beauty of such popularity that, confidentially, she accepted twelve separate invitations to a fancy dress ball and asked each suitor to wear an outrageous costume. They all arrived attired in an identical shade of pea-green, but the joke was accepted and, we are told, she danced with them all. She died in 1779. The most famous monument and one of the most original is a spiral column enriched with roses, to Rose Aylmer. The elegy written in her memory by Walter Savage Landor, the poet who loved her, was added to her tomb much later, but it poignantly describes the human misery, the waste of young lives, which was so often the price of Empire:

> Ah, what avails the sceptred race!
> Ah, what the form divine!
> What every virtue, every grace!
> Rose Aylmer, all were thine.
>
> Rose Aylmer, whom these wakeful eyes
> May weep, but never see
> A night of memories and of sighs
> I consecrate to thee.

She died of dysentery in 1800, aged 20, and the distraught poet lingered on, for sixty-four empty years. Hers is just one of the two million European graves which lie in this land.

When Lord Valentia visited Calcutta in 1803 he considered 'the hearts of the British in this country seem expanded by opulence: they do everything on a princely scale.' His views were influenced by the splendour of the inaugural ceremony for the opening of the new

(Left) *Pyramid tomb of Elizabeth Barwell.* (Right) *The famous spiral monument to Rose Aylmer.*

Government House, which had been built by the Governor-General, the Earl of Mornington, the future Marquess Wellesley and elder brother of the Duke of Wellington.

Wellesley had arrived in India in 1798. A departure from previous incumbents of the post, he was a highly cultured aristocrat at ease in the sophisticated grand salons of Europe. He was affronted by the 'stupidity and ill-bred familiarity of Calcutta Society'. His first step towards transforming the whole tone and emphasis of his position from that of 'primus inter pares' to a quasi-monarchical role was the creation of the most splendid Georgian building in India, exceeding even Lord Clive's new edifice, then in the process of construction in Madras.

His predecessors, including Warren Hastings and Cornwallis, had lived in a variety of houses. Some used the Fort House in Fort William which survives in a much altered form as the Outram Institute. When not in use by the Governor-General, it was occupied by the officer commanding Fort William and after 1803 it was used occasionally as a residence for state guests. In 1823 Bishop Heber stayed there and left a detailed description which accurately portrays a typical house interior of the period:

> The house consisted of a lofty and well-proportioned hall, 40 feet by 25 feet, a drawing room of the same length, and six or seven rooms, all on the same floor, one of which served as a chapel, the lower storey being chiefly occupied as offices or lobbies. All these rooms were very lofty with many doors and windows on every side; the floor of plaister, covered with mats; the ceilings of bricks, plaistered also, flat, and supported by massive beams, which were visible from the rooms below, but being painted neatly, had not at all a bad effect. Punkhas, large frames of light wood covered with white cotton, and looking not unlike enormous fire-boards, hung from the ceilings of the principal apartments, to which cords were fastened, which were drawn backwards and forwards by one or more servants, so as to agitate and cool the air very agreeably. The walls were white and unadorned, except with a number of glass lamps filled with cocoanut oil, and the furniture, though sufficient for the climate, was scanty in comparison with that of an English house. The beds instead of curtains had mosquito nets; they were raised high from the ground and very hard, admirably adapted for a hot climate.

However, the Fort House was used rarely, the principal residence being Old Government House on the Esplanade which was a rented two-storey building with an arcaded frontage set behind an open courtyard, enclosed on two sides by single-storey wings. The house was set on a rusticated podium and had a shallow pyramidal roofed belvedere, probably a bedroom for use in hot weather. It is depicted in illustrations with balustraded parapets punctuated with dies and urns.

Wellesley considered these existing facilities wholly inadequate and complained to the Court of Directors that 'the Apartments ... were inferior to the apartments in the most ordinary houses of individuals, exposing the health of the Governor-General to the most serious injury from the effects of the climate.' He went on to berate the lack of suitable rooms for public entertainment and even for family accommodation, and argued that the rent far exceeded the value of the building.

Within a month of his arrival the Engineer Officer, Captain Charles Wyatt, and Edward Tiretta, the Civil Architect, were instructed to prepare plans, and the Chief Engineer, Major General Cameron, to furnish estimates. Tiretta, was a free-booting Italian who had been an associate of the notorious Jacopo Casanova. As a result of his amorous adventures Europe had become too hot for him and he drifted to India, where we are told 'he became, in turns, respectable, versatile, wealthy and bankrupt'. For many years he held the post of Superintendent of Streets and Buildings or Civil Architect to the Company and he was responsible for numerous public buildings including the remodelling of St John's Church in 1811. Fortunately Wyatt's designs were preferred to Tiretta's, but the Civil Architect retained a close involvement in the construction of the new edifice.

Wyatt hailed from a great family of English architects. He was born in 1758, the son of William, elder brother of the famous James Wyatt, and he entered the army in 1780. He arrived in India in 1782 and by 1800 he had risen to Captain and Commander of Police and, by 1803, Superintendent of Public Works.

Wyatt's scheme was adapted from Kedleston Hall in Derbyshire, which had been built by Robert Adam between 1759 and 1770, on the basis of earlier designs prepared by James Paine. Wyatt's choice of model for the new Government House was not fortuitous. His uncle, Samuel, had supervised Kedleston's erection, and undoubtedly Wyatt had access to the detailed designs which had been published in Robert Adam's *Works of Architecture, Vitruvius Britannicus* and most current text books on architecture.

Government House in about 1870. Built by Charles Wyatt for the Earl of Mornington, elder brother of the future Duke of Wellington, it is based on Kedleston Hall, Derbyshire.

Although inspired by Kedleston, Wyatt's designs were not a muted plagiarism of the original, but a thoroughly worked out conception well-adapted to the vicissitudes of the Bengal climate. The similarities are obvious – the basic shape, plan and dimensions, the central block with quadrant corridors linked to corner pavilions, the domed bow on the garden frontage, and the concentration of state rooms in the main block are all common elements. However, the Calcutta house has wide verandahs, a semi-circular projecting portico and colonnade on the south front and, more importantly, it has all four pavilions rather than the two completed at Kedleston. The corridors linking the central block with the pavilions are full height, whereas at Kedleston they are two-storeyed and subordinated to the mass of the principal central range and pavilions. Overall the use of painted plaster creates a quite different character from the textural subtlety of Derbyshire sandstone.

Internally the major difference is the absence of any grand staircase at Calcutta and the substitution of four small staircases in each corner of the main block, a mean arrangement which attracted great criticism. The satirist, Sir Charles D'Oyly, wrote in *Tom Raw the Griffin*:

> In such a palace one might have expected
> A splendid staircase, as at home we find
> In noble edifices well erected,
> And made in spacious turns and sweeps to wind,
> But here, forsooth, there's nothing of the kind.
> It certainly a strange and very rare case is,
> One must suppose the architect was blind,
> When there was so much room, and lots of spare places
> To build four little dingy miserable staircases.

The dome over the south portico was added in about 1814 to increase the impact of the elevation, but in its original form it was not very successful and it too fell foul of D'Oyly's caustic wit:

> One word about the dome – 'tis so superior
> In every way to domes of brick and stone.
> It covers nought below! but ripens sherry or
> Madeira – a wood box, perched up alone,
> To aid proportion and for dumpiness to stone.

In 1824 it was replaced by a shallow dome crowned by a figure of Britannia with spear and shield but this was struck by lightning and eventually a new cast-iron structure was added in 1852. The dome is entirely decorative, but it does provide a point of balance to the south elevation which might otherwise be regarded as excessively horizontal. Lord Elgin added a small gallery to crown the summit in 1863, but as late as Curzon's time it was used as a store for timber. Indeed Curzon had the unique distinction of having resided in both houses and considered that 'the differences greatly exceed the points of identity', and that there was no comparison between Calcutta and the exquisite Adam detailing at Kedleston. Nevertheless Curzon loved Calcutta and

The south-east frontage of Government House by J. F. Bordwine shows the ornamental dome which so amused Sir Charles D'Oyly.

paid for several improvements to the building out of his own pocket. The balustraded parapet was enhanced by the provision of urns, the tympanum to the north front was filled with the royal coat of arms, and the original arms on the south front, with 'both the lion and the unicorn transcending all bounds even of oriental imagination', were replaced by cast-iron devices from Macfarlanes of Glasgow. It was Curzon too who first painted the house white instead of the dirty umber or yellow which had been preferred, and which accounted for early references to similarities with St Petersburg.

The new building was set in its own extensive twenty-six acre compound and the principal approaches were adorned with monumental neo-classical gateways which recall Adam's screen at Syon House. These four external gateways comprise masonry arches surmounted by sculptured lions and sphinxes, which were made locally in wood by a carver called Woolaston. Later these were replaced in brick and plaster. It is alleged that the sphinxes were rather amply endowed and that their plaster breasts were cut off on the orders of an ADC who thought Lord Wellesley might be shocked at their over-exuberance, but if the story is true, it is more likely that the reference is to the sphinxes flanking the northern staircase which are far more prominent.

The concept of monumental gateways added to the imperial flavour of the design and provided impressive vistas from the surrounding streets. The idea proved influential and they were copied for government houses elsewhere in India, notably at the Residency in Hyderabad and at Mysore, where similar screens survive.

Originally the compound was bare. In 1818 Lord Hastings imported the best Bayswater gravel for surfacing but it remained devoid of vegetation until the late 19th century when Lord and Lady Mayo and the Northbrooks implemented a proper planting scheme, which improved privacy and amenity at the expense of architectural impact on the city.

The interior of the building is striking. The ceremonial steps on the north front lead to the first of three state apartments on two floors: the Breakfast or Tiffin Room resembling a gallery, which was used for informal gatherings with screens of columns at either end; a similar room, later the Throne Room, balances the south front; and the two are

66

joined by the Marble Hall designed on the model of a Roman atrium and used as a state dining room. The plan repeats on the floor above with a spectacular ballroom enriched with an Ionic order. The southern wings were used as private apartments, one northern wing as a Council Chamber and one for guests.

The building is beautifully functional with vistas in all directions — straight through the principal rooms and curved along the corridors. The ceilings have simple painted beams and, in the principal rooms, coffering to designs prepared by H. H. Locke of the Calcutta School of Art, which replaced the original canvas ceilings in 1865. Affinities to Kedleston recur — in particular a line of busts of twelve Caesars. Their origins are obscure but they were a familiar ornamental theme in Palladian houses of the 18th century. The ballroom is the most spectacular space in the house and it was here that the great state balls were held, including the inaugural ball attended by Lord Valentia in January 1803. Valentia described the scene vividly:

> The state rooms were for the first time lighted up. At the upper end of the largest was placed a very rich Persian carpet, and in the centre of that, a musnud of crimson and gold, formerly composing part of the ornaments of Tippoo Sultan's throne. On this was a rich chair and stool of state, for Lord Wellesley ... About ten, Lord Wellesley arrived ... The dancing then commenced, and continued till supper. The room was not sufficiently lighted up, yet still the effect was beautiful. The rows of chunam pillars, which supported each side, together with the rest of the room, were of shining white, that gave a contrast to the different dresses of the company. Lord Wellesley wore the Orders of St Patrick, the Crescent in diamonds. Many of the European ladies were richly ornamented with jewels ... The side of the citadel facing the palace was covered with a blaze of light, and all the approaches were lined with lamps suspended from bamboos.

The ballroom was renowned for its mirrors and glass chandeliers, some of which were purchased from the sale of General Claude Martin's

Entrance screen, Government House: Architectural allegory — the British lion triumphant.

The ballroom, Government House. Scene of the inaugural ball and countless state occasions showing the chandeliers which once decorated Claude Martin's fantastic palace-tomb at Lucknow. The coffered plaster ceiling replaced the original canvas one in 1865.

effects and taken from his fantastic palace of Constantia at Lucknow. Miss Emma Roberts noted in 1835: 'handsome sofas of blue satin damask are placed between the pillars, and floods of light are shed through the whole range from a profusion of cut glass chandeliers and lustres.'

Although the new house was generally admired, opinions varied widely. Lord Valentia was firmly in favour:

> The sums expended upon it have been considered as extravagant by those who carry European ideas and European economy in to Asia, but they ought to remember that India is a country of splendour, of extravagance and of outward appearance; the Head of a mighty Empire ought to conform himself to the prejudices of the country he rules over . . . In short I wish India to be ruled from a palace, not from a country house; with the ideas of a Prince, not with those of a retail-dealer in muslins and indigo.

This was clearly a passing swipe at the mercantile ethos of the

68

A view of the eastern Esplanade in 1859.

Company. Bishop Heber, always damning with faint praise, thought it 'narrowly missed being a noble structure', dismissed the columns as 'in a paltry style', and concluded 'it has three storeys, all too low, and is too much pierced with windows on every side.' Miss Emma Roberts considered 'it is altogether, whatever may be the fault of its details, a splendid pile.' The architectural historian James Fergusson was well qualified to judge its qualities in a more detached way in 1873. Although he complained of the 'solecism of the order running through two storeys, while standing on a low basement', he concluded 'but, taken altogether there are few modern palaces of its class either more appropriate in design, or more effective in their architectural arrangement and play of light and shade, than this residence.'

Notwithstanding the architectural nuances of the design, the Directors of the East India Company were the most astringent of all critics. Fury at the extravagance and at Wellesley's high-handed style of government led to his recall in July 1805. They maintained they had been kept in total ignorance of the project and its colossal expense (£167,359) but there was little they could do from such a distance. The house was open and in use by the time Wyatt presented the plans in London in October 1804, but a protracted row broke out over financial accountability, which rumbled on long after Wellesley's recall.

The erection of Government House was of seminal importance in the history of Calcutta for it created a focus for the subsequent development of the city. A whole series of classical perspectives were formed with vistas terminated by prominent public buildings and monuments. European ideas of planning, townscape and layout were imposed on an Asian city on a scale which had never before been witnessed, and which was to give Calcutta its name 'city of palaces'. The scale of Government House with its huge open compound, the monumental entrance screens and the grandeur of its colonnaded façades created a centrepiece for the subsequent development of the city and a magnificent focus for British power in India. British aims were no longer mercantile but overtly Imperial.

Mrs Maria Graham arrived in 1809: 'We felt that we were approaching a great capital. On landing I was struck with the general appearance of grandeur in all the buildings; not that any of them are according to the strict rules of art, but groups of columns, porticos, domes and fine gateways, interspersed with trees and the broad river crowded with shipping, made the whole picture magnificent.'

St Andrew's Kirk was designed to close one of the newly-created vistas down Old Court House Street. Placed symmetrically on the axis it was deliberately intended to be a focus in the townscape to upstage the nearby Anglican Church of St John's. The rivalry between Dr Bryce of the Kirk and the Bishop of Calcutta was intense. Bishop Middleton used his influence to prevent the Kirk from obtaining government sanction for a spire. Bryce had travelled with Middleton from England and found him even worse than his other main enemy, the 'prickly heat', and he retorted by declaring he would have a steeple higher than St John's on which a cock would be placed to crow over the Bishop. He succeeded in spite of government opposition and the parlous financial state of the Kirk.

Ironically St Andrew's owes much of its architectural inspiration to St John's, which was widely admired in spite of its architectural and functional deficiencies. The Doric order and frieze are similar, but the steeple is a more successful adaptation of Gibbs's original prototype, and altogether it is a more coherent architectural statement than the loose amalgam of classical detail which characterises St John's. Built by Messrs Burn, Currie & Co, it was opened in March 1818. An early engraving by James Fraser shows its original impact with the entrance portico standing proud of the monotonous façade of Writers' Buildings, a welcome punctuation of the townscape.

The Palladian style, which had been so eloquently expressed in Wellesley's new Government House, continued to prevail and when in 1804 a lottery was held to fund a new Town Hall on the site of the Old Court House, it is no surprise to find that a Tuscan-Doric style was used, firmly in the Palladian tradition. It was designed with a large first-floor saloon for public entertainments and organised meetings with supper and card rooms on the ground storey. The architect was Colonel John Garstin, Chief Engineer for Bengal, whose tomb is preserved in Park Street Cemetery. The building was fraught with problems. During construction the portico collapsed and huge cracks developed in the walls. Two years after its opening in 1813 the ballroom floor developed a spring and the pillars began to crack again. The foundations were blamed, probably rightly, as semi-fluid quicksand caused a history of building collapses in the area. It was overhauled at Garstin's expense in 1818, but he was lampooned by Sir Charles D'Oyly:

When pillars bulged, and their foundations gave
And the Great builder (not to be disgraced)
Commenced anew, folks still were heard to rave
And shunned its tottering walls, as one would shun the grave.

The building complemented Government House and it reflects the adaptation of the Palladian style to an Indian context. The south front has a monumental elegant façade set on a low plinth with the by now characteristic hexastyle portico facing the Maidan. The north portico serves as a carriage entrance.

During the 1820s a number of buildings were erected in India for the purpose of producing a more uniform currency. In Calcutta the new

St Andrew's Kirk, consecrated in 1818.

The hexastyle portico of John Garstin's Town Hall, one of the finest buildings of the period. Its demolition has been agreed.

71

complex marked a substantial departure from the Palladian tradition. The Silver Mint was designed in the latest Greek Revival style, a neo-classical composition creating a striking impact of mass and power. The building is square in plan with a quadrangle in the centre. After the structural failure of the nearby Town Hall, it was built to last with as much brickwork below the soil as above. It was designed by Major W. N. Forbes and took six years to complete, longer than Government House. The building stands on a high platform or stylobate which enhances its impact. The central portico, a copy in half size of the Temple of Minerva in Athens, is set forward from the colonnaded wings, but the authenticity of the building is let down by its clumsy detailing, and in particular, by the manner in which the junction between the abacus and architrave is fudged. In fact the detailing is far crisper on the Mint Master's house opposite, which is a delightful little Greek bungalow with columns in antis enclosing a central verandah. This house demonstrates perfectly two common concessions to the climate – green painted louvred screens between the columns, and *jhilmils*, projecting wooden fretwork canopies over the windows, which have no glass, just louvred shutters.

Given the usual time-lag between European and Indian fashions, the Greek Revival reached India early, but it remained influential for some time. One of the best examples in Calcutta is Metcalfe Hall started in 1840 and opened in 1844. It was founded in honour of Sir Charles Metcalfe, officiating Governor-General between 1835 and 1836, to

The Mint Master's house, facing the old Silver Mint, is a remarkable Greek Revival bungalow. Note the fretwork valances and louvred shutters to the windows.

house the Agricultural and Horticultural Society and the Calcutta Public Library. Later it was intended by Lord Curzon to house the Imperial Library. The building takes the form of a Greek temple with the portico to the principal west front being copied straight from the Tower of the Winds in Athens. The design was chosen by the architect C. K. Robison for its lightness and durability. Colonnades surround the building on three sides, but much of its original impact has been lost by the erection of a high boundary wall which truncates the principal elevations and screens the building.

The conscious pursuit of the Picturesque continued throughout the early 19th century and the classical vistas of Calcutta were progressively enriched with monuments and statuary combining visual amenity with Imperial dignity. In 1824 the northern view from Government House was closed by a stone screen enriched with a beautifully detailed Greek portico enclosing a marble statue of the Marquess of Hastings by John Flaxman. This structure had no functional purpose but was part of a deliberate policy of imparting Imperial grandeur to the capital. In 1866 it was incorporated into the Dalhousie Institute, an Imperial Valhalla, since demolished. A vast column 152 feet high, was raised on the Maidan in honour of Sir David Ochterlony, who had served in every Indian war from the time of Clive onwards, culminating in the conquest of Nepal in 1816. Designed by J. P. Parker in 1828 it is an extraordinary affair – an attenuated Greek Doric column standing on an Egyptian-style plinth and crowned by an upper stage derived from Syrian precedents with a metal cupola of Turkish origin. Inside a circular stone stair winds upward to two narrow viewing platforms.

These major focal points were complemented by public statuary to British figures. Since Independence most have been relocated in the

Metcalfe Hall: The west front is based on the Tower of the Winds in Athens. This fine Greek Revival building is now neglected, the facades truncated by a high boundary wall. C. K. Robison, City magistrate and architect of Metcalfe Hall, is typical of the enlightened amateurs responsible for many British buildings. The book on the table is a copy of Stuart & Revett's Antiquities of Athens, *a standard reference work on Greek architecture.*

vicinity of the Victoria Memorial. The most eminent sculptors of the time were commissioned and works by Westmacott, Thomas Woolner, Onslow Ford, and J. H. Foley are common. Westmacott's statue of Lord William Bentinck is particularly noteworthy for its effusive inscription to this evangelical radical who abolished suttee. The lower panel depicts a widow-burning ceremony and it is inscribed:

The Ochterlony column designed by J. P. Parker in 1828.

> Who during seven years
> Ruled India with eminent providence,
>   integrity and benevolence,
> Who, placed at the head of a great empire,
>   Never laid aside
> The simplicity and moderation of
>   a private citizen.
> Who never forgot that the end of Government
>   Is the welfare of the governed,
>   Who abolished cruel rites,
> Who effaced humiliating distinctions,
> Who allowed liberty to the expression of
>   Public opinion
> Whose constant study it was to elevate
>   The moral and intellectual character of the
>   Nation committed to his charge.

Lord William Bentinck's statue by Richard Westmacott. The bronze panel depicts a suttee. Bentinck remains highly-regarded in India.

Ironically Bentinck's cultivation of a low-key gubernatorial style so outraged local society that he was compared by one observer to a 'Pennsylvania Quaker', but he did encourage wealthy Indians to sponsor public works. As a result there is a handsome Doric colonnade erected by Raj Chandra Das at Babu's Ghat on the river front. An Ionic pavilion was raised by private subscription at another ghat or landing point to commemorate James Prinsep, the Orientalist.

Bentinck's low-key style remained the exception rather than the rule and, in its accentuation of the martial qualities which underlay the foundation of the Raj, Lord Ellenborough's Gwalior Monument of 1847 is much more typical. This is faced in Jaipur marble and crowned by a cupola made from the metal of guns seized from the enemy during the 1843 war. It was designed by Colonel Goodwyn of the Bengal Engineers. Perhaps the most high-handed expression of these qualities was the dismantling of an entire pagoda from Prome in Burma in 1854 and its trans-shipment and re-erection in Eden Gardens, as a memorial to the First Burmese War. The most eccentric manifestation was Lord Curzon's remodelling of the gardens at the northern end of the Maidan on the plan of the Union Jack.

One of the best-known buildings of the mid-19th century is La Martinière School. The girls' school was designed around a remodelled 18th-century house complete with elephant porch, but in 1835 the boys' school was erected to the designs of J. P. Parker and Captain Hutchinson, a military engineer. It is a rectangular block with Ionic columns which could have been taken straight from Nash's Regent's Park. Faced in chunam, there is a central rotunda now lacking its original dome, with two-storey wings terminating in higher pavilions. The style of public buildings remained firmly in the classical tradition with the ubiquitous use of chunam over a rough brick core. However, by the mid-19th century the heaviness of touch which characterised many of the earlier 18th-century public buildings had been overcome, and over the past hundred years public buildings had multiplied alongside private houses to create a spectacular Imperial capital which engendered civic pride. But there was another side to the city, an appalling underworld of poverty and despair which Kipling portrayed in 'The City of Dreadful Night', where thousands of people slept each night in the gutters outside the palaces of the rich. This was the darker side of mercantile wealth, urban squalor breeding pestilence and disease, the harrowing human price paid by the poor in the 19th century, from Birmingham to Bengal. It was as much a part of the reality of the city as the glittering balls and the sumptuous ceremonial.

> Me the Sea-captain loved, the River built,
> Wealth sought and Kings adventured life to hold.
> Hail England! I am Asia – Power on silt
> Death in my hands, but Gold!

CHAPTER 4

CANTONMENT AND RESIDENCY

By the late 18th century the British controlled such large areas of India that a new military strategy was evolved based on the rapid deployment of troops and artillery. This had profound consequences for settlement patterns and for the actual form and layout of urban areas. The concentration of troops in city centres was replaced by separate camps, cantonments, on the periphery of the main cities. From 1800 onward real military power resided in the tree-lined avenues and neatly clipped compounds of these suburban settlements rather than in the formidable bastions of the city forts, which were reduced to mere symbols of Imperial power. It was no coincidence that in the Great Mutiny of 1857 the British were invested not in their old fortified strongholds, but amongst the bungalows and residencies of the European quarters. The origin of cantonments may have been dictated by military necessity, but they had a profound impact on the whole social and spatial structure of British India. They represented the first stage in the physical separation of the rulers and ruled which characterised the Raj; a phenomenon which at its best promoted an aloof incorruptible government and at its worst, arrogant ideas of racial superiority. Insulated from the teeming bazaars of the native quarters, cushioned from the chaos and squalor of native life, the British created a wholly separate existence which bore little relation to the real India. Thus the growth of the cantonment marks a parting of the ways between European and Indian societies. The easy-going familiarity and cultural and social miscegenation which characterised the early settlements was superseded, and the first steps were taken down the road of misunderstanding which led to the charnel house of 1857.

The concept of the cantonment arose from the Moghul practice of peripatetic government. Sir Thomas Roe had noted as early as 1616 that on tour the royal camp covered an area of twenty square miles and that it was organised like a town with regular streets where each nobleman or tradesman had his allotted place, topographically and socially. Like so many other institutions, the British merely adapted this established pattern of life to their own ends, and it suited the hierarchical nature of English society as well, if not better than Moghul India. In reality the actual cantonment was a petrified military camp. Indeed the early cantonments were little more than organised avenues of military tents, and in some areas they remained so when the military presence was likely to be temporary. However, where a permanent garrison was kept, tents soon gave way to thatched bungalows, which in turn were replaced by permanent facilities of mess-rooms, barracks, officers' bungalows, clubs and garrison churches.

Barrackpore cantonment in the 1870s showing individual bungalows and outhouses in separate compounds. The physical separation of the Europeans into their own cantonments fostered ignorance and racial arrogance as well as aloof incorruptibility.

The layouts and plans of British cantonments tend to differ in the juxtaposition of their constituent parts, but a common pattern may be discerned. Generally they lay five or six miles from the city which they guarded; between city and cantonment were placed the lines of the Indian regiments. This careful segregation of the Indian lines was far more common after the Mutiny had demonstrated the danger of billeting Indian troops within the European quarter. Within the cantonment the civil and military lines were usually kept apart. Most stations were laid out on a grid-pattern of spacious avenues lined with pretty classical bungalows. Each bungalow, designed with a verandah on three sides, was set in its own garden compound and shaded by bougainvillaea, climbing plants and elaborate trelliswork. Large open areas were laid out as parade grounds for drill and training, whilst the bigger garrisons had their own clubs, racecourses and parks. The focus for most cantonments was the church.

Agra and Benares have typical cantonment churches of a very similar design and pattern. Both are set in large grass enclosures studded with decaying monuments to forgotten men and women, and both follow the same architectural precedent with steeples based on St John's, Calcutta.

St George's, Agra was built in 1826 to the designs of Colonel J. T. Boileau, Royal Engineers, although the tower and spire were added later. Boileau and his brother were an eccentric pair. Many years later in Simla they astonished polite society by receiving the Commander-in-Chief at their house, each brother standing on his head beside the main

78

pillars of the central porch, like a pair of inverted statues. Surprisingly the church is conventional and restrained, the entrance being approached through a small vestibule with niches. The interior is divided into a central nave and side aisles by six Ionic columns carrying a slightly vaulted roof. The chancel at the east end has been Gothicised at a later date with a carved white sandstone screen, whilst the altar and reredos are enriched with the marble inlay work for which Agra is famous. The internal ornament is predictable – a heavy dentilled cornice to the nave and aisles and simple reeded architraves with corner rosettes to the doors and windows. Its interest lies in the external treatment. The aisles have louvred doors in the place of windows, a common enough expedient, but the alternating segmental and triangular pediments over each opening are applied straight onto the bare plasterwork like eyebrows, without any supporting pilasters, frieze or order beneath. At the west end the chancel wall is treated in a similar fashion with an implied portico, but it is all surface detail with no structural or functional role. The result is rather delightful; the contrast of white plaster ornament on yellow ochre walls accentuated by the glare of the Indian sun, the crisp horizontal emphasis of the parapet cornice, the repetitive rhythm of pediments to the window openings and the simple rectangular fanlights over, coalesce to form a composition of elegance and charm which would hold its own in Europe.

St Mary's, Benares is similar. The steeple, entablature and frieze are

(Above) *St George's, Agra: a typical cantonment church in Upper India designed by Colonel J. T. Boileau in 1826* (Below).

common themes, but St Mary's has a portico, clumsily infilled later. The external treatment of the aisles shows several important differences. The flank elevations are divided by pilasters into seven bays, the two outer bays having blind doorcases enriched with blocked surrounds and keystones in the manner of Gibbs, whilst the five central bays are played down, three with simple louvred doors beneath plain cornices alternating with two bays each with white plaster niches. Above each doorway is a rectangular fanlight protected from the glare of the sun by a plain timber canopy, a simple innocuous device, but one which has a major architectural impact. The frieze has been severed to accommodate each hood and their projection is thrown into sharper relief by the sun than is the case with the elaborate blocked doorways at each end.

Agra and Benares exhibit typical variations on the same ecclesiastical theme, which recurs in many of the up-country churches erected by the British in the early part of the nineteenth century. Nor was this just confined to Bengal. For instance St Mary's, Poona follows a similar pattern. Indeed the character, layout and ambience of the English cantonments share a common flavour, so that from Bangalore to Peshawar, and from Poona to Dum Dum the quintessential Englishness of it all shows through in spite of regional variations.

Barrackpore, fifteen miles from Calcutta, is different. Although it was founded as a cantonment in 1775, it was not typical as it housed the summer residence of the Governors-General. Unlike most cantonments Barrackpore grew up piecemeal in response to changing needs and circumstances. In the mid-1770s it comprised a few crude bungalows interspersed amongst tents, but within fifty years it had become a nerve-centre of the British Empire in India.

The importance of Barrackpore was due to the enthusiasm of Wellesley, who did so much to transform English interests in India from the solely mercantile to the Imperial. Not content with the extravagant expenditure on Government House, Calcutta, he was anxious to find a suitable residence for the hot season. In 1801 he took over the use of the Commander-in-Chief's bungalow, and Captain Charles Wyatt was appointed to supervise repairs and improvements. It is depicted by Henry Salt, the artist, as a simple villa with an Ionic portico, but it became unsafe and in 1804 Wellesley ordered a far more impressive structure to be built. Wellesley's vision of a summer residence was as grandiloquent as his concept for the new Government House. It is alleged that a grand avenue was planned to link the two houses. This is not proven, but he was responsible for planting an avenue of trees at twelve-foot centres all along the Grand Trunk Road from Calcutta to Barrackpore. In 1856 Lady Canning noted: 'The last ten or twelve miles of the road are as straight as an arrow and bordered all the way with beautiful trees, planted in Lord Wellesley's time, mango, banyan, indian-rubber, peepul-like white poplars – teak, with enormous leaves, laurel of several sorts, mimosas, tamarinds etc.' The avenue was devastated by a cyclone in 1864, but it was replanted subsequently, and it is visible to this day.

Wellesley's summer palace had only reached plinth height when he

was recalled to London by the Court of Directors for the extravagance of Government House. They were incensed when they heard of Barrackpore and its estimated cost of £50,000. Sir Charles D'Oyly in *Tom Raw* put it to verse:

> Wellesley first stampt it his. He was the boy
> For making ducks and drakes with public cash,
> Planned a great house that time might not destroy;
> Built the first floor, prepared brick, beam and sash,
> And then returned, and left it in this dismal hash.

The flank elevation of St Mary's, Benares, showing the blind doorcases and blocked surrounds. The frieze has been designed to accommodate the hooded ventilators.

The building lay a melancholy ruin for some years, before Lady Hastings built a conservatory on the site.

Barrackpore remained a favourite resort, and during the ten-year rule of Lord Hastings (1813–1823), one of Wellesley's temporary buildings was remodelled into a summer residence for the Governor-General. The architect was Captain Thomas Anbury, who had succeeded Wyatt; he created an imposing country mansion with a deep entrance portico of eight Tuscan columns on the north façade, and with colonnaded verandahs to the other three sides.

The house was never large and always lacked space for guests, who stayed in bungalows dispersed in the park. An immense drawing room occupied the *piano nobile*, designed for balls and receptions, and there was a dining room and billiards room. Although grandly conceived, the

The country retreat of the Governor-General at Barrackpore designed by Captain Thomas Anbury.

house always had an air of decrepitude with a shortage of suitable furniture. In the words of Emily Eden, Lord Auckland's sister, there were 'no glass windows in the lower storey, and there are no doors whatever to the interior of our part of the house – nothing but open jalousies and (this) spoils our comfort' . . . 'The furniture is worse than that of any London hotel.'

One of the greatest delights of the house was its setting, on an open sweep of the Hooghly with distant views of the Danish colony of Serampore on the opposite bank. Wellesley had enlarged and landscaped the park into an Arcadian vision. Great mounds of earth had been formed to break up the flat ground into an undulating landscape. A series of walks were laid out through gardens designed on English lines, each new incumbent of the house adding their own special contribution. Lord Hastings imported a marble basin and fountain, part of the Royal Baths from the palace at Agra. Lady Canning laid out an Italian garden and planted many more exotic species – bougainvillaea, convolvulus, palms and tropical plants, but the strangest feature of the park was the menagerie which provided amusement for many visitors. This had its origin in an abortive scheme of Wellesley's to form a Natural History Institution, but the animals ended up at Barrackpore. The cages in which the animals were kept were treated as ornamental garden features and were designed as neo-classical temples and pavilions, the water birds being kept in delightful Gothic arcades erected over tanks of water. In its heyday the park and grounds must have been an exotic sight. Bishop Heber confronted some lynxes being taken for a stroll in the park in 1823, whilst the elephant stud provided opportunities for evening rides along the river bank on beasts bedecked in magnificent state hangings of scarlet and gold.

Wellesley's pursuit of the Picturesque in the form of an English country retreat on the banks of the Hooghly was fulfilled by his successors, albeit on a less lavish scale and in a more relaxed form than he envisaged. Over the years a number of ancillary buildings and monuments were added to the grounds to enhance its attractions. From the earliest days the round semaphore tower was a conspicuous feature of the grounds, part of a chain of stations for signalling up-river, but the first Lord Minto provided a more elegant and evocative monument in the form of a Greek temple dedicated to the twenty-four officers who had fallen in the conquest of Java and the Île de France (Mauritius) between 1810 and 1811. The Temple of Fame, as it is known, was designed by George Rodney Blane in about 1815. The ends are pedimented hexastyle Corinthian porticos, and the flanks have colonnades of a similar order. The memorial chamber is a simple barrel vault with four black tablets and wall panels commemorating the fallen. With its inscription 'To the Memory of the Brave', it is reminiscent of an 'Heroum' of the Ancient World, but one transplanted to an Oriental setting of palm trees and lush tropical vegetation. Since its erection a plaque has been added to commemorate the battles of Maharajpur and Pannier in the Gwalior Campaign of 1843. Recently the Indian authorities have re-erected some of the discarded equestrian statues from Calcutta on brick plinths alongside the Temple, a remarkably sensitive and practical solution to the problem posed by Imperial statuary in a post-Imperial world. Here on the banks of the Hooghly stand King George V, Peel, Minto, Mayo, Lansdowne, Roberts, Woodburn and Lord Napier of Magdala, assembled as if about to participate in some Viceregal handicap. Napier's statue has a replica at Queen's Gate, London.

One of the most poignant monuments of all is the grave of Lady Charlotte Canning, who died at Calcutta on 18th November 1861 at the age of 44. This sweet and charming lady contracted malaria whilst returning from Darjeeling across the fever-ridden Terai. It was decided to lay her to rest in the gardens she loved and which she had done so much to enhance. Her distraught husband haunted the grave day and

(Above) *Barrackpore: The circular semaphore tower, one of a chain of stations for signalling up-river.*
(Left) *The Temple of Fame, Barrackpore, commemorates those who fell in the conquest of Java and Mauritius. The statue in the foreground is of Field Marshal Lord Roberts of Kandahar. King George V may be glimpsed between the columns on the right of the picture.*

The pedimented front elevation of the Temple of Fame recalls the memorials of classical antiquity.

night in an anguish of despair. He died seven months later and lies in Westminster Abbey, 7,000 miles from his devoted wife and companion. The delicacy of feeling shown by the Indian authorities is such that Canning's statue has been moved from Calcutta to Barrackpore, where he stands on a newly-erected pedestal overlooking his wife's grave, a fitting tribute to a man whose clemency did much to reunite India and to salve the wounds inflicted by the Mutiny.

Lady Canning's distinctive memorial crowned by the cross of St Andrew is a replica. The original designed by George Gilbert Scott on a theme suggested by her sister Louisa, Lady Waterford was transferred to St Paul's Cathedral, Calcutta, and thence to St John's Church where it stands in the north portico, the beautiful marble inlay work pitted by the monsoon rains. The original iron enclosure to the tomb, designed from the intertwined initials of her name (C.C.), survives at Barrackpore.

Today Barrackpore has lost much of its original character. The house is used as a police hospital. The great drawing room is a typhoid ward, where a scoreboard shows the number of patients, recoveries and deaths, like some bizarre cricket match:

> For when the One Great Scorer comes
> To write against your name
> He marks — not that you won or lost —
> But how you played the game.

The marble fountain from Agra is cracked and ruinous, the house dilapidated and the grounds given over to the police and army. But it's all still there — The Temple of Fame, the bungalows, the Great Banyan

tree from which the first mutineer Mangal Pande was hanged, and even the memorial to *Myall King*, Lord William Beresford's racehorse, three times winner of the Viceroy's Cup, Calcutta, who died on the racecourse in 1893 and who lies in the garden of Lord Kitchener's former bungalow.

The grave of Lady Charlotte Canning beside the Hooghly river, designed by George Gilbert Scott in collaboration with her sister Louisa, Lady Waterford. The ornamental ironwork of her intertwined initials (C.C.) may be seen in the background.

With the expansion of British political power in the late 18th century, Europeans became a common sight throughout Bengal, Bihar and Orissa. They aroused no more interest than the numerous waves of conquerors who had preceded them. As the administrative and revenue-collecting arms of the Company were consolidated, European dwellings sprang up in rural areas and provincial towns to house a growing number of officials and merchants. In the early years most were content with simple vernacular dwellings, but their growing political and personal prestige coupled with the desire for European standards of comfort led to new residences on European lines.

In rural areas most follow a recognisable pattern based on the country residences outside Calcutta, a plain plastered rectangular block with an entrance portico and verandahs set in a large garden compound, but there are delightful exceptions. At Bankipur outside Patna there is a fine Gothick house with crenellated parapets, rusticated staircase towers and pointed arched windows decorated with hood moulds. The entrance portico is a beautiful hybrid, neither wholly European nor Indian in conception. In the mofussil often grander structures were built to convey the power and authority of the Company to the local population.

Benares, the religious centre of Hindu India, came under British control in 1775 and it delighted British antiquaries. One such man was

James Prinsep who was Assay Master to the Mint between 1820 and 1830. He was a gifted Orientalist and scholar with a profound interest in and respect for the astonishing architectural heritage of the city. He carefully surveyed many historic buildings and monuments and instigated a programme of restoration and repair. It was an important step in the interpenetration of two cultures, which fostered a fascinating exchange of cultural and artistic values. From 1815 onward the Indians learnt European painting techniques, depicting Hindu ceremonies and practices for the British, whilst the British acquired a far deeper knowledge of the complex social and religious customs of their subjects. One unusual result of this was the erection of an Indian well in the English village of Ipsden in the Chilterns. The Maharajah of Benares became a close friend of the Commissioner Edward Anderton Reade between 1846 and 1853. On Reade's retirement to England the Maharajah wanted to give to a charity and, recalling how Reade compared the water problems of Benares to his own native Chilterns, he donated funds for a well in his village. The cast-iron well, designed by Reade with a Saracenic dome, bears witness to the warmth of the personal relationships which often bridged the two cultures.

There are two typical buildings of the early 19th century in Benares — the Mint, designed by James Prinsep, and the Nandeswar Kothi opposite. The Mint has been altered extensively from Prinsep's original design and is now given over to a carpet showroom and airline offices, but interior details of the period survive including reeded architraves, raised and fielded six-panel doors and a few pretty chimneypieces with fluting and corner rosettes.

The Nandeswar Kothi stands in its own grounds opposite the former Mint and is owned by the Maharajah. King George V and Queen Mary stayed here in 1906, as the Prince and Princess of Wales, and the house has been altered little since. Today a new hotel and the shops of the bazaar have encroached upon the compound, but the interior lingers on in a state of splendid decay. The watercolours decorating the walls are spotted with mould, the pictures of the Viceroy Lord Lytton, turned yellow with age, whilst the drapes and hunting trophies are eaten by moth and worm. It was in this house that Mr Samuel Davis, the Judge and Magistrate, was besieged by the followers of Wazir Ali, the deposed Nawab of Oudh in January 1799. The mob killed the British resident nearby and attacked the house. The Judge sent his family on to the roof and successfully defended the staircase single handed with a spear, until the cavalry galloped to the rescue from the old cantonment.

If life could be precarious for up-country Europeans, it was far more so for the native cultivator, who often not only was oppressed by local native landowners and banias, or money-lenders, but also suffered from the unpredictable vicissitudes of the climate. Crop failure and famine were endemic and in the late 1770s this prompted Company intervention with the idea of erecting 'golas' or storehouses for grain for use in times of famine. Accordingly in 1786 a monumental conical structure was erected at Bankipur, near Patna.

The Gola is probably the most extraordinary building erected anywhere in the British Empire. It was designed by John Garstin, later

Nandeswar Kothi, Benares: Venetian window. The roof above was defended by Samuel Davis in 1799.

The Gola, Patna: Designed by John Garstin in 1786. The cantilevered stone platforms are resting places for sacks of grain on the long climb to the top.

Surveyor-General of Bengal and the architect of Calcutta Town Hall, but in 1786 a humble Captain of Engineers. He was born in Manchester Square, London and was one of the most gifted military engineers in India. His tomb in Park Street Cemetery, Calcutta is one of its finest surviving neo-classical monuments and it is a fitting tribute to a man whose work did much to raise the architectural quality of Anglo-Indian buildings.

The drawings of the Gola are preserved in the British Museum and they show a vast beehive-like structure over ninety feet high. The shape is conical with symmetrical spiral ramps up the outside to an opening at the top where the grain was thrown in. Cantilevered stone platforms recur every ten feet or so on which to rest the sacks of grain. The scale is gigantic – 426 feet round at the base, a diameter of 109 feet internally and walls over 12 feet thick. Murray's *Handbook to Bengal*, a fascinating repository of obscure facts, alleges that Prince Jang Bahadur of Nepal once rode a horse up the ramp to the summit, whilst inside 'a blow on a tin case there fills the air with a storm of sounds, which can be compared to nothing so well as to the hurtling of volleys of tent-pegs thrown from every quarter with great violence'. A contemporary of

Major-General John Garstin, Surveyor-General of Bengal, by John Opie.

88

Garstin's who visited the Gola in 1806 was more direct on its acoustics. 'It has so good an echo that it repeats 32 times', she noted.

Architecturally this bizarre structure has been compared to the superhuman, neo-classical visions of Nicholas Ledoux and the megalo-maniac schemes of his French associates, but this seems rather fanciful. Its importance lies in another direction. The symbolic beehive form is dictated by its function and it is entirely devoid of any superfluous ornament. Its origins probably lie in the circular godowns and conical storehouses which were once common in the area, but the scale has been transformed to the monumental. Whether or not Garstin was attempting to make any sort of architectural statement it is difficult to say, but it is unlikely that as a military engineer he was motivated by anything deeper than functional necessity. The building was rarely used, as it could not contain more than a day's ration for the local population, and the expansion of the chain used in the structure was a design fault which led to the cracking of the brick and plaster shell. Today it is as much a curiosity as when it was first built, but glimpsed from the river it is an evocative landmark and one well worth preservation. At sunrise the views from the summit are truly magnificent with distant prospects of the sails of the river traffic framed by the palm-fringed shores of the Ganges.

Imperialism implies control, but the Company tried where possible to consolidate its position through indirect influence rather than direct rule. Even at the height of the Raj, over two-fifths of India was administered by native princes. In the late 18th century Oudh and Hyderabad were regarded as the most important native allies where it was essential to maintain English suzerainty. The idea of a controlled native state was not new. It had influenced Clive in his handling of the situation in Bengal, and the French in Hyderabad,

The Nawabs of Oudh were renowned for their fabulous wealth and for their sybaritic court. In the last quarter of the 18th century the Nawab was Asaf-ud-daula, a man 'mild in manners, polite and affable in his conduct', possessing no great mental powers, but well-disposed towards the English. He was fascinated by the new technology of the age and expended over £200,000 each year on English goods, often with little idea of how they worked or should be displayed. 'Without taste or judgment, he was extremely solicitous to possess all that was elegant and rare ... and his museum was so ridiculously displayed, that a wooden cuckoo clock was placed close to a superb timepiece which cost the price of a diadem.'

During this crucial period of expansion and consolidation, an English Resident was maintained at the capital in Lucknow to advise and, where possible, to exert influence over foreign policy. The Nawab paid for and erected a splendid Residency as part of a wider programme of civic improvements, which reflected the magnificence of his court. He enjoyed over twenty palaces and a hundred gardens and parks. However, it was a Frenchman in the service of the Company who acted as its unofficial agent and who was responsible for maintaining a smooth relationship with the Court, often acting in trusted liaison between the Nawab and Resident. He was Major-General Claude

Colonel Mordaunt's Cockfight *by John Zoffany. Claude Martin is on the sofa, holding his calf.*

Martin, a charismatic figure, who served initially as a French soldier under Lally. After capture at Pondicherry in 1761 he formed a company of chasseurs and served the English East India Company. From 1760 onwards he worked for the Surveyor-General of Bengal in a variety of capacities and learnt a wide range of skills from ballistics and cartography, to engineering and architecture. Most engineer officers were expected to undertake a wide range of tasks, and many were more than adept in a variety of different fields out of sheer necessity. Thus when Martin retired from active service through ill-health in 1779 it is no surprise to find him as a watchmaker, gunsmith, balloonist, amateur diplomat, surveyor and architect with novel ideas on design and construction. In 1782 he was promoted to Lieutenant-Colonel by the Company for his efforts in dissuading the Nawab from supporting the rebellion by the Raja of Benares the year before. In 1784 we find him mediating between the Court and the Resident and indigo farming with the Frenchman De Boigne. As late as 1792 he returned to active service and served Cornwallis well in Mysore, for which he was made a full Colonel, before returning to Lucknow, where, by a combination of astute money lending and business acumen in the indigo trade, he amassed a huge fortune which he lavished on his two houses – the Farhad Baksh and Constantia.

Thomas Twining visited his town house, the Farhad Baksh, in January 1795:

> In the afternoon we were introduced to Colonel Martin, an officer who had acquired considerable celebrity in this part of India . . .

90

We found him in a large and elegant mansion, lately built by himself, on the banks of the Goomty ... The house had the appearance of a fortified castle, and was indeed constructed with a view to defence, with draw-bridges, loopholes and turrets, and water, when desired, all round ... The most handsome room was one which he had constructed over the river itself, the exterior walls resting upon pillars placed in the middle of the Goomty.

Claude Martin by Renaldi.

Today the Farhad Baksh is unrecognisable, having been extensively altered and incorporated into a later palace, but it does illustrate Martin's idiosyncratic tastes in architecture and an obsession with defence, which are the hallmarks of his surviving palace-tomb, Constantia. Constantia is an extravagant architectural fantasy in a city with a reputation for architectural exuberance. Today it houses La Martinière Boys' School, a foundation established from some of the proceeds of Martin's will. This adds a further bizarre dimension to the whole edifice, for the speech, slang, interests and uniforms of the boys are those of Edwardian Harrow or Eton. It was here that Kipling's boy-hero Kim was supposed to have been educated, but India hardly intrudes at all. Here is an English public school, endowed by a parvenu French General, and housed in a fabulous mausoleum in the heart of India. The names of the boy's houses – 'Hodson', 'Cornwallis', Lyons' and 'Martin' – evoke an ethos long since vanished from the mother country.

As a work of architecture it is a real hybrid, a disturbing restless building of the most peculiar design. Situated on an immense podium it is a symmetrical pile with an arcaded lower storey from behind which rises a huge central tower formed from four octagonal corner turrets linked by bridges. The first storey has corner pavilions and lines of sculpture figures in full silhouette on the skyline. Vast heraldic lions, taken from the Company coat of arms, loom over the ground storey, and the whole resplendent mass faces a large lake from the centre of which arises a substantial fluted pillar. The curved side wings were added in 1840, and these enhance the impact. Unfortunately flood precaution measures and a large earth dyke have severed the house from the lake, radically impairing the composition. The building was completed over thirty years after Martin's death by R. H. Rattray, but the Calcutta architect J. P. Parker supervised and it is no coincidence that the fluted column in the lake resembles the Ochterlony Column, for he designed them both.

Lord Valentia visited the house in 1803 and thought it:

A strange fantastical building of every species of architecture, and adorned with minute stucco fret-work, enormous red lions with lamps instead of eyes, Chinese mandarins and ladies with shaking heads, and all the gods and goddesses of heathen mythology. It has a handsome effect at a distance, from a lofty tower in the centre with four turrets; but on a nearer approach, the wretched taste of the ornament only excites contempt. A more extraordinary combination of Gothic towers, and Grecian pilasters, I believe was never before raised.

91

The interior is equally lavish. The original reception rooms are now used by the school as a library and chapel. They are covered in a riot of bastardised rococo ornament executed by imported Italian craftsmen. Hundreds of real Wedgwood plaques and bas reliefs are pegged into the plasterwork which is moulded into myriads of arcane shapes and devices, including Martin's own coat of arms. In the central tower the rooms are linked by a circular purdah gallery half-way up the walls. Martin devised his own ingenious air-cooling system. Great pillars run from the top to the bottom of the building in the centre of which are air shafts with holes to each room, allowing warm air to rise and cooler air to descend. Beneath the great podium lies the *tykhana*, a characteristic feature of houses in Oudh, a whole complex of underground rooms for use in the hot weather. These were provided beneath the new Residency built by the Nawab for the English Resident, but Thomas Twining believed them to be experimental when he visited Martin in 1795. The palace was still under construction. He was critical of the smoke and heat from the number of lamps needed to light the subterranean chambers, but Martin seemed undeterred and already he had planned to site his tomb there.

Martin died of bladder stone on 13th September 1800. His tomb lies beneath the tower in a vaulted chamber, approached through huge iron doors. Originally the stone figures of four life-size sepoys stood sentinel over the tomb, but these were destroyed in 1857 when the building was occupied by mutineers and Martin's bones were scattered. The bones were later reinterred, but the sepoys never resumed their silent vigil.

Martin is a mysterious figure, grown more so with the passage of time. Undoubtedly he acted as a sort of double agent in the interests of the Company, but spiritually he was a Renaissance man – a condottiere, artist, man of science, banker, engineer, craftsman and liberal benefactor. Even more strange is the vehement attack mounted on him after his death by Lord Valentia. In a scurrilous passage he wrote: 'a more infamous or despicable character than the late General Martin never

(Left) *Constantia, Lucknow: The fantastic palace-tomb of Claude Martin erected to his own peculiar designs. It now houses La Martinière School. The column was built by J. P. Parker after Martin's death.*

existed. He had not a single virtue, though he laboured to assume the appearance of several.' The precise reason for this vitriolic attack on Martin is unclear, but doubtless his Oriental lifestyle (he kept four wives) was partly to blame. There were also wild allegations about the origin of his wealth motivated as much by jealousy as anything else. His portraits by Zoffany, Chinnery and Renaldi show a person of refinement, a tall man with a fine figure, open countenance, and keen and vivacious eyes. The contents of his will bear witness to the essential goodness of his character. It is partly a profession of faith, and partly an apology for his life as well as a final testament. The greater part of his fortune went towards the foundation of educational institutions for boys and girls in Lucknow, Calcutta and Lyons, his home town, the rest went to a trust for the poor of all faiths in Calcutta, Lucknow and Chandernagore. He left handsome pensions for his wives and the many dependent women and children whom he took under his wing, who had been deserted or abandoned as orphans by Europeans, so the aura of impropriety that attaches to his name seems undeserved. Unfortunately his great library and art collection and much of his furniture were dispersed at auction on his death, the chandeliers from Constantia ending up in Government House, Calcutta.

If the Company owed its favoured position in Oudh to the work of the Resident and the court activities of Martin, at Hyderabad in the Deccan it owed as much to a similar charismatic figure, but one made in a very English mould. He was James Achilles Kirkpatrick.

Kirkpatrick was born in 1764 at Keston, near Bromley, Kent, the youngest of three brothers. Educated at Eton, he arrived in India as a cadet in 1779, but after ten years he was invalided home. His brother, Colonel William Kirkpatrick, was Resident at Hyderabad, and when James returned to India after convalescence he assumed a position on his brother's staff as translator to the Nizam. The post was important for Hyderabad was one of the largest native states – a fragment of the old Moghul Empire covering an area the size of mainland Britain with the Nizam at its head.

In 1797 William Kirkpatrick was relieved of duty through ill-health. His younger brother succeeded him, and over the next nine years he negotiated three important treaties. By a combination of personal charm, diplomatic guile and a lightning *coup de main* he prevailed upon the Nizam to replace his French troops with a British subsidiary force. In a dramatic confrontation with 14,000 French-trained sepoys and over 120 French officers, the Nizam's resolve wavered but Kirkpatrick retained his nerve and secured the surrender of the entire French force without bloodshed. With the French departure British suzerainty was established and the last major centre of French influence in Southern India vanished. For establishing effective British paramountcy, at minimal cost, and for removing a persistent nuisance from the British flank, Kirkpatrick was made an honorary aide-de-camp to the Governor-General.

Under his brother and his predecessors the Residency had been housed in a small villa and group of bungalows, but James Kirkpatrick

The former British Residency at Hyderabad with the Company's arms over the south front.

94

was given a sixty-acre site on the river Musi by the Nizam for a new house. It is alleged that when Kirkpatrick first presented his request for the site on a large-scale plan, the Nizam refused, as he did not understand scaled plans and thought that the Resident was asking for the entire Kingdom. When the plan was redrawn on a small card, the Nizam agreed immediately. An immense new house was begun in 1803. It was designed and supervised by Lieutenant Samuel Russell of the Madras Engineers, the son of the Royal Academician John Russell. Conceived in a Palladian style, the house stands as the centrepiece of a wider composition of arcaded walkways, colonnades, wings and stable buildings approached via a triumphal archway from the river frontage. The river approach is a formal processional route calculated to impress on the visitor the magnificence and power of the Resident. Something of its original splendour can be seen from an aquatint drawn by Captain Grindlay around 1813 showing a grand procession entering the Residency. The magnificent architecture, the slow ascending processional way from the river, the imposing entrance portico and the sumptuous interior exemplify the astonishing bluff by which the British maintained their Empire abroad. Paid for by the Nizam, the house was an architectural expression of supreme power intended for political ends. More than one contemporary argued that in a country where power was expressed outwardly and openly, the Company's hegemony could only be sustained by similar measures. In fact in 1811 the Resident wrote:

Major James Achilles Kirkpatrick by George Chinnery.

The splendour of a ceremonial procession approaching the Residency from the river, depicted by Captain Grindlay around 1813.

They can judge of power and authority by no other standard than the external marks of it; and if they saw a Resident with less state than his predecessor nothing would convince them but that he had less power too. The keeping up of an outward appearance of power will in many instances save the necessity of resort into the actual exercise of it. The Resident's authority must either be seen or it must be felt.

Externally the building is influenced by Wellesley's newly completed Government House, Calcutta. The Corinthian entrance portico with the Company's arms in *alto rilievo*, the domed Ionic semi-circular bay on the south front, the grand entrance screen enriched with sphinxes and trophies all recall Wyatt's recent composition. Internally the impression is quite different. It is strikingly neo-classical in conception with oval saloons flanking a large Durbar hall and a central staircase which divides at a landing and ascends in two elegant sweeps. The staircase is reminiscent of Robert Adam's interior at 20, Portman Square or William Kent's earlier staircase at 44, Berkeley Square. The parallels are striking in form and detail, but the Hyderabad interiors are more plainly treated, though none the less creditably executed by native craftsmen.

The lavish architectural ornament of the house was complemented by the opulent lifestyle of the Resident, who travelled in great state on richly-caparisoned elephants escorted by two companies of infantry and a troop of cavalry. Mountstuart Elphinstone, later Governor of Bombay, arrived in 1801 and left a description of Kirkpatrick in his diary: 'Major K. is a good-looking man; seems about thirty, is really about thirty-five. He wears mustachios; his hair is cropped very short, and his fingers are died with henna. In other respects he is like an Englishman. He is very communicative, and very desirous to please, but he tells long stories about himself and practises all the affectations of which his face and eyes are capable.'

His rather exotic appearance may be accounted for by his marriage to one of the ladies of the Nizam's court, a liaison which caused an uproar in Calcutta and nearly lost him his post. The story of his marriage has gained much in its repeated telling, and it may be apocryphal. Kirkpatrick's love of story telling was well-known, but it is a strange tale with unexpected architectural implications.

It is alleged that Kirkpatrick, known in the Nizam's Court as Hushmat Jung (Magnificent in Battle) was renowned for his good looks. During a court entertainment a young girl, Khair-un-Nissa (Beautiful among Women), had watched him through the purdah and fallen hopelessly in love. Kirkpatrick was sitting alone one night on the terrace when to his astonishment he was visited by an old woman, an emissary, who pleaded the passion of Khair-un-Nissa. At first he repelled the advances made to him, but the princess would brook no denial. After repeated but unavailing overtures through her emissary, the girl resolved to take the matter into her own hands. A veiled figure was ushered into the Residency and pleaded her suit so passionately that the Englishman's heart melted. In a letter to his brother, William, now Military Secretary to the Governor-General, James wrote: 'I, who was but ill-qualified for the task, attempted to argue this romantic young creature out of a passion which I could not, I confess, help feeling myself something more than pity for. She declared to me again and again that her affections had been irretrievably fixed on me for a series of time, that her fate was linked to mine, and that she should be content to pass her time with me as the humblest of handmaids.'

Kirkpatrick relented and married her under Muslim law and the Nizam made him his adopted son. Allegations of bribery, corruption and abjuring his religion descended upon him and, at one point, the Governor-General sent a man to supersede him, but he was headed off by a squadron of cavalry and potential damage to British interests was avoided. After a lengthy inquiry he was exonerated, and was allowed to live in peace.

As a Muslim, Khair-un-Nissa remained in strict purdah, so Kirkpatrick built separate quarters as a zenana. It was enclosed by high walls with pavilions, fountains, galleries and terraces ornamented in a richly Oriental manner with gilding, painting and trelliswork. Unfortunately no trace of the Rang Mehal remains, for it was here that the wives of visitors were entertained, whilst the male guests were received in the Residency. As his wife never left her zenana, Kirkpatrick built a model of the newly-completed Residency in the Begum's garden, where it survives to this day, a miniature replica of the main house complete in every detail. However when I visited the garden in 1981 part had been crushed by a tree, and it is unlikely to be repaired.

The romantic story of Kirkpatrick and his passionate wife has a postscript. One of their two children, Catherine Aurora, born in 1802, was the inspiration for the heroine Blumine in *Sartor Resartus*, a novel by Thomas Carlyle. Blumine is 'a many tinted radiant Aurora', 'the fairest of Orient light-bringers'. Catherine Kirkpatrick haunted Carlyle for the rest of his days – 'a strangely complexioned young lady, with soft brown eyes and floods of bronze red hair, really a pretty looking, smiling, and amiable, though most foreign, bit of magnificence and kindly splendour, by the name of "dear Kitty"'. She was an exotic creature, 'placid and sensuous who loved perfumes; a half-Begum in short', but she spurned Carlyle and married into an eminent West Country family, the Winsloe-Phillips. She died at the villa Sorrento in Torquay on 2nd March 1889.

To the South of Hyderabad lies Mysore, the territory of Hyder Ali and Tipu Sultan, whose ferocious resistance to British expansion did not finally end until the fall of Seringapatam and the death of Tipu in 1799. In Mysore city a Residency was erected in 1805 as a focus for British influence in the area, but whilst it shares several common features with the Hyderabad Residency, and Government House, Calcutta, it is wholly different in plan and form.

It was designed by Colonel Wilks in a Tuscan Doric style. The compound is approached by two roads, each with a triumphal entrance arch. The main entrance has a long axial carriageway punctuated by cast-iron lamp columns, but the entrance from the city is a winding avenue boarded by brightly-coloured shrubs and trees. The setting is delightful, situated on a low rise overlooking the city, and the triumphal screens assert the authority of the building long before it is reached. The house is single-storey, but the formal layout and size of the compound serve to diminish rather than accentuate its presence, so that the initial reaction after the splendid approach is one of disappointment rather than architectural climax. Fortunately the feeling is not sustained close-to. The whole complex has great charm and is scrupulously maintained by a staff of thirty for government guests. In plan the rooms are disposed around a landscaped central atrium which is colonnaded on all sides. Green-painted valances reduce glare to the rooms, which are approached off the colonnades through half-height louvred swing doors, whilst the outer walls are screened by arcaded loggias and umbrageous shrubbery. There is a substantial projecting *porte-cochère* fringed with palms and climbing plants. The bedrooms are beautifully maintained with brass beds and many of the original fittings. Like many Moghul houses it is impossible to say where the inside of the house begins or ends, as the central atrium and open vestibule mean that a great deal of the floorspace is essentially outdoors, which provides ample light, but not glare, and cool refreshing breezes to every corner of the house. The house may be conceived along the lines of a Greek or Roman villa, but the plan and practical adaptations to the climate owe much to native sources.

Government House, Mysore: The entrance screen designed to proclaim British power and authority to the city.

98

Internally the most distinctive feature of the building is the large semi-circular bay room on the south front which was added by Sir John Malcolm to designs prepared by Thomas Fiott de Havilland, the architect of St Andrew's Kirk, Madras. The ornament is neo-classical with Venetian arches and plasterwork enriched with festoons and paterae, but the most interesting aspect is the roof, which covers one of the largest rooms in South India without intermediate support. We have seen how de Havilland experimented with wide structural spans in the curious arch which he built in his garden at Seringapatam, and clearly he used the experience here.

Elsewhere in India the Palladian and neo-classical impulses emanating from the great centres of activity in Madras and Calcutta were sufficiently strong to influence the form and design of European buildings in the remotest areas of the mofussil, but over on the west coast in the third Presidency, Bombay, there was no significant European architectural heritage until the second decade of the nineteenth century when two major buildings were erected in a conscious attempt to create an urban impact – the Town Hall and the Mint.

Since 1718 the town had been dominated by St Thomas's Church and its distinctive low belfry was the principal landmark on the skyline behind the brooding ramparts of the Fort. With the establishment of the See of Bombay, it became the cathedral church and the low belfry was converted into a loftier tower of no particular architectural merit. The only other building of any significance was St Andrew's Kirk, a more modest variation on the usual Gibbs theme, but with a heavy Doric portico which creates a rather leaden impact.

Catherine Aurora (Kitty) and William Kirkpatrick in Oriental dress shortly before their departure to England by George Chinnery.

Government House, Mysore: The semi-circular bay room added to the south front by Thomas Fiott de Havilland.

The Town Hall was commenced in 1820, but took over fifteen years to complete. It cost over £60,000, most of which was defrayed by the East India Company, and the remainder by private subscription and a fortunate lottery ticket, which yielded £10,000. The intention was to house not just civic offices for the Legislative Council, but a library and museum for the Asiatic Society. The idea for a major public building on the Green was long-standing and the fact that it took over twenty years to come to fruition is a reflection of the relative insignificance of Bombay when compared with the great cities on the east coast, Madras and Calcutta.

The building was designed by Colonel Thomas Cowper, Bombay Engineers, and completed after his death in 1825 by various others, principally Charles Waddington. It is the finest neo-classical building in India with several unique adaptations to the climate. The façade is a massive composition in a Greek Doric order. There is a central octastyle pedimented portico, with columns in antis approached by a wide cascade of steps. Each wing is embellished with a subsidiary portico, and the whole edifice is raised high on an arcaded basement to accentuate the impact. The end result is magnificent – a composition of power and massive solidity, an austere uncompromising statement of the growing might of British India, and it is no coincidence that it was commenced just three years after the defeat of the Peshwa at the Battle of Kirkee in 1817. The huge projecting *jhilmils* or window canopies are part of the original composition, intended to provide shade and cool to the rooms within. They are elaborate structures contained within the

100

(Above) *Town Hall, Bombay about forty years after its completion. The building exudes the power and confidence of the rising British Empire in India.* (Below) *Fine original detail of the side portico. The huge projecting jhilmils form part of Cowper's original design.*

expression of each window opening, so that, unlike many others which were added to buildings, they enhance rather than diminish the architectural effect, and Cowper tried to integrate them by enriching each valance with a frieze of Greek palmettes.

The Doric columns were made in England and carried out in an East Indiaman as freight. Originally it was Cowper's intention to group them in pairs, but on arrival they were so massive that, fortunately, the idea was dropped and the supernumerary columns were diverted for use at Christ Church, Bycullah, then in the course of erection. The interior of the building was completed by Waddington with a Corinthian order and a large entrance hall immediately behind the central portico. However, in the rooms for the Medical Board on the ground floor he indulged in a piece of antiquarian whimsy and installed four splendid Ionic columns copied from a Greek Temple on the banks of the Ilyssus. Elsewhere in the building is some excellent statuary with figures of Mountstuart Elphinstone, Sir Charles Forbes, and Sir John Malcolm, all by Chantrey. Malcolm stands in a flood of light at the head of a fine elliptical staircase which is approached through the north portico, and the strong interplay of light and shade accentuates the neo-classical austerity of the design.

The Mint was commenced in 1824, and was operational by 1827. It was erected on the Fort rubbish dump to designs prepared by Major John Hawkins, Bombay Engineers, who was sent to England to study minting techniques in the office of Boulton and Watt with Major William Nairn Forbes, the architect of the Calcutta Mint. Architecturally it is an elegant composition, a plain rectangular building enriched with an Ionic portico complementing the Town Hall nearby, although today it is hidden in the Dockyard area and access is restricted.

Christ Church, Bycullah, the fortunate recipient of Cowper's unused Doric columns, was consecrated in 1835, but its principal interest lies in the handsome monument to Sir Robert Grant, the Governor, who died in 1838 at his country retreat at Dapuri. It is related that he walked a favourite path every sunset, but on the day of his death a sentry saw a cat leave by the same door and down the same path as the stricken Governor. The guard were convinced that the Governor's soul had transmigrated to the cat, and as no one was sure later which of the many cats there had been blessed with gubernatorial status, for the next thirty years each time one trotted out of the house, the guard presented arms. No wonder the British love India.

CHAPTER 5

BUNGALOWS
AND HILL STATIONS

In a loop of the river Cauvery at Seringapatam stands a bungalow set in a garden of great beauty, but the house is lonely and isolated, haunted by memories of a past tragedy. Here in April 1817 Colonel Scott, the Commandant of the British garrison, returned from parade to find his wife and daughter dead from cholera. It is alleged that he walked from the house in quiet despair, waded into the river, and slipped beneath its waters to drown his sorrows forever. Actually he did not drown himself, but resigned his appointment and returned to England where he died at his home at Lovel Park, Berkshire in January 1833. On the orders of the Maharajah of Mysore the bungalow lay untouched, as if one day the souls of the departed would return to their last place on earth. In the nearby cemetery lies the tomb of Catherine Isabella Scott (and infant child) who died in childbed on 19th March 1817. In 1875 'Aliph Cheem' wrote:

> The mouldering rooms are now as they stood
> Nearly eighty years ago,
> The piano is there
> And table and chair
> And the carpet rotting slow;
> And the beds wheron the corpses lay,
> And the curtains half time-mawed away.

The house was repaired in the 1920s, and the furniture is preserved now by the State Directorate of Archaeology and Museums in Mysore.

Few bungalows have such romantic associations, although many have had their share of human tragedies. Their origins are more prosaic. Bungalows originated in Bengal. In 17th-century Hindustani the word 'bangla' or 'bangala' referred to local village huts, and it was from these crude prototypes that the bungalow developed. There were two possible originals. Both share a rectangular plan and raised floor, but one had a curvilinear roof with crescent-shaped eaves, often sweeping over the walls to form a verandah supported on rough-hewn posts. The other was a double-roofed house with a pitched, tiled or thatched roof, the upper part resting on the walls and the lower part dropped to form a verandah around the edge of the walls.

With the arrival of the British and other Europeans in large numbers the word was soon corrupted and applied to any single-storey building with a verandah. The increasing numbers of officials, planters, and soldiers stimulated demand for a form of mass housing that was quickly built, using local materials, but that was more comfortable than the tent

The Scott Bungalow, Seringapatam.

and better adapted to the climatic extremes of Bengal. Vernacular structures had been used as out-buildings and privies to the grander classical compositions in the main towns, but out in the mofussil or in the remote tea plantations of Assam these simple structures were the principal form of European housing.

In the early 19th century many Englishmen arrived in India imbued with a Romantic nostalgia for rural life, then currently in vogue in Europe. In England this had been given eloquent expression in the *cottage ornée* and with the development of the first London garden suburb at St John's Wood from 1820 onwards, where small Picturesque villas were set in an Arcadian landscape. It was natural that nostalgic and romantic concepts of the mother-country should be grafted on to the simple indigenous structures of Bengal, which were cheap and flexible. The result was an exotic Anglo-Indian hybrid – the bungalow, and its appeal was obvious when compared with the chaotic squalor of Indian towns. As a native structure it was perfectly adapted to the climate; the wide verandah provided shade from the harsh Indian sun and protection during the monsoon rains, whilst the plan form, layout and voluminous interior promoted a cool flow of air.

In 1801 an observer described the English as living in 'what are really stationary tents which have run aground on low brick platforms. They are "Bungalows", a word I know not how to render unless by a Cottage. These are always thatched with a straw on the roof and the walls are sometimes of bricks and often of mats.' By 1824 the name and house type were in common usage. Bishop Heber wrote: 'Bungalow, a corruption of Bengalee, is a general name in this country for any structure in the cottage style and only of one floor. Some of these are spacious and comfortable dwellings, generally with high thatched roofs, surrounded by a verandah, and containing three or four good apartments, with bathrooms and dressing rooms, enclosed from the eastern, western or northern verandah. The south is always left open.'

Clearly by Heber's time the bungalow had developed into a far more

104

comfortable house type than its vernacular antecedents. The British rapidly took up the bungalow as an ideal form of tropical housing and exported it all over the world. In one of those peculiar cultural distortions of Empire, which gave the British dungarees and mulligatawny soup and the Indians blazers and banana custard, the bungalow was adopted as the universal form of colonial housing throughout the Empire – from Rangoon to Adelaide, and from Durban to Toronto. With the development of planned suburban cantonments, the bungalow came into its own and acquired more European characteristics. The bungalow should have been a great social leveller. Everyone lived in them regardless of status from the Governor of Bombay in his double-roofed bungalow on Malabar Hill to the lowliest peripatetic official in his dak bungalow, but with the development of an English caste system in India as rigid and arcane as the Indian, the bungalow soon began to acquire elements which portrayed social status. Wooden posts gave way to Doric and Tuscan columns, tiles displaced thatch, and roof pitches were screened behind ornamental balustrades. The English love of gardening was taken to its limits. Each bungalow was set in its own large landscaped compound, promoting the growth of widely dispersed settlements, which were serviced by cheap native labour. Urban expansion tended to occur horizontally rather than vertically, spreading across the flat open landscape of Bengal and Upper India. In order to create points of interest in these huge suburban cantonments entrances were accentuated by the addition of elaborate carriage porches. The superimposition of classical detailing over these indigenous structures reflected a desire to emulate, in miniature, the grand town residences of Calcutta and, still more deep-seated, a desire to maintain a European identity and values in a heathen land. Mud was replaced by brick and plaster or chunam. As the European population

Barrackpore: Early 19th-century bungalow with fluted Doric porte-cochère.

expected higher standards of comfort and accommodation local Indian techniques of 'cutcha' construction using sun-dried bricks gave way to English methods of 'pukka' building using kiln-baked bricks, bonded by a mortar made of brick dust, water, sand and cut hemp.

Bungalows were affected by the same architectural fashions as public buildings, so it is no surprise to find in a typical cantonment, such as Barrackpore, a variety of popular motifs and styles – fluted Doric, plain Tuscan, Adamesque fans over arches, Venetian windows and Regency Gothick quatrefoils. Common devices were used to control temperature and light – Venetian shutters to the windows and doors, cane tatties suspended from verandahs, and latticework screens simulating the elaborate carved screens of *moucharabya* work found on Moghul buildings. Internally the pitched roof was usually screened by sheets of stretched muslin which aided proportion, and maintained air circulation. Often in hot weather these were soaked with water to cool the atmosphere. These diaphanous ceilings provided a useful barrier against snakes, spiders and other unwelcome intruders, who otherwise were prone to drop from the thatch onto the disconcerted occupants beneath. Air circulation was aided by the punkah, a large cloth or glass fan suspended from the ceiling and drawn to and fro by the punkah-wallah. Mechanised fans or 'thermantidotes' were introduced in about 1780 in Calcutta and they were widely adopted soon afterwards in Bombay and Madras.

The plan form of many classical bungalows is similar. The house is entered through a colonnaded portico which functions as a *porte-cochère*. Here carriages could wait for guests in the shade rather than in the glare of the outside compound. This leads to a wide colonnaded verandah, part of which is sometimes enclosed to form a study or office. Usually the drawing room leads straight off the verandah, a lofty

Bangalore: A mid-19th century bungalow overlain with later Gothic details.

spacious room with the roof structure exposed. Generally the dining room lies behind the drawing room and they are connected by an open archway or classical screen beyond which lies the rear verandah which functions as the main delivery entrance and centre of household activity. Usually kitchens were kept away from the house in a separate outbuilding.

There was, and still is, a time lag between fashions in England and India, and architecture was not an exception. It was not until the 1870s that classical forms of architecture for bungalows gave way to more romanticised Gothic styles. Frequently in the case of vernacular buildings, the two styles overlapped to create delightful hybrid designs of great charm and refinement. Nowhere was this more evident than in Bangalore and Mysore in Southern India. Here a particular local tradition was developed which cultivated the Picturesque long after it had been superseded in England. Wide porch roofs and gables were enriched with elaborately carved bargeboards and fretwork canopies known as 'monkey-tops'. These distinctive features usually took the form of projecting, pointed hoods over windows and doors, or canopies enclosing verandahs and porches. From being accessories to the design, they became the focus of the design itself. They were made of a close trelliswork of vertical slats, usually measuring about one and a half inches by half an inch and painted dark green and white which, when combined with cascades of brightly-coloured bougainvillaea, created a fairy-tale atmosphere, a Gothick Arcadia. Usually the secluded verandahs were used for informal entertainment. Cane and bamboo furniture was manufactured to complement the architecture of a tropical Elysium, untarnished by the impact of corrugated iron which later disfigured so many of the hill stations. The verandah acted as a sort of private territorial buffer zone around each house where the European occupants could come to terms with the country about them.

Often classical and Gothick details were combined in wonderful flights of imaginative fancy. One particularly popular design was that of a classical colonnaded portico set between two crenellated and gabled wings with quatrefoil windows, and window and door openings embellished with 'monkey-tops' and carved bargeboards. Frequently the serrated profiles of the monkey-tops were complemented by elaborately detailed bonnet tiles employed as crestings to the roof. The whole effect was enhanced by the choice of colour, which was usually red-oxide, yellow-ochre or cream with the ornament highlighted in white. The plaster was usually chunam, applied to give the impression of a stone façade, usually with rusticated quoins, but further points of brilliant colour could be achieved by stained glass fanlights and windows. In Bangalore and Mysore floors were made of cool local slate or unglazed terracotta tiles.

In Bangalore the increasing density of occupation and rising land prices saw a gradual reduction in the size of garden compounds and there was pressure to expand vertically rather than horizontally. Often bachelor officers and officials shared accommodation in 'chummeries' where individual rooms were let off and sanitary facilities were communal. By the early 1900s many houses had two storeys enriched

with the same architectural detailing of lattice-work, monkey-tops and crested tiles. Frequently these houses boasted hexagonal or octagonal bays, providing additional facets to the already highly fragmented form and mass of the structure. In the suburbs of Mysore there are a number of well-preserved officers' 'bungalows', which have long since lost the single-storey form of their Bengal prototypes, and which most resemble detached Victorian villas, yet they retain elaborately carved bargeboards, verandahs and crested roofs. The carriage entrances have been replaced by gravelled drives for automobiles.

The Indian bungalow was regarded as the perfect house for all tropical countries and its success was allied to the growth of prefabricated building techniques which were pioneered by the British in the early part of the 19th century. The basic concepts of industrialised building — standardisation of parts, mass production, flexibility and ease of assembly on site — were available by the mid-century, and for the next fifty years these were developed and explored all over the Empire, particularly in South Africa, North America and Australia. The most essential component of this process was the use of iron. The principle of increasing the rigidity of sheet iron by fluting or corrugating had been known for a long period, but the first patent was not granted until 1829. This was acquired by Richard Walker, who pioneered its application to practical building construction. Sheet iron painted green or red had been used as a roofing material in St Petersburg, for instance, since 1814. An ordinary London town house of 1820 in Wilmington Square has a similar sheet iron roof, and it was used in the colonies from this date, but it was only with the advent of hot-dip galvanising patented by Craufurd in 1837 that durability

Monkey-tops and crestings in Bangalore.

Difficult to tell where hat stand ends and antlers begin on this typical verandah. The punkah hangs stationary above the table.

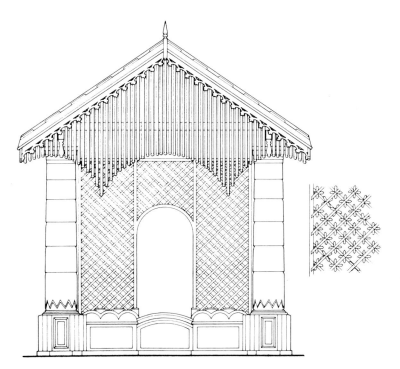

Typical trellis-work details in Bangalore.

was obtained. In 1843 John Porter's works in Southwark was the first to manufacture corrugated iron in the United Kingdom, and a year later the Phoenix Iron Works in Glasgow went into mass production. The advantages of prefabrication became allied with the idea of a cheap, portable form of housing for emigrants and iron houses, churches, hotels and arcades were exported all over the world. The Great Exhibition of 1851 held in the vast prefabricated iron and glass Crystal Palace in Hyde Park added impetus to the movement, and a portion of Paxton's palace itself later ended up as a sugar store in Commercial Road, Durban. An iron lighthouse was exported to Barbados, a customs house to Peru and Matthew Digby Wyatt designed an iron church for Rangoon. In the Crimean War many of the barrack buildings were prefabricated, and later an iron bungalow was designed for Bombay. In India the availability of cheap supplies of timber meant that generally iron was used more as a roofing material. An advertisement in the *Bombay Builder* for 1865 advertised sectional portable wooden buildings with double skin walls and roof to permit a free flow of air, demonstrating the common application of prefabrication techniques to local materials. However, iron remained a popular and durable form of construction. By 1891 British production of corrugated iron exceeded 200,000 tons, of which 75 per cent was exported, and when new government offices were erected in Simla, they were constructed entirely from prefabricated iron parts which could be transported up to the hills with relative ease.

The Indian bungalow arrived in England in 1869 when, unobtrusively, it invaded Kent at Birchington-on-Sea. Its introduction can be attributed to John Taylor, a pupil of J. P. Seddon, the eminent

110

architect, who later collaborated in the venture. The Birchington bungalows incorporated the latest sanitary appliances and structural techniques. Taylor's were rather utilitarian – some were even portable wooden structures – but Seddon's were more substantial affairs with squat towers and sgraffito work by George Frampton. They proved immensely popular as coastal retreats for the wealthy infirm. Dante Gabriel Rossetti took one and died there in 1882. He lies in Birchington Churchyard, his bungalow demolished. The novel concept of the bungalow proved so influential that by 1928 Clough Williams-Ellis was aghast at the 'bungaloid growth' which had spread across much of Southern England, and believed that it 'constitutes England's most disfiguring disease'. To this day its popularity remains and the bungalow lives on, the exotic product of an intermarriage of cultures, a sort of architectural tart from poor rural origins, taken up by the colonial middle classes only to be discarded far from its original home, briefly loved but now disdained, providing temporary solace for the urban masses in pursuit of leisure and the status of a second home.

In the later part of the 19th century the second home was a very characteristic aspect of Anglo-Indian life. With the development of the bungalow as the ideal form of colonial housing came the search for the ideal form of colonial settlement, and being an English ideal it was one imbued with many of the attributes of the English provincial resort. The development of the hill station was a peculiar and unlikely phenomenon, but one which exerted enormous influence over the pattern and nature of colonial life. Annual furlough in the hills was all that kept many officers and wives from premature demise in the intolerable heat of the plains. As Kipling noticed, it often came too late:

> Ay, lay him 'neath the Simla pine –
> A fortnight fully to be missed,
> Behold, we lose our fourth at whist,
> A chair is vacant where we dine.

Between 1815 and 1947 the British created over eighty hill stations on the lower mountain ranges of India at levels varying between 4,000 and 8,000 feet. They fall into four main regions, each providing rest and recreation for great urban centres of European population. The foothills of the Himalayas contain the largest number: Simla, Mussoorie, Naini Tal, Murree and Dalhousie were among the most favoured, although in later years the ornate 'Swiss Chalet' houseboats of Kashmir became popular alternatives. In the north-east the incomparable Darjeeling with its views of Kanchenjunga and the Everest range, and further east Shillong in Assam, remained favourite resorts for Calcutta. Over in the west, lay Poona and Mahabaleshwar serving Bombay, and in the south the stations of the Nilgiri Hills – Ootacamund, Coonoor, and Kodaikanal served Madras. Although each station has a highly distinctive character of its own, they all share common features – an Arcadian setting, an informal layout and a strict social hierarchy – a nostalgic

recreation of English upper-class values in the Indian hills.

In the north Simla was the summer capital from 1864 onwards. Here, for six months of the year, perched 7,000 feet high in the foothills of the Himalayas the temporary capital of the most powerful rulers in Asia lay in celestial isolation. But the military realities were never apparent. The prevailing atmosphere was one of relaxation and calm; recuperation from the searing heat of the plains below with dream-like visions of the snow-capped Himalayas beyond.

English attention was drawn first to the area during the Nepalese War in 1815. Two years later a government survey of the Sutlej valley was carried out. In 1821 Major Sir William Lloyd reached Simla. 'It is impossible that Simla and its sublimity can ever be effaced from our minds', he recalled. In 1822 Captain Charles Kennedy was appointed Superintendent of the Hill States. It was he who erected the first house at Simla in 1825, a pretty little gabled cottage with a cruciform plan and central chimney stack surrounded by a Gothic verandah. As early as 1824 Europeans, chiefly invalids from the plains, had permission to establish themselves in the locality rent-free from the Maharajah of Patiala and the Rana of Keonthal. The station rapidly acquired a reputation as a sanatorium, and this together with Kennedy's reputation as an effusive host, led to the visit of the Governor-General Lord Amherst in 1827 and the erection of over sixty houses by 1831. It was Amherst who once rebutted an over-zealous aide with the retort: 'The Emperor of China and I govern half the human race, and yet we find time to breakfast.' The fashion for retreat having been set, the Commander-in-Chief Lord Combermere came the following year accompanied by his ADC, Captain Mundy. According to Mundy, conditions were primitive:

Three late 19th-century bungalows on the outskirts of Mysore. The one at the top left was used in the T.V. series The Jewel in the Crown.

113

The wooden pent-roof ... only admitted of my standing upright in the centre ... though this canopy of planks was lined with white-washed canvas it by no means excluded the rains ... so peremptorily as I, not being an amphibious animal could have wished; and during some of the grand storms the hailstones rattled with such stunning effect upon the drum-like roof, that the echo sung in my ears for a week after. [He shared his accommodation with] an eternal carnival of rats ... I soon grew tired of these four-footed Pindarees, became callous to their nocturnal orgies and kept a cat.

Combermere laid out a road around Mount Jakko, the highest peak in Simla, and Lord William Bentinck, Amherst's successor, became a regular visitor, residing at his own house, Bentinck's Castle. Many houses were let for the season and all had chimneys and fireplaces to compensate for the altitude. Most had fanciful homely names – Swiss Cottage, Fountain Hall, Daisy Bank, Woodbine Cottage and Sunny-bank, but all were erected on common structural principles entirely unlike those used in the plains. In 1839 Charles French noted:

The walls of the houses are erected after a singular fashion unlike anything in the plains. Cement is seldom or never used except in the outer coatings. Instead of this a brittle kind of stone resembling slate, and which is procured in great abundance in the hills, is in the first instance shaped in to squares or parallelograms. These stones are then adjusted or laid down in layers of two or two and one half feet in thickness, and this they do regularly and neatly without the aid of lime or mortar. At every two, three or four feet of the height of the wall, the adjusted pile of stones is bound down with long pieces of timber laid horizontally over the edge of each side and connected by cross bars of wood. It cannot well be conceived how this plan can lend much strength to the walls or promote their stability, but practically it has been found to succeed.

He went on to mark how the roofs were either slated or shingled in a shallow angular form; one or two were thatched, but none tiled. The slating was crude and not brought to any great perfection. Ample supplies of pine and fir were available from the Mahasu forest nearby, but demand was so high and felling so uncontrolled, that soon the exposed soil was washed away into the valley.

French's description of construction techniques is important, because it demonstrates that the form and structure of the hill residences were based on long-established vernacular principles and not on imported European know-how. Many of the local temples and native houses demonstrate a traditional technique of construction, one dictated by the availability of materials and the exigencies of the climate. Heavy winter snowfalls necessitated pitched roofs, whilst common design features such as fretwork bargeboards were employed to protect the eaves from wind and to carry off meltwater in spring. The

British merely developed these indigenous structural elements into design features from their own architectural experience: wooden tie beams became exposed timber framing, and fretwork eaves and canopies became ornamental carved bargeboards, often in the style of the alpine cottage.

Emily and Fanny Eden accompanied their brother, Lord Auckland, to Simla in 1838–39. They lived in Auckland House, which still survives as part of a much wider complex of buildings. The original house was single storey with a compressed-earth roof, which Emily described as 'a jewel'. Everything was brought with them from Calcutta including carpets, chandeliers, and wall-shades. To improve the decor she 'got a native painter into the house, and cut out patterns in paper, which he then paints in borders all round the doors and windows'. She found that 'It makes up for the want of cornices and breaks the eternal white walls of the houses'. The hill on which the house stood was christened 'Elysium' in honour of the stunning sisters who resided there. Perhaps less appealing was 'Bentinck's Nose', a landmark which bore a noticeable resemblance to the Governor-General's remarkable protuberance.

In 1839 Simla residents were favoured with a glimpse of Mrs James, then 15 years old, 'who looked like a star amongst all the others'. Emily Eden thought her 'undoubtedly very pretty, and such a merry, unaffected girl', but with far-sighted prescience she noted that 'she is very young and lively, and if she falls into bad hands she would soon laugh herself into foolish scrapes'. It would be an understatement to describe her life as one of 'scrapes', for as the notorious dancer Lola Montez she went on to become the courtesan of King Ludwig of Bavaria, until scandal forced her to flee in disguise to England, where she remarried. Prosecuted for bigamy, she fled to Spain where her new husband died. She proceeded to the United States, and married yet again. On a tour of Australia she burst into the offices of the *Ballarat Times* and horse-whipped the editor for libel. Back in America she lectured on the Art of Beauty and spent the last years of her life ministering to reformed prostitutes. She died in New York in 1861 aged 38.

One of the delights of Simla was the pleasure ground at Annandale, a large flat clearing in the forest surrounded by an amphitheatre of hills. It was used for all major social occasions including a brilliant *fête champêtre* for Prince Waldemar of Prussia in 1835. A cricket ground was laid out in 1847. Gymkhanas and race meetings were the most popular diversions, even though 'rarely does a meeting pass without some serious accident, such as a rider rolling down a precipice either with, or without his horse, into the valley below'.

Not all social events were organised successfully. In a satirical piece in *The Delhi Sketch Book* Stiggins, writing from 'The Hovel', Simla referred to the 1851 Annandale Flower Fete:

> Now all sage committee men, take my advice,
> When you get up a flower fete, provide something nice, . . .
> Be careful that whenever Englishmen meet
> They never depart, without something to eat.

115

Simla around 1870.

It is an indication of the extraordinary confidence that pervaded the Raj that the British could consider seriously the idea of ruling one-fifth of mankind from a remote Himalayan village whose only connection with the outside world was one tortuous and precipitous road. With the outbreak of the Mutiny in 1857, after a few initial alarums, all remained quiet in Simla and the Hill States. Had it not, virtually the entire government would have been cut off. The crisis of confidence induced by the rebellion did not curtail the practice of retreating to the hills. In fact from 1864 onward Lord Lawrence positively advocated the wisdom of removing the government to Simla on strategic grounds, although by then communications had been much improved as part of a grandiose project of Dalhousie's to form the Great Hindustan and Tibet Road. It was preposterous, as though the whole of Whitehall moved lock, stock and barrel to St Moritz for the summer, but until the advent of air conditioning it was essential if work was to be sustained. Kipling put it to verse in 'A Tale of Two Cities':

> But the rulers in that City by the Sea
> Turned to flee –
> Fled with each returning Spring & tide from its ills
> To the Hills.

As a result of the annual diaspora to the hills Simla changed. There were two distinct societies – the official and the social, the bees and the butterflies, and the station was no longer just a resort; physically it

116

changed into an eccentric suburb of Calcutta, 700 miles away, adding further incongruity to its already idiosyncratic appearance.

From 1862 to 1888 the Viceroy lived in Peterhof which was generally regarded as unsuitable for a Viceregal establishment and which Lord Lytton thought 'a pigstye'. Like most of Simla it was perched high on a precipice with hardly any grounds to front or rear, and it was not until Lord Dufferin pressed energetically for a more appropriate residence that a new Viceregal Lodge was built in 1888. Peterhof survived until 1981 when it was gutted by fire. The site chosen for the new house was entirely appropriate for the residence of the Viceroy of the Indian Empire for it was a natural watershed, the drainage on one side flowing down to the Sutlej and on to the Arabian Sea, and on the other into the Jumna and out into the Bay of Bengal.

> Queen of these restless fields of tide,
> England! What shall men say of thee,
> Before whose feet, the worlds divide?

Dufferin had long cherished dreams of building a great romantic house under his own direction. He had tried before at his seat at Clandeboye in Ireland and later when Governor-General of Canada, in Quebec, but at Simla he was given the resources to fulfil his fantasies. The designs were prepared by Henry Irwin, based on earlier proposals advanced by Captain Cole, but Dufferin himself suggested the plan of the building and interfered at every opportunity. He constantly modified and examined all the drawings, visiting the site daily, usually with his wife, who shared his enthusiasm for the building. She was amused by the appearance of the native labourers, particularly the women who 'walk about with the carriage of empresses, and seem as much at ease on the top of the roof as on the ground floor; most picturesque masons they are.'

The design is a free interpretation of the Elizabethan or English Renaissance style with few concessions to India in its detailing or form. It could be transposed to the Highlands and function perfectly well as a country house. Indeed later residents compared it somewhat unkindly to a 'Scotch hydro', and even to Pentonville Prison, with its crenellated tower and forbidding blue and grey facings of local limestone and sandstone. Nevertheless the Dufferins loved it and the spectacular views to the north and north-east more than compensated for its unyielding elevations.

Internally the great entrance hall and gallery are the principal feature around which the main rooms are disposed. A huge teak staircase provides access to the upper floors and the gallery; rising full height through the house, it gives a sense of space and grandeur to the building. The state dining room is panelled to a height of ten feet, enriched with pierced Elizabethan strapwork carrying the armorial bearings of former Governors-General and Viceroys. Curzon with his scholarly mind and obsession for historical accuracy later corrected several of the armorial devices and altered the decorations, which had been provided by Messrs Maple & Co, London. More significantly he

Viceregal Lodge: Entrance Hall. The overbearing teak panelling and sombre ornament oppressed many occupiers of the house. Subsequent Vicereines made considerable efforts to improve the decor. The Viceroy's state howdah can be glimpsed on the left of the picture.

also raised the external tower which was thought to be out of proportion, and spent considerable sums on correcting defects in the structure.

Architecturally the house is a creditable composition and compares favourably with many similar Victorian country houses of the period. It incorporated several innovations including electric light and even a separate indoor tennis court, similar to that built by Dufferin at Rideau Hall, Ottawa, as well as older salvaged treasures such as the mirrors from King Thebaw's palace in Mandalay. Today it is used as an Institute for Advanced Studies, but it is a sad, eerie place. It was never homely and it exudes that peculiar melancholy of departed greatness which hangs like an aura over many grand buildings which have outlived their original function. When I visited it in 1981 the building was shrouded in mist which added to its forbidding aspect. A lone watchman guarded the interior, the smoke from his fire lit in the middle of the entrance hall floor wreathing insubstantial patterns amongst the dust sheets.

By the time the walls of Viceregal Lodge were erected, the quintessential character of Simla had been firmly moulded. Most of the principal public buildings were concentrated along 'The Ridge', which was dominated by Christ Church: an adequate Gothic composition enhanced by its crowning position on the skyline. Designed by Colonel J. T. Boileau, it had been commenced in 1844, but it was not consecrated until 1857 after a series of incremental additions including the tower. It was always a small church, and where once the vicar preached a sermon berating the ladies on the space occupied by their voluminous crinolines, the congregation has now dwindled to less than ten.

Viceregal Lodge, Simla: a grim, forbidding edifice in quasi-Elizabethan style designed by Henry Irwin for the Viceroy, Lord Dufferin.

The timber-framed Post Office buildings were another landmark on 'The Ridge', a little above its junction with 'The Mall', the legendary 'Scandal Point' of Kipling's Simla. They still survive in a style which can best be described as Wild West Swiss. Beneath The Mall and The Ridge, which were exclusively European preserves, lay the bazaars of the native quarters cascading down the hill in a vertiginous warren of alleys and shacks. 'A man who knows his way there can defy all the police of India's summer capital, so cunningly does veranda communicate with veranda, alley-way with alley-way, and bolt-hole with bolt-hole', wrote Kipling. In its heyday it was one of the spy centres of the world. The model for Lurgan Sahib of Kipling's *Kim*, a certain Mr Jacob, actually ran a curio shop similar to Lurgan's in between his more furtive activities as political agent, mesmerist and spy in the 1870s and 80s, a local figure around whom many mysterious tales revolved.

With the consolidation of Simla as the summer capital, several older residences were used by the great officers of state – 'the heaven-born', so that Simla acquired the soubriquet 'the abode of the little tin gods'. The Private Secretary to the Viceroy resided at Observatory House, once the home of the eccentric Colonel J. T. Boileau, the architect of Christ Church, Simla and St George's, Agra, a keen astronomer, who built his own observatory here in 1844 and gave his name to the locality – Boileaugunge. The Lieutenant Governor of the Punjab occupied Barnes Court, one of the most famous houses in Simla, a half-timbered neo-Tudor pile where Lord Napier, Colin Campbell, General Anson and Sir Hugh Rose had lived, with an extravagant Moorish ballroom enriched with decoration designed by John Lockwood Kipling, Rudyard's father, and Principal of the Mayo School of Art in Lahore. Lockwood Kipling also designed the fresco around the chancel window of Christ Church. From 1885 onwards the Commander-in-Chief resided at Snowdon. In the early 1900s, as a diversion from his quarrels with the imperious Curzon, Kitchener enlarged and stamped his own personal flavour on the house. A huge walnut staircase was installed embellished with trophies taken from the dervishes at Omdurman and from the Boers in the Transvaal, including a curious oak coat of arms removed from the back of the canopy under which Kruger used to sit in Pretoria. An oak chimneypiece was installed in the billiards room inscribed with the motto 'Strike and fear not', a maxim dear to Kitchener's heart.

Elsewhere new buildings were erected to accommodate facilities and offices for the 'heaven-born' of the administration. A new civil secretariat arose on the site of Gorton Castle on The Mall, a gaunt, sinister edifice built in a style resembling Scottish baronial. The designs were prepared by the eminent Sir Samuel Swinton Jacob, an enthusiastic advocate of Indo-Saracenic styles. He left a remarkable legacy of fine buildings in Lucknow, Jodhpur and Jaipur, but alas not in Simla for the Secretariat is rather a monster, looming above the fir trees. Perhaps more typical of the local style is the old Hotel Cecil, which is built on a precipice so that the entrance from the road is near roof level and one descends to the principal rooms. It incorporates all the familiar nuances of the Simla style: exposed timber framing, balustrated terraces

The timber-framed Post Office buildings above 'Scandal Point' still survive in a much-altered form.

hanging high over precipitous chasms, canopied balconies and serrated profiles of fretwork and crestings.

The most imaginative manifestation of timber-framed building is the Ripon Hospital designed by Henry Irwin in 1885 and built by Campion and Learmouth. It is interesting because it demonstrates the extent to which Gothic detailing could be adapted to accommodate the inherent constraints of timber-framed construction. It is a delightful building with a very distinctive open staircase, which is clearly influenced by the great mediaeval staircases at Blois and Chambord and Scott's much later use of the same element in the University Hall in Bombay. Here it is executed in open timber framing crowned by a corrugated iron roof, but it has charm, originality and vitality, elements which are rare architectural attributes in Simla, where the ubiquitous use of corrugated iron creates a transient, ramshackle character. Later the architects T. E. G. Cooper and A. Craddock did much to improve the artistic flavour of the station in a series of well-built business premises, and James Ransome's work, as consulting architect to the government of India, raised standards still higher.

However, the great government and commercial buildings were, and still are, the exceptions in Simla. It is the modest villas once inhabited by the ordinary officials and colonials which mark the place. Constance Cumming described them in 1884 as 'a good deal like Swiss chalets with a strong family likeness to each other'. Here under the shaded verandahs of Oakwood, Sunnybank or Woodbine Cottage the mem-

Snowdon, the Drawing Room. The traditional residence of the Commander-in-Chief was remodelled by Kitchener, whose portrait hangs over the mantelpiece. The lavish interior was a thinly disguised attempt by Kitchener to challenge the status of the Viceroy, Lord Curzon.

The sinister Gorton Castle by Sir Samuel Swinton Jacob once housed the Civil Secretariat.

sahibs met to chat and gossip about the latest affairs or the unreliability of their servants, who shuffled discreetly to and fro with cups of tea, lemonade, and other essentials of colonial life. Such pleasant interludes were punctuated only by the occasional crash of a monkey leaping across the iron roof in pursuit of mischief or a discarded sandwich.

As the Imperial sun reached its zenith in the skies of Asia, communications with Simla were transformed by the construction of an astonishing mountain railway. It was one of the outstanding feats of British Imperial engineering and was a matter of justifiable pride. It cost over £1 million and was designed by H. S. Harington, the chief engineer of the Kalka–Simla railway. It runs over sixty miles in a series of tight reverse curves with gradients of over three feet in every hundred. Five miles is entirely underground in a series of 107 tunnels. Nearly two miles are out across precipitous viaducts balanced over yawning chasms, but it was not built without mishap. Suddenly in November 1903 all work stopped amidst great excitement amongst the native work force. The bones of a great snake had been discovered embedded in one of the tunnels, but on careful investigation the wonderful serpent was revealed to be an iron pipe carrying fresh air to the workings.

With the arrival of the railway in 1903, Simla society became less

(Left) The Old Hotel Cecil was built, like much of Simla, on a precipice. The entrance is at roof level and one descends to the main rooms. (Right) Ripon Hospital: an inventive adaptation of Gothic detailing using available local materials.

123

closed and introverted. Hotels and boarding houses sprang up to accommodate an increasing number of visitors, and now there were too many people for the Vicereine to meet. In summer over 7,000 Europeans made the journey up from the plains, but the trip was now in the narrow-gauge carriages of the railway and, in later years, by the elegant electric railcar, which still glides serenely through the hills. Emily Eden's world of caparisoned jampans and palanquins had gone forever, submerged in a confused jumble of over 1,400 European dwellings.

If Simla is like some fading insubstantial dream, far to the south in the Nilgiri Hills, Ootacamund, the Queen of Hill Stations, evokes an altogether different response. It is a pastiche of rural England preserved in aspic, a window on a forgotten world.

Ooty, as it was popularly known, was a paradise for the exiled Englishman. In 1818 two surveyors, Whish and Kindersley, returned from an expedition in the Nilgiris with wonderful tales of a lost world — a hidden plateau over fifty miles across and eight thousand feet up in the hills. Here, it was said, the soil was rich, the air fresh and the moors and thicket teemed with wildfowl and game. The local collector at Coimbatore, John Sullivan, listened attentively to the story and determined to see for himself. The following year he set off with a French naturalist. When finally they broke out on the plateau, the Frenchman, who had been on the verge of death from fever, recovered miraculously, fortified by the buoyant air and equable climate. Sullivan returned in 1820 with a passionate interest in the development of Ooty. The government of Madras were almost as enthusiastic as Sullivan at the prospect of a restorative sanatorium in the hills where invalid officers could go to recuperate, instead of the long voyage to the Cape of Good Hope, which further debilitated already infirm constitutions.

In 1823 Sullivan built the first house in Ooty. The plans and elevation survive. They show a long, low single-storey bungalow raised on a shallow stone platform. The verandah is carried on a series of Ionic columns and the windows appear glazed with casements in the manner of Georgian sashes. Unusually the building was constructed entirely of stone, hence the name 'Stonehouse', and it survives embedded in part of a later building now used as government offices. Sullivan appears to have moved here permanently from this date onwards with his wife and children, much to the disapproval of the Madras authorities.

In 1826 the enlightened Sir Thomas Munro, Governor of Madras, visited Sullivan at Stonehouse for four days, access from Coimbatore having been improved by the construction of a road through the hills built by convict labour. At this time Sullivan was in sole control of Ootacamund and its development, and he used the opportunity to acquire as much land as possible for himself. By 1829 he held five times more than any other European resident. It was he who introduced the first European species into the region, English apple and peach trees, as well as strawberries and potatoes. Soon after, oak, fir, pear, walnut,

John Sullivan, founder of Ootacamund.

124

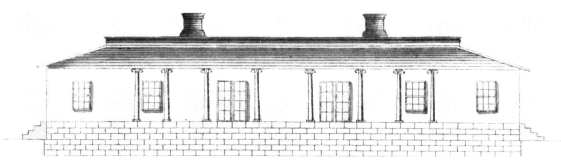

chestnut and pine arrived with English flowers: roses, dandelions and honeysuckle. The climate was such that English species grew in great profusion, and with far more vigour and abundance than at home. Each new resident became an enthusiast, so that in a comparatively short space of time the landscape acquired the characteristics of Sussex or even Westmorland, for Sullivan had dammed the local streams and created an ornamental lake.

Stonehouse: The first house in Ootacamund built by John Sullivan in 1823.

Eventually Sullivan's grip was weakened when a Military Commandant was appointed in 1830, but Ooty continued to blossom and expand in all directions. The then Governor of Madras, Stephen Lushington, became a regular visitor residing either at his brother's house, Lushington Hall, or at the house of Sir William Rumbold, which is now the Club. To Lushington it all resembled 'Malvern at the fairest season'. Soon eucalyptus and Australian wattle were introduced to replace the rapacious felling of the local forests, and these spread across the open downland imparting a more wooded and secluded look.

In 1830 St Stephen's Church was consecrated by the Bishop of Calcutta. Named in Lushington's honour, it was designed by Captain John James Underwood of the Madras Engineers, who had already been active in building a sanatorium for invalid officers. The building timber was removed from Tipu Sultan's Lal Bagh Palace at Seringapatam, and to economise the pillars to the nave were constructed in the same salvaged teak but plastered over to resemble stone. However, as usual the economies, while not enough to placate the Court of Directors in London who complained about being kept in the dark about the whole project, were sufficient to cause later structural problems. In a few years the roof needed repair and there were complaints of dim light and poor ventilation. Today St Stephen's, like much of Ooty, looks like a pasteboard parody of itself. This is accentuated by the flat yellow ochre colouring of the external walls, the light and the absence of any significant moulded stucco ornament. But imagine it in stone, and it would grace any English village without much adjustment – crenellated parapets, buttresses and finials. Only the deep carriage entrance gives it away, but like all English parish churches it has grown incrementally over the years. The pews were added in 1842, the clock and bell in 1851, and the ubiquitous plaques and monuments of English ecclesiastical life mark the way of all flesh. But it is the churchyard and its tombs straggling back up the steep hill behind the church which impart a feeling of continuity and age. This is no longer a new resort. It is a town with its own roots, home to generations who lived, loved and

died here, and the cemetery is not haunted by the bitter-sweet romantic melancholy which pervades many in this land. It is calm, peaceful, timeless – a real place of rest for exiles who once held dominion over palm and pine.

Over the next hill from the church stands the Club, that singular repository of English values. The building was erected in about 1830 as a hotel for Sir William Rumbold, and the work was supervised by his butler, Felix Joachim, who later ran the hotel. Although trusted implicitly by his master, he was 'an unmitigated scamp' who lined his own pockets at Rumbold's expense. Rumbold was a partner in William Palmer & Co, a notorious firm who lent vast sums of money to the Nizam of Hyderabad at extortionate rates of interest. Rumbold's house was the most comfortable in the station at this time. Here in 1834 those two giants of British India – Lord William Bentinck and Thomas Babington Macaulay met for the first time, Macaulay passing the time making early jottings for his great Indian Penal Code.

When the Club was convened in 1843 it took over Rumbold's house and steadily expanded into one of the most eminent in India, the social centre of 'snooty Ooty'. The basic form and appearance of Rumbold's early house remains with its central Ionic portico and low wings. The style is typical. It reflects the form and massing of 'Stonehouse' on a slightly grander scale, and the elongated façade seems an early design feature recurring on other surviving buildings including the school, which I suspect is Underwood's original. The nearby Savoy Hotel (formerly Sylks), built as a school for the sons of those in the Church Mission Society, is almost certainly by Underwood, for the roof has similar salvaged teak beams to those used in the church, and later, in 1841, Underwood acquired the house for his own use.

An aura of timelessness pervades the club. Interspersed amongst the flayed tigers and animal trophies are stirring prints of Rorke's Drift and Tel-el-Kebir. It is beautifully maintained, as always, for its declining clientele; the brasswork gleams, the leather shines, and the kitchen can still rustle up baked fish and lemon tart for the infrequent visitor. It was here in the club in 1875 that a young subaltern of the Devonshire Regiment, Neville Chamberlain, perfected snooker, the game he had conceived in the officers mess at Jubbulpore, and on the walls of the billiards room the first rules were posted, but the fun, the laughter and the *esprit de joie* have departed, and the club, like Ooty itself, lives on past memories and nostalgia.

Homesickness and nostalgia for England run as common themes through most of the diaries and letters of the expatriate British. Lady

St Stephen's, Ootacamund, built by Captain John James Underwood in 1830 using salvaged timbers from Tipu Sultan's palace at Seringapatam.

St Stephen's Churchyard.

Sir William Rumbold's House: The original building is now incorporated into the Club. The Ionic centrepiece remains a recognisable feature.

The single-storey pilastered school has all the hallmarks of an early building and is probably Underwood's original.

Betty Balfour wrote of a day in 1877: 'The afternoon was rainy and the road muddy, but such beautiful English rain, such delicious English mud. Imagine Hertfordshire lanes, Devonshire downs, Westmorland lakes, Scotch trout streams and Lusitanian views.'

Not all shared her enthusiasm for this distorted dream of an English Eden. Edward Lear thought it resembled Leatherhead and that the light made it undrawable. Richard Burton, the great explorer, arrived as a young officer in 1847 and reserved his most astringent comments for the Ootacamund soirée, which 'happens about once in twelve months to the man of pleasure, who exerts all the powers of his mind to ward off the blow of an invitation.' He went on to describe the 'scene of unfestivity' and other 'similar horrors . . . He must present Congo [tea] to the ladies, walk about with cake and muffins, listen to unmelodious melody and talk small . . . in spite of all efforts [he] will occasionally give vent to half or three-quarters of some word utterly unfit for ears feminine or polite.'

The prevailing social mood was that set by the Ooty Hunt out after jackal on Wenlock Downs, the regular picnics in nearby beauty spots, like the Tigers Cave, the morning stroll down grassy lanes past Charing Cross and on to the Botanical Gardens, but somehow the whole town is a curiously distorted vision of England, an anachronistic reflection in an Oriental mirror. One recalls Kipling:

> If England was what England seems
> And not the England of our dreams . . .

If the prevailing social mood was the English country set, the prevailing architectural character was, and still is, Gothic, but a Gothic which eschews the architectural canons in favour of charm and eccentricity. On a knoll near the church stands the Civil Court, which was enlarged from Breek's Memorial School in 1899, to provide for civil litigation. It has a dumpy little staircase tower and spire, crested corrugated iron roofs, diamond paned windows, carved bargeboards and a needle-thin clock tower crowned by a pyramidal roof, all executed in dark red

128

The Law Courts: Erected in 1873 this ramshackle courthouse was once Breek's Memorial School.

brick. The rambling Lawrence Asylum is modelled on Osborne House, and like the Nilgiri Library (1865) is by the excellent Madras architect Robert Fellowes Chisholm. The latter opened with a ball, the lofty Reading Room lit by five arched windows and a tall Gothic window at the far end, providing a charming setting for the occasion. It is a pretty red brick building with stucco dressings and little scrolled gables flanking a central chimney stack. Rapidly it became a favourite meeting place. Today it's as though the clock stopped in 1935 with old copies of the *Illustrated London News* left out for the casual visitor to thumb through. Now its entire membership is less than fifty.

As Ooty became the summer social centre of Southern India, native Indian princes acquired their own houses in the area. Fernhill Palace was the residence of the Maharajah of Mysore. The original house, built in 1842, was transformed by the addition of large ballrooms and suites for private entertainment. In a sunken hollow in the grounds an indoor

129

badminton court was built for the relaxation of guests and visitors. The whole complex is a riot of carved bargeboards, ornamental cast-iron balustrading, trelliswork and verandahs set in a compound studded with firs, cedars, palms, and monkey puzzle trees. The house is painted deep red oxide with green painted timberwork, and it is the culmination of the Swiss chalet style which pervades much of the architecture of Ootacamund.

Over to the north Arranmere, once the residence of the Maharajah of Jodhpur looks distinctly Home Counties with an Arts and Crafts air, mullioned and transomed windows and beautifully manicured lawns. Inside there is an underground passage, a direct link between the main house and the separate quarters of the Maharani, which enjoy breathtaking views of the blue-tinged horizons of the Nilgiri Hills.

Other palatial residences survive either as hotels or government colleges. Woodside has two handsome marble chimneypieces in its reception rooms taken from the huge mansion built at Kaiti by Lord Elphinstone. The Cedars belonged to the Resident at Hyderabad, Baroda Palace, to its eponymous owner, and high upon Elk Hill, Elk Hill House was built by George Norton for his own use in 1836.

In the 1860s the bare hills surrounding the town were given over to plantations of cinchona imported from Peru and eucalyptus brought from Australia. Today these impart an exotic look and smell to the countryside, complemented by the luxuriant growth of other imported species in the Botanical Gardens, which rise up the side of the hill to the

The Nilgiri Library, 1865, by Robert Fellowes Chisholm.

130

Fernhill Palace: The Maharajah of Mysore's private badminton court. The carved bargeboards of the palace may be seen in the background.

entrance to Government House. The Gardens were laid out by Mr MacIvor who was sent out from Kew to supervise in 1848. He introduced Persian vines, mulberry trees, cascades of camellias, and countless other shrubs and trees.

Government House was erected for the Duke of Buckingham and Chandos during his tenure as Governor of Madras in 1877. It is a large, Italianate mansion in cream-coloured stone with a projecting round-arched central portico and paired columns, copied from the Duke's family seat at Stowe in Buckinghamshire. There is an elegant frieze beneath the eaves, but little else to distinguish it from many other late Victorian Italianate mansions. Nearby and below stands the older, more modest original Government House. The road into the estate skirts the Botanical Gardens and the entrance is marked, not by a triumphal entrance screen in the manner of Mysore, Hyderabad, Lucknow or Calcutta, but by a half-timbered and roughcast lodge suitable to the prevailing vernacular style of the station. Today the house is untenanted for most of the year, other than by the millions of rock bees which have set up home in the portico, as they have at the former Residency at Hyderabad, as though they had a penchant for gran-diloquent lodgings.

Unlike Simla in the north, Ooty never succumbed to the onslaught of the great offices of state, and there remains an identifiable continuity of style and ambience. As late as 1896 the little Union Church was erected in a pretty Regency Gothick style, fifty years after it went out of fashion

131

Government House: Gate Lodge. The Arts and Crafts style is rare in India in spite of its nostalgic associations. This Voyseyesque Lodge marks the entrance to Government House from the Botanical Gardens.

elsewhere. To Whish and Kindersley, Ooty seemed a little unreal, a sort of lost world, and a trace of that remains to this day, although its isolation is no longer a reliable bulwark against change and the twentieth century.

The development of the hill station occurred at a point when British power was consolidated sufficiently for settlements to be developed in remote and inaccessible areas in the confident knowledge that British troops could be called upon to cope with any emergency, an assumption that nearly proved fatal during the Mutiny. The hill station grew up as a response by Europeans to life in India. They were essentially resorts developed to provide rest and recreation, an alternative to the inhospitable towns and cities of the plains. The principal beneficiaries were the women and children, but the price paid was stultifying boredom. Deprived of any effective domestic, economic or political role the memsahib lived a static existence where time hung heavily on her hands. The hill station was just a welcome consolation for those who lived their lives in exile. They were always pale imitations of life at home, and never more than wistful reflections of the real thing, which is why today they seem so forlorn and rather sad. Conceived in nostalgia, they seem destined to decline into melancholy, for old empires don't really die, they just fade away.

CHAPTER 6

THE DEVIL'S WIND

In the early 1850s India was undergoing a period of acute stress as the changes of the past thirty years pressed hard upon the traditional social structure of the country. The high-minded liberal innovations of Bentinck, Macaulay and the evangelical radicals had altered native perceptions of British rule. It was no longer a disinterested instrument of control over-ruling the factional, fissiparous structure of Indian society, but one with a passionate belief in its own role, driven by all the remorseless moral rectitude of the Victorian social conscience. Government was seen to be partial, bestowing patronage and benefits on those who collaborated with the new forces of innovation.

Technological changes such as the introduction of the telegraph and railway, and the development of irrigation and road works disturbed the ultra-conservative basis of Indian society. The great revenue assessments of northern India displaced many traditional land-holding communities and individuals, fostering the growth of usury and a crisis within the village structure. It was no coincidence that when the military mutiny broke out in 1857, the banias or money-lenders were the first to suffer in the civil insurrection that followed in its wake. The most obvious focus for the welter of grievances was the political doctrine of 'lapse' adumbrated by the Governor-General, the Marquess of Dalhousie. Under this expedient British rule was extended to those territories without direct heirs and persistent political mismanagement of native states was used as a valid excuse for annexation. With the takeover of the huge Muslim state of Oudh, the activities of the British began to alarm the entire Indian ruling class.

As early as 1833 Sir John Shore remarked with considerable foresight: 'I do not imagine that this [revolt] will be effected by a combination among the native princes, or by a premeditated insurrection; it is more likely to happen when totally unexpected, and to have its origin in some petty disturbance.' Richard Burton, the great explorer, was more forthright and warned of 'the forthcoming St Bartholomew's Day in the east'. Contrary to popular belief the Indian Mutiny was neither a war for Indian independence, nor a religious conspiracy, nor a populist revolt based on agrarian grievances, although there were elements of all these in its complex origins. Essentially it was a post-pacification revolt falling between periods of primary and secondary resistance. The response was compartmentalised, reflecting the uneven impact of colonial rule and the diverse development of various social groups. It involved only parts of Upper India, and portions of the population, splitting the decaying fabric of Indian society into bloody civil war. Paradoxically, often social tensions were far greater in areas that did not revolt or which remained loyal to the British. The spark came not from within the peasantry or from amongst the displaced magnates, but from within the Company's own army, inflamed by rumours that cartridges for the new Enfield rifles were smeared with pigs' and cows' fat, an affront to Muslims and Hindus alike. However, the disaffected sepoys did not attempt to lead the rural insurrection which followed the breakdown of government control; they concentrated in Lucknow, Cawnpore and Delhi, where the old Moghul Emperor, Bahadur Shah, became a puppet figurehead for all the various factions. The rising occurred at a point when the British were powerful enough to disturb the traditional structure of Indian society, but when they lacked the effective instruments of social control. It promoted a resurgence of the old ways, a wild, atavistic spasm of violence against the steadily advancing new order of Westernised values and institutions, but it was unco-ordinated with no expressed aims, no real unity and no fundamental driving purpose. It marked the death throes of old India and the dawn of the nation state.

The ferocious storm of violence which engulfed Upper India in 1857 has left many evocative monuments and sites which, curiously, remain largely unknown in England. The Mutiny came as a profound shock to the British. It left a mark deep in the Imperial consciousness, a sense of betrayal, leading to a change of emphasis and eventually to policies designed to extricate Britain from India rather than to found an Asiatic society based on liberal ethics of utility and education. The Mutiny was a nightmare to be forgotten, but one which haunted the official mind for the duration of the Raj.

The first suggestions of incipient mutiny occurred as early as 26th January 1857 when the 19th Native Infantry refused the new Enfield cartridges and were marched to Barrackpore to be disbanded. In March a young sepoy, Mangal Pande, intoxicated by drugs, ran amok firing on his British officers until the redoubtable General Hearsey himself seized and disarmed the man. Pande was hanged from the branches of the great banyan tree at Barrackpore. The flashpoint occurred at Meerut, 48 miles north of Delhi, on 8th May. The mob swept through the cantonments looting and burning everything in sight. White women and children, cornered in their own homes, were cut to pieces by the razor-sharp tulwars of the cavalry or were beaten to death with iron cudgels, their mutilated bodies left sprawling in the gardens of their own bungalows. The fate of many was horrific. The pregnant wife of one officer was butchered by the market slaughterhouse keeper; another, infected with smallpox, was burned alive by firebrands tossed at her clothes. It was a scene which repeated itself in station after station all over Bengal and Bihar. The British were taken completely unawares and there was a fatal delay in responding. Within a month the British were dislodged from Delhi and most of the surrounding area, and invested in Lucknow and Cawnpore. Elsewhere prompt or decisive action won the day. The Bombay and Madras Presidencies held, but Bengal went up in flames, and with the entire area between Calcutta and Delhi denuded of European troops it seemed to many that the days of the British were numbered.

At Cawnpore the situation was dire in the extreme. Here the British under General Wheeler had retreated into a shallow earth entrenchment only four feet high, an exposed position incapable of stopping even musket fire. One of the major reasons why the Mutiny made such an impact on mid-Victorian England was that for the first time large numbers of English women and children were in the forefront of events and liable to the most brutal treatment. Their sudden exposure to the ferocity of siege and insurrection, often at the hands of those they trusted most, released deeply-suppressed racial tensions. The pangs of childbirth came upon some in the midst of the most dreadful discomfort, and in the worst possible season. The June sky was like a great canopy of fire, and shade of any sort was impossible. 'Some saw their children slowly die in their arms, some had them swept away from their breasts by the desolating fire of the enemy. There was no misery which humanity could endure that did not fall heavily upon our English women.'

By day and by night the raking fire of muskets and artillery never ceased. There was not a single place immune from bullets or round shot. Shells rolled and hissed across the entrenchment exploding in a hail of lethal splinters to spread mutilation and destruction in all directions. A single shell killed seven married women of the 32nd Foot crouched in a trench. A round shot took off the head of General Wheeler's son, Lieutenant Wheeler, before the eyes of his horrified mother and sisters. A rare account of the siege written by one of the handful of survivors, Amy Horne, was published in Calcutta in 1893. After the first week the thatched roof of the barrack building caught fire and all vestiges of relief for the sick and wounded, and shade for the women and children, went up in flames.

A few were dragged out regardless of their excruciating wounds, but the rest were burnt alive . . . Great God, was it thus to be, was it possible that human beings could endure so much! . . . The whole place was nothing but a ruin, the walls were perforated and it would be vain to describe the havoc this fire caused, the walls

A grisly view of Wheeler's entrenchment at Cawnpore.

retained the heat for several days and were unapproachable, the Doctors warned us not to go in, that we would die, or lose our reason, some went in preferring the heated rooms to the sun. Mrs Belson and child, Miss Campbell, Colonel Williams' daughter, Miss Yates, Mrs Christie and child, these all died of a maddening fever, Rev Haycock was bereft of reason, a perfect maniac ... Death was everywhere. Two little girls of eight and nine years of age had been left by their mother for the night in one of these rooms; you can imagine her feelings when she came back in the morning and found that a shell had burst in the room and killed them, their bones and flesh were gathered in a sheet and thrown into the well outside, which was the grave of our dead.

The swarm of flies were a plague and the offensive smell from the dead animals unbearable. They mostly prowled near the well, where they were shot, fragments of their flesh falling in and polluting the water ... Words cannot describe our wretched condition and misery.

The position at Cawnpore was completely untenable, and when Nana Sahib, the rebel leader, offered safe passage to Allahabad if the garrison capitulated, Wheeler had no choice. On the morning of 27th June the garrison marched out to the Suttee Chaura Ghat on the river for embarkation into the boats, a straggling column of men, women and children, highly suspicious of the whole affair. Their suspicions were justified for during the embarkation into the boats fighting broke out, some say accidentally, most that it was planned. The great majority were shot or cut to pieces in the water. The survivors were hauled from the river. The men were shot a few days later, and the women and children incarcerated in the city at the Bibigarh. There were few exceptions. One was Ulrica Wheeler, youngest daughter of the General, who was carried off by a sowar and was discovered years later living in Ambala. The remainder were less fortunate. When it became clear that a relieving force under General Havelock was nearing the city, the remaining captives were slaughtered, and their dismembered bodies put down a nearby well. Havelock described his entry into the city in his memoirs:

The troops now advanced to the Sevada Plain, East of Cawnpore. Some of them hastened to Wheeler's entrenchment, and to the building where the women and children had been confined, and were struck with horror at the sight which met their eyes. The pavement was swimming in blood and fragments of children's and ladies' dresses were floating in it. They entered the apartments and found them empty and silent but there also the blood lay deep on the floor, covered with bonnets, collars, combs and children's frocks and frills. The walls were dotted with the marks of bullets, and on the wooden pillars were deep sword cuts, from some of which hung tresses of hair. But neither the sabre cuts nor the dents of bullets were sufficiently high above the floor to indicate that the weapons had been aimed at men defending their

The Bibigarh, Cawnpore: scene of the massacre of the women and children.

lives, they appear rather to have been levelled at crouching women and children begging for mercy. The soldiers proceeded with their search when in crossing the court yard, they perceived human limbs bristling from a well and on further examination found it to be choked up with the bodies of the victims, which appeared to have been thrown in promiscuously. The dead with the wounded till it was full to the brim.

Surgeon General Munro discovered a large sharp hook six feet from the floor around which were found a child's prints. 'Evidently a wounded child had been hung upon the hook, and the poor thing in its feeble struggles, had left the impress of its little bleeding fingers on the wall. This was horrible to think of or look at, so I hurried from the room.'

The well was covered to form a grave and a terrible vengeance was enacted under the dreadful Brigadier Neill. Each miscreant apprehended was forced to lick the blood from the Bibigarh floor before being defiled and hanged.

For those who gaze with misty-eyed nostalgia on the days of the Company and the Raj, it is as well to recall the terrible passions which lurked beneath the surface of Anglo-Indian society, and the latent theme of communal violence which erupted again during partition in 1947. It is hard to convey to the modern reader the traumatic effects of the massacres at Cawnpore and the lamentable events of the Mutiny, but they left a permanent mark on the Anglo-Indian mind and it is no surprise to discover that the sites of these melancholy events were revered.

At Cawnpore little has changed in over one hundred and thirty years. Although the passions are long spent, there is still an evocative aura about the place. The Suttee Chaura Ghat remains unaltered from the fateful day. One can wander from the site of the entrenchment down a dry winding path to the river and summon up images long since forgotten in England. At the river the little hexagonal temple to Shiva is still there, but there is nothing to mark the spot save a small plaque by the roadside erected in 1930. The principal monuments are concentrated in the old entrenchment which is marked out with stone boundary posts around the Cawnpore Memorial Church, which was raised in honour of the fallen at the north-east corner of Wheeler's defences.

The church was designed by Walter Granville, architect to the East Bengal Railway and later consulting architect to the government of India. It was commenced in July 1862, but not completed until December 1875, the conciliatory climate prevailing after the Mutiny rendering fund-raising difficult. The original designs were modified substantially, but the completed structure in a Lombardic Gothic style is handsome, executed in bright red brick with polychrome dressings. It is dominated by a lofty campanile and spire and the rose window over the western entrance is filled with fine stained glass which dapples the polychrome interior. The apsidal east end has a series of marble tablets on which are inscribed the names of the fallen. The walls are studded with memorials including a canopied tablet to the engineers of the East Bengal Railway and a captivating brass plate in memory of John Robert Mackillop who sacrificed himself procuring water from the well for the distressed women and children. Galleries run around the upper half of the church lit by arcaded clerestory windows.

The church is a peaceful place in which to indulge in quiet contemplation of the terrible tragedies which occurred in and around this consecrated ground, but the most evocative of all the monuments erected in India lies outside in the churchyard, where the screen and memorial, which were raised over the Bibigarh well, have been moved from the Memorial Gardens to a more discreet and appropriate place. No Indian was allowed inside the original enclosure and it is an extraordinary tribute to the maturity and magnanimity of the Indian people that the monument was carefully relocated in 1948 and not merely swept aside as one of the more gruesome trappings of imperialism.

The Memorial is approached through two gateways over which are inscribed the moving words – 'These are they which come out of great tribulation'. The centrepiece is a beautiful carved figure of an angel by Baron Carlo Marochetti with crossed arms holding palms, a symbol of peace. It was paid for by Lord Canning, and is surrounded by a handsome carved Gothic screen designed by Henry Yule of the Bengal Engineers in 1863. The enclosure is rarely visited now, and an elegiac mood hangs over the place accentuated by Marochetti's mournful seraph which stands in permanent reproach to the folly of man.

Forty-nine miles to the north stands Lucknow. In 1857 it lay at the eye of the storm and here amongst the shaded lawns of the Residency compound was played out one of the most compelling dramas in the history of the British Empire. The defence of Lucknow became the British Thermopylae, an epic, heroic struggle against overwhelming

The tall campanile of Walter Granville's Memorial Church, completed in 1875. The interior is a shrine to the fallen.

138

The most poignant image of the Great Mutiny. Baron Carlo Marochetti's mournful seraph marked the location of the well at the Bibighar. Now it stands in the Memorial Churchyard with Henry Yule's Gothic screen.

odds. Lord Canning's words, later inscribed in stone, bear witness to the extraordinary hold which the siege had on the Victorian collective mind: 'There does not stand recorded in the annals of war an achievement more truly heroic than the defence of the Residency of Lucknow.' For a nation which prided itself on understatement, that is a measure of the awe in which the whole episode came to be viewed.

In 1857 Lucknow was the capital of the newly annexed state of Oudh. It was seething with discontent, a seedbed of sedition and anti-British feeling. The outbreak at Meerut and the collapse at Delhi had undermined British authority in the whole region and on 30th May, the native regiments in the Lucknow cantonment burst into revolt in a frenzy of looting and killing. But the British were more fortunate than at Cawnpore for the Commissioner Sir Henry Lawrence had made preparations to resist a possible rising. The Residency compound had been quietly but steadily fortified for the previous month, and large stocks of grain and food had been collected.

The Times correspondent, W. H. Russell described Lucknow as 'a fairy-tale city, more vast and brilliant than Paris; a vision of palaces, domes azure and golden, cupolas, colonnades, long façades of fair perspective in pillar and column, terraced roofs – all rising up amid a calm still ocean of the brightest verdure ... Spires of gold glitter in the sun. Turrets and gilded spheres shine like constellations.' This was not an exaggeration for the Nawabs of Oudh had lavished crores of rupees on civic improvements and extravagant palaces to create a city unequalled in opulence and grandeur in the East, an Oriental vision of magnificence recalling Kublai Khan's fabled Xanadu. As part of this vast dream-like vision the Residency occupied a privileged position on a raised plateau close to the river commanding views of the city and the river crossings including Rennie's famous iron bridge.

The actual Residency building had been commenced in the 1780s, but it had taken several decades to complete so that, architecturally, it lacked cohesion, acquiring something of the air of an English country house with wings and ranges added on at various points in time. The building enjoyed the usual extensive verandahs and porticos. Contemporary sketches show the windows screened by canvas blinds, but the really distinguishing feature was an octagonal corner staircase tower crowned by a shallow cupola. Beneath the principal rooms was a suite of tykhanas or underground rooms for use in the hot weather, elements which Thomas Twining thought were the innovation of Claude Martin at Constantia, but which were common expedients in Oudh. The basement had enormous walls thick enough to accommodate niches and cupboards, and a huge underground swimming pool.

Throughout the first half of the 19th century a whole complex of European buildings arose around the house to provide a conclave of houses, buildings and offices commensurate with the political power of the Resident. The area was entered through an impressive triumphal gateway and guardhouse, The Baillie Guard, named after Major John Baillie, the Resident between 1811 and 1815. Architecturally the archway was in the tradition of Government House, Calcutta and the Residency at Hyderabad, a classical screen designed as a public

statement proclaiming the power of the British Resident to the whole city. Nearby lay a detached Banqueting Hall, not dissimilar to that erected in Madras, standing on a rusticated plinth and carrying paired columns punctuated by Venetian windows. Adjacent stood the Treasury and Council chamber. The building, later known as Dr Fayrer's house, also dates from the early 19th century. This was a handsome structure with excellent neo-classical detailing of Adam-esque fans over the rectangular door openings. Quite who was responsible for the actual design and construction of this fine complex of European buildings is difficult to know, but they have been attributed to William Tricket, architect and engineer to the King of Oudh in the early 1820s, and it would be surprising if he hadn't had a hand in them.

Today the whole area stands as a romantic ruin, preserved in aspic like an Oriental Pompeii, the classical columns and thin red brick structure beneath accentuating the Roman analogy; an oasis of Western civilisation overtaken not by natural calamity, but by events so terrible that henceforth they were christened 'The Devil's Wind'.

After the open insurrection of 30th May discretion was thrown to the winds and the defensive position around the Residency was strength-ened into a continuous chain of buildings, walls, trenches, palisades and ramparts. Pits were dug and filled with sharpened stakes and batteries were sited to provide overlapping fields of fire. The siege began in earnest on 30th June, the day after a sizeable British force of infantry and cavalry went out to meet the mutineers at Chinhat only to

The Residency, Lucknow: The Baillie Guard Gate was designed in the manner of the great entrance screens at Calcutta and Hyderabad. Only the brick core survived the siege.

141

be defeated and very nearly annihilated by an overwhelming number of mutineers. If the situation had been grave before Chinhat, it was parlous after.

Few thought that they could last a week, let alone eighty-seven long days of ferocious fighting. When at last Havelock and Outram broke through to the beleaguered garrison on 25th September, the relieving force had been bled so white that it too was invested for a further fifty-three days before it was finally evacuated by Sir Colin Campbell on 25th November. The city was not retaken until March 1858, and only then at a fearful price. Amongst the fallen lay Havelock, who died at the Alam Bagh shortly after the relief of the Residency, and also Major Hodson of Hodson's Horse, killed in the fighting at La Martinière, where his grave lies outside the gates. Tennyson put it all to verse:

> Banner of England, not for a season, O banner of Britain
>   has thou
> Floated in conquering battle or flapt to the battle cry
> Never with mightier glory than when we had rear'd thee
>   on high,
> Flying at the top of the roofs in the ghastly siege of
>   Lucknow
> Shot thro' the staff or the halyard, but ever we raised
>   thee anew,
> And ever upon the topmost roof our banner of England blew.

The subsequent preservation and veneration of the ruins as a lasting monument to British stoicism have sterilised the site, so that now it is difficult to invoke the images of suffering and hardship which raged here amongst the manicured lawns and shady walks of the garden areas; except that is for the tykhana. Here deep in the underground room, the women and children of the 32nd Foot were kept, and from the cool, chill atmosphere and dark, dank walls emanates a curious kind of melancholy which haunts the casual visitor. Here twenty feet below ground 1857 seems very close indeed.

> But the Ruins remain, which still speak of the past!
> The stranger now treads, with full reverence, the ground,
> Where the sleepers will sleep till the last Trumpet's sound.

Outside the epicentres of revolt at Cawnpore and Lucknow, the Mutiny seems as remote as any other historical event. At Arrah the little house defended by twelve Englishmen and fifty Sikhs for eight days against over 2,000 mutineers is now an historical monument, but one which is rarely visited. Only at Delhi do a few reminders linger on to convey the drama of the great siege and storming of the city. There the British had been swept out by the influx of the first mutineers from Meerut. They clung precariously to the Ridge outside the city where gradually sufficient forces were mustered to carry the city by storm between 13th and 20th September 1857.

North of the Kashmir Gate stand two country houses which were

erected in the early 19th century – Hindu Rao's and Metcalfe House. Both acquired a reputation during the siege of Delhi as salient points in the British lines, and both survive. The former was erected in 1830 for William Fraser, as a country retreat outside the city, and it shares the usual classical features – verandah, pilasters and a deep plinth. Architecturally Metcalfe's House is more interesting. Situated by the river Jumna the verandah faces south in the form of a terrace, beneath which is a subterranean room under the actual river bed to provide cool shelter during the summer. Although this was common in Oudh, it was very unusual in Delhi. Emily, Lady Clive Bayley, the daughter of Sir Thomas Metcalfe, recalled the house vividly in happier days:

> The rooms were so large, so lofty, and there were so many of them, all on one floor, and all twenty-four feet in height. Study, library and Napoleon Gallery in one line faced the north portico; then the drawing room and banqueting-room behind them facing east and west; then the day-room and small drawing room, the dining-room and serving-room. These opened in to the oratory and lobby, off which opened the large spare bedrooms and dressing-room. Then facing the south verandah, my Father's bedroom, my Mother's sitting-room and my bedroom.

"Whilst retrieving china from the Residency drawing room, Susanna Palmer was mortally wounded early in the siege. After suffering the agonies of amputation, and considerable suffering, bravely borne, she died later, her only thought for her surviving father." Tragedies such as these were commonplace and horrified Victorian England.

Externally the house followed common established themes. 'Round all four sides of the house was a splendid verandah, twenty to thirty feet wide and very lofty, the roof supported by magnificent stone pillars.' The house was badly damaged during the siege as it was the site of Metcalfe's Battery and the scene of heavy fighting.

Elsewhere along the Ridge stand the Flagstaff Tower around which the British survivors of the insurrection gathered on the night of 11th May shocked and confused, and the octagonal spire of the Mutiny Memorial. This was erected by the army shortly after the Mutiny and it takes the form of a Gothic memorial cross reminiscent of the Eleanor

SUSANNA PALMER
KILLED IN THIS ROOM
BY A CANNON BALL ON THE
1ST JULY 1857,
IN HER NINETEENTH YEAR

crosses in England. Set on a high platform it contains a staircase from the summit of which can be obtained a spectacular view of the city. The cross has three principal stages crowned by a low spire, and around the base are panels inscribed with the names and regiments of those who died in the recapture of the city.

Many of the fallen are buried outside the Kashmir Gate in a small overgrown cemetery. Here lies Brigadier-General John Nicholson, perhaps the most charismatic of all the figures thrown up by the Mutiny, a giant of a man of enormous physical strength and talent who held down the North-West Frontier and the Punjab, before arriving outside Delhi to a tumultuous welcome, escorted by his personal guard of devoted Multani horsemen. Nicholson was a legend in his own lifetime and it was his presence and driving force, more than any other single factor, that carried the city. He was a lonely, tortured character full of contradictory impulses, yet he was venerated as a deity by a sect who thought 'Nikkul Seyn' was the reincarnation of Brahma. They rejoiced when he beat them, believing it to be a sign of his true divinity rather than the manifestation of a dark, sadistic streak. He was adored by his followers and fell mortally wounded at the hour of triumph, shot through the chest as he led his men forward through the alleys of the city. When he was buried his personal band of tough Multani cavalry were inconsolable, throwing themselves to the ground in a spontaneous outburst of hysterical grief.

An early photograph of Brigadier-General John Nicholson, mortally wounded in the storming of Delhi on the night of 17th September 1857.

Just inside the Kashmir Gate, through which the British stormed on the night of the 13th September, stands St James's Church, a local landmark both now and in 1857, its distinctive dome appearing strangely incongruous in a city of more exotic forms. The church was consecrated in 1836 and it was erected at the sole expense of the legendary Colonel James Skinner, of Skinner's Horse, in fulfilment of a vow made while lying wounded on the field of battle. Architecturally it is a most unusual departure from the established pattern of Gibbs derivatives which recur throughout India. In plan it resembles a Greek cross, with Tuscan porticos to three of the arms, the fourth forming the choir. The dome is carried on an octagonal drum, but the symmetrical appearance is offset by a low clock tower placed between two porticos. Internally, it is surprisingly spacious, enriched with Ionic pilasters and modillioned cornices. The walls are relieved by niches and circular recesses. Outside in the compound a small railed enclosure is dedicated to the Skinner family, and there is a memorial to William Fraser, agent to the Lieutenant-Governor at Delhi and builder of Hindu Rao's house, who was murdered in 1835. The area around the church was subject to fierce fighting. Contemporary photographs show the extent of the damage it sustained. The golden orb crowning the dome was used by the sepoys for target practice, but it was reinstated after the Mutiny and the church stands to this day as a resplendent monument to that curious mixture of martial and pious qualities that pervaded Anglo-India and which reached its most distasteful extremes during the Mutiny.

As the Mutiny petered out into the sporadic lawlessness of 1859, it became clear that things could never be the same again. The days of the

The octagonal spire of the Mutiny Memorial on the Ridge outside Delhi.

St James's or Skinner's Church, Delhi. The scene of fierce fighting in 1857, the original orb and cross over the Baroque dome were used by the rebels for target practice.

Pale women who have lost their Lord Will kiss some relics of the slain – Some tarnished epaulette – some sword – Poor toys to soothe such anguished pain.

Cawnpore Cemetery: The price of Empire was never cheap.

Company and its army were over. The Crown assumed direct control through the instrument of the Viceroy, and this new personal relationship accounted for the extraordinarily close bond that was to develop between the Queen and her Indian subjects. British administration was reorganised into a mould which was to last more or less unaltered until 1947. Far greater emphasis was placed on respect for India's complex socio-religious systems. The army was completely reorganised. The financial base of the administration was overhauled. But the single most important change was the call for greater contact and understanding between the two communities, which had been diverging since the early 19th century. British interests which were once identified with social engineering and policies of Westernisation and change, went into reverse. The *ancien régime* of the princes, maharajahs and liege chiefs, which the evangelical radicals regarded as a barrier to change, became the main bulwark of the British Raj. Those who had remained loyal were showered with rewards, decorations and status in the new order, but in the long term it was contrary to India's real interests and the Raj became identified as reactionary and backward-looking, unable to come to terms with the new forces of the age. The future lay in the great new urban centres, not in the old princely courts where privilege and nepotism reigned, and it was no coincidence that in the aftermath of the Mutiny the focus of commercial activity and expansion shifted to the west coast and the emergent commercial centre of Bombay, which was destined to grow from a forgotten backwater to a great Imperial city within three decades.

146

CHAPTER 7

BOMBAY:
URBS PRIMA IN INDIS

In 1781 Samuel Pechel wrote in his *Historical Account of Bombay*:

> The island of Bombay is the antient property of the English East
> India Company; it hath hitherto been of all her settlements the
> most conducive to the greatness of the nation in Asia; yet through
> the splendor of achievement, great acquisition of territory and
> immense harvests of wealth in Bengal and the Coast of Coroman-
> del, it hath been in some measure overlooked and, as if in a corner
> of the world unnoticed.

In the early years Bombay was rivalled by Surat to the north where the
first English factory had been established. Until the early 19th century
it was only the success of the Bombay ship building yards run by
Parsees which made its existence worth while. The town was renowned
for the extraordinary quality of its ships, constructed in Malabar teak,
and it enjoyed the signal honour of constructing numerous ships-of-
the-line for the Admiralty, the first orders ever placed outside England.

Bombay was isolated from contact with the east coast across the
mainland by the Maratha tribes, and their general hostility accentuated
the insularity of the island colony. The independent merchants of
Bombay maintained a valuable, if limited, commerce in raw silk, pearls,
dates and perfumes with Muscat and Arabia, in spices, sugar and
ambergris with Java, Malacca and the East Indies, and in cotton and
bullion with China. This commercial contact created an unusual social
system, which remained a distinctive local quality throughout the Raj.
Bombay society was more cosmopolitan and liberal in its attitudes,
unlike the rather rigid social hierarchies which characterised Madras
and Calcutta. The Parsees, Sephardic Jews and the British associated
freely and without prejudice, sharing a mutual interest in the
warehouses, counting houses and shipyards that were the commercial
raison d'être of the city. A quality of informal intimacy and open-
handed friendship characterised the place, but the actual English
population was minute – only 250 resided within the walls in 1813.

In the early 19th century the chains which had bound the potential
commercial vitality of the town were severed one by one. On the night
of 17th February 1803 the town was devastated by a great fire. The real
importance of the fire lay not in the improvement of the town within
the walls, but the inducement to construct a new town outside with
wider, regular streets, relieving the congestion of the old Fort area. The
expansion of the trading community was given an enormous boost in
1813 when the insidious trade monopoly of the Company was

abolished. Trade with England was transformed. Between 1809 and 1816 the annual trade in raw cotton trebled from thirty million to ninety million lbs. Finally in November 1817 the power of the Peshwa, titular head of the Marathas, was broken at the Battle of Kirkee and the constraint on trade and communications across the mainland was lifted. English supremacy was assured and the old-established trade routes across the Deccan plateau were drawn into the economic hinterland of Bombay. The town became the commercial centre of the Arabian Sea and in 1819 it stood poised to expand further under the enlightened guidance of the new Governor, Mountstuart Elphinstone.

Elphinstone was an unpretentious liberal man of considerable prescience and charm, extending an easy familiarity to natives of all ranks. He fostered the expansion of trade, the moderate and uniform settlement of the revenues and the education of the people. 'On this side of India there is really more zeal and liberality displayed in the improvement of that country, the construction of roads and public buildings, the conciliation of the natives and their education, than I have yet seen in Bengal,' exclaimed Bishop Heber.

By 1830 the road to the Deccan had been opened and improved. Visually the town gained immeasurably from the construction of Cowper's Town Hall and Hawkins's Mint (see page 100) and systematic land reclamation did much to transform Bombay from an unwholesome swamp into a salubrious residence. Economic growth was sustained throughout the 1830s by a steady rise in American cotton prices. By 1830 annual exports of Indian cotton to England exceeded one million bales. At last in 1835 Bombay became a bishopric, and in 1838, a city, with the Church of St Thomas raised to cathedral status. However, unlike Madras or Calcutta, the city had little of the architectural ambience of a great metropolis.

A description of the city appeared in the *Asiatic Journal* of May to August 1838:

> The town or city of Bombay is . . . nearly a mile long . . . the houses are picturesque, in consequence of the quality of handsomely-carved woodwork employed in the pillars and verandahs, but they are inconveniently crowded together, and the high conical roofs of red tiles are very offensive to the eye, especially if accustomed to the flat-turretted and balustraded palaces of Calcutta.

More than one visitor thought that the only building with any architectural charm was the Cathedral. It is certainly worthy of veneration, not so much for its architectural merit, which is slight, as for its age and historical associations. The Cathedral was begun by Gerald Aungier in 1672 but it was not formally opened until 1718. Built in stone the plan is simple, with a vaulted roof. Like all cathedrals, it is a repository of fascinating monuments which bring alive the glorious feats of Imperial arms. Consider Major Eldred Pottinger's, the hero of Herat who defended the Afghan city against all odds, dying a few years after, aged 32, or Bacon's monument to Captain Hardinge RN, the

BOMBAY: URBS PRIMA IN INDIS

younger brother of Lord Hardinge, who died in 1808 in a brilliant engagement in which his undermanned and outgunned frigate captured the French cruiser *Piedmontese*. Of the civil monuments, that to Jonathan Duncan, the Governor, is delightful, depicting him receiving the blessings of young Hindus, a reference to his successful repression of infanticide in certain districts of Benares and Kathiawar. A noble fellow, he was inspired by the now unfashionable belief in absolute rather than relative moral values, a belief so irresistible that it swept away slavery from the Empire and motivated the evangelical radicals who abolished suttee, thuggee and other native practices abhorrent to the European mind. Katherine Kirkpatrick, the mother of James Achilles Kirkpatrick the Resident of Hyderabad, died at 22 and is commemorated in a marble mural by the younger Bacon raised by her sons:

> Image of Truth! In Mind by few surpassed
> In Beauty's mould by Nature chastely cast . . .
> That thy own Sons, asserting Nature's claim
> Join to commemorate a Mother's Name;
> And hallowing with their Fears the votive stone
> Record her virtues and attest their own.

Such memorials marking the passage of time and the vanity of all human endeavour culminate in a small memorial tablet to Henry Robertson Bowers, 'noble Birdie Bowers', of the Royal Indian Marine, who died with Scott in the Antarctic on the ill-fated expedition of 1912.

In the 1840s two churches were commenced in India, St Paul's Cathedral, Calcutta, and St John's Church, Bombay. They are of seminal importance in the architectural history of Anglo-India. A new enthusiasm was being transmitted from home – Gothic – but in terms of style these two manifestations of it were quite different.

After eight years in construction, St Paul's Cathedral, Calcutta, was completed in 1847 and was regarded with justifiable pride as a handsome edifice. The style chosen was suitably Christian, English Perpendicular Gothic adapted to the vicissitudes of the climate. The tower and spire were modelled on Norwich Cathedral with certain modifications cribbed from Canterbury. Much of the external and internal detailing was copied from the finest carving to be found in York Minster. The architect was William Nairn Forbes, the military engineer who designed the Calcutta Mint, as the Church Building Committee were unable to afford an architect from England.

Forbes was a gifted man, but not a genius. If the Calcutta Mint was flawed by architectural solecisms and a certain clumsiness of detailing, then the Cathedral also lacks that essential spark which separates the work of an inspired professional from the military dilettante. More importantly it was conceived in a whimsical Gothic style which was essentially backward-looking and conservative. It belongs to the same era of pretty, picturesque Gothic as St Peter's Church of 1835 in Fort William (page 51). It was conceived at a point just prior to the

formulation of new principles of Gothic architecture by Pugin and Ruskin and promoted by the Cambridge Camden Society (later the Ecclesiological Society) but it is a noble structure for all that and it is important, for it broke the mould of Gibbs derivatives which hitherto had dominated church design in India. Bishop Wilson was the 'first to intimate discontent with the style of churches previously built in India', and Forbes gave it visible expression.

The constraints were considerable. Funds were short, the sub-soil poor and available materials limited, but Forbes received valuable assistance from C. K. Robison, the city magistrate and designer of Metcalfe Hall, and also from Major Fitzgerald both of whom served on the Building Committee. The building was constructed in a peculiar brick especially prepared for the purpose, which combined lightness with compressional strength; the dressings were of Chunar stone, and the whole edifice was covered inside and out with polished chunam. The adaptations to the climate and the site are self-evident. The lancet windows in the choir and transepts are carried down to plinth level to increase ventilation. There is no nave, as the soil was considered incapable of supporting the mass of clustered columns, arches and side aisles, and also their presence would have reduced ventilation and impaired the view. The roof is unusual. It is a shallow curve spanned by iron trusses adorned with Gothic tracery, and, when built, it was one of the largest spans in existence.

The original east window was the gift of the Dean and Chapter of Windsor to whom it was presented by King George III for use at St George's Chapel. It depicted the crucifixion after a design by Benjamin West, but was destroyed by a cyclone in 1864. The present design by Clayton and Bell is extremely fine. However, the *tour de force* of the entire composition is the magnificent west window designed by Burne-Jones in 1880 as a memorial to the Viceroy Lord Mayo, who was assassinated in the Andaman Islands. It is the finest piece of stained glass in India, a panoply of exquisite colours and Pre-Raphaelite figures.

The reredos is also High Victorian and can be attributed to Sir Arthur Blomfield. It is executed in alabaster with panels of Florentine mosaic depicting the Annunciation, the Adoration of the Magi and the Flight into Egypt. The Willis organ is one of the finest ever made by the firm. In common with most of the public buildings of Calcutta, the Cathedral suffered from the vagaries of the climate. An earthquake brought down the upper stage of the steeple in June 1897. It was restored but after another earthquake in 1934 it was rebuilt to the design of Bell Harry tower at Canterbury.

Forbes lies buried in the church to which he devoted many of the last years of his life. He was a Scot born in 1796 at Blackford, Aberdeen and he died a Major General on his way home at Aden in 1855. His body was brought back to Calcutta and interred beneath a fine mural tablet, surmounted by his bust, and flanked by female figures, one bearing a trumpet and laurel wreath, the other a pen and scroll.

The Afghan Memorial Church of St John the Evangelist at Colaba, Bombay was commenced in 1847 and consecrated eleven years later. Its

Major William Nairn Forbes, architect of St Paul's Cathedral and the Silver Mint.

St Paul's Cathedral, Calcutta. The tower was recast without the original spire after the 1934 earthquake.

Afghan Memorial Church, Colaba, Bombay. The first church in India to embody new principles of Gothic architecture.

building history is confused. The architects J. M. Derick and Anthony Salvin were instructed to prepare drawings, but the plans eventually adopted were those of Henry Conybeare, son of the Dean of Llandaff, and Town Engineer of Bombay at the time. Architecturally it is not outstanding, but historically it is most important for it was the first church erected in India along the lines laid down by the Ecclesiological Society, embodying the new principles of Gothic architecture advanced by Pugin. In style it is Early English with a tower and thin spire, nave and aisles and some fine stained glass by William Wailes. The interior is lit by a series of narrow lancet windows and the chancel is lined with marble memorial tablets to the fallen of the First Afghan War. If much of the interior seems rather plain, then this was due to the absence of a skilled labour force versed in the arts of Western carving. To modern eyes it all looks conventionally straightforward, but in 1858 it was revolutionary, particularly in India, and it pointed the way forward to those High Victorian Gothic buildings, secular and ecclesiastical, that were to become the hallmark of the late Victorian

152

Raj. When new it was considered 'unrivalled among the churches of the East', and it remained a local landmark long after more ebullient Gothic buildings rose in the city.

As early as 1846 *The Ecclesiologist* had argued for two basic colonial styles – Hyperborean and Speluncar, one intended for the north and one for the southern parts of the Empire. The northern, Hyperborean style should, it argued, be based partly on the native vernacular style for whichever country the building was designed. For the southern regions a variation of Lombardy Gothic was advocated, 'the mother of mediaeval architecture' and a style associated with warm climates. Speluncar (literally cave-like), a name as pretentious as the ideas it conveyed, should have monumentality, with heavy planes, massive piers and brilliant polychrome masonry.

Outlandish as the names may be, the ideas were influential and permeated the intellectual establishment. Great thought was given to the adaptation of European styles to an Indian or colonial context in a way which would combine architectural integrity with functional refinement. In 1868 T. Roger Smith, a Bombay architect, wrote: 'Now the proper corrective is not, I hold, the direct imitation of Asiatic types, but the adoption of those European styles which have grown up in sunshiny regions. Such styles are ancient Roman, or even Greek . . . or the Renaissance and Gothic of Southern Italy or the Early Gothic of Southern France.'

Henry Conybeare's original drawings of the Afghan Memorial Church. The design was simplified in the course of construction. A comparison with the photograph shows the altered broach spire.

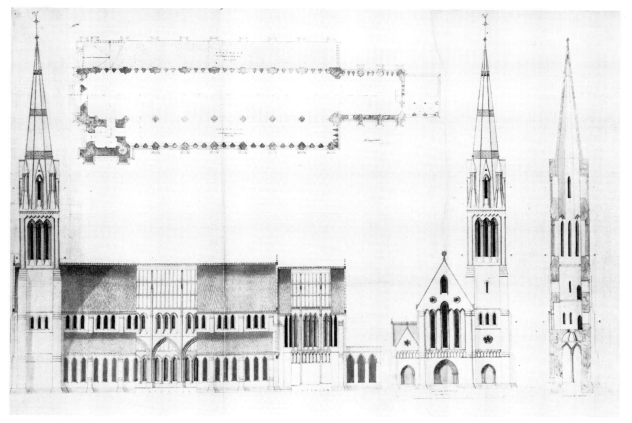

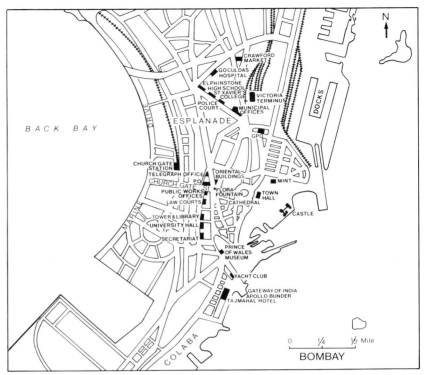

In this and other lectures he went on to claim that 'the style native to England – English Gothic – is not fitted to be transferred to India without large modification' and 'a leaning towards the peculiarities of the best Oriental styles is desirable.' These 'peculiarities' he thought were 'walls of ample thickness, covered with a profusion of delicate surface ornament, absence of vertical breaks, prevalence of horizontal cornices, and walls often replaced by lines of piers or columns'.

The debate was never resolved and continued right through to the 1920s with stormy exchanges of views over the style adopted for New Delhi, but it is easy to see how the enthusiastic promotion of new principles of Gothic architecture coincided with the search for a more successful form of tropical construction, and the history of Bombay for the next fifty years was dominated by the quest for an effective synthesis between the two.

The steady consolidation and expansion of Bombay's fortunes which characterised the 1830s gathered momentum in following decades, facilitated by the rise of the Great Indian Peninsula Railway which reached Thana in 1853. The first stage of the rival Bombay, Baroda and Central India Railway opened in 1860, reaching Broach and Baroda in 1861, Ahmedabad in 1863 and Bombay in 1864. The East India Company resolutely refused to finance railways on its own and it remained unimpressed by Dalhousie's dream of a unifying network of lines welding together a nation out of the scattered villages of the sub-continent. However the suppression of the Mutiny had demonstrated the enormous strategic advantages conferred by the railway and telegraph, and with the abolition of Company rule in 1858, the way lay clear for the construction of a rail network which would become one of the most enduring symbols of British rule.

The latent forces of commercial and economic prosperity which had been accumulating in Bombay for over four decades were unleashed in a sudden frenzy of activity. By 1864 there were thirty-one banks, sixteen financial associations, eight land corporations, sixteen printing press companies, ten shipping companies, twenty insurance companies and sixty-two joint stock companies. In 1855 there had been none. In 1857 the first cotton mill opened. By 1860 there were seven. Investors, developers, speculators and entrepreneurs were swept along on a tide of enthusiasm made irreversible by the sudden slump in the supply of American cotton to the Lancashire cotton mills on the outbreak of the American Civil War. Bombay was 'cottonopolis', a vast clearing house for all the great cotton fields of India. Irrespective of quality, prices climbed to staggering levels, earning an additional £75 million over pre-war prices in five years. Sir George Clerk wrote to the Governor, Sir Bartle Frere: 'Everything is at famine prices in Bombay just now, while [men] in trade and profession are making fortunes, our government servants are pinched for food.' Later the Municipal Commissioner Arthur Crawford simply remarked: 'no one ever drank anything but champagne in those days.'

Of course it was all too good to last. Land values rose fourfold as speculation in land became frenetic and land reclamation schemes became the order of the day. 'Financial associations formed for various purposes sprang up like mushrooms; companies expanded with an inflation as that of bubbles; projects blossomed only to decay.' When the crash came only two old-established land companies survived intact, but the general enthusiasm for land reclamation and improvement impelled a continued interest in urban expansion.

The influx of unprecedented wealth coincided with the arrival of a new Governor. Sir Henry Bartle Edward Frere was one of the most dynamic Imperial figures of his day. After a distinguished record in the Mutiny, he was appointed Governor in 1862, and under his enlightened tutelage the city was transformed into the Gateway to India. On his arrival Frere made his intentions plain. 'I look forward with the utmost confidence to the time when we shall hear that Bombay has taken her place among cities, owing as much to art as she does to nature and position.'

One of his first major civic improvements was the removal of the old town walls which surrounded the Fort area, a project which had been mooted as long ago as 1841, when a letter to *The Times* exclaimed: 'The maintenance of the Fort of Bombay is not only useless. It has become a downright and most serious nuisance to the inhabitants at large.' In 1864 the ramparts were demolished and most of the city's roads were widened and improved as part of a strategic plan prepared by James Trubshawe, architect to the Ramparts Removal Committee. A few years earlier the Municipal Commissioner, Charles Forjett, had been responsible for the laying out of Elphinstone Circle on the site of Bombay Green, the first example in the city of civic planning on a grand scale to a scheme conceived by Frere's predecessor Sir George Clerk. Forjett was an extraordinary individual. As Deputy Commissioner of Police in 1857 he was largely responsible for saving Bombay from insurrection. He personally haunted the most dangerous bazaars and slums in disguise, apprehending all who muttered anything remotely seditious, and the culmination of his career was his elevation to Municipal Commissioner in 1860. It was a new appointment replacing the earlier Conservancy Board in which 'obtuseness, indifference and party spirit appeared to have completely overcome whatever modicum of public spirit was still conserved among its members.'

Elphinstone (now Horniman) Circle bears eloquent testimony to the ideals of the new administration. Planned around the focus of the Town Hall, it comprises a circus with central gardens surrounded by ornamental iron railings imported from England. The site was bought by the Municipality and sold in building plots to English firms at a large profit, but the design of the buildings was controlled to create a unified composition of Italianate façades. On the western edge of the circle is a magnificent Venetian Gothic palazzo transplanted from its spiritual home on the Grand Canal to more exotic climes, complete with bracketed eaves, arcaded storeys and interlacing arches, all executed in warm brown sandstone.

Frere maintained the impetus of civic improvement generated by his predecessor and seized the opportunity to give Bombay a series of buildings worthy of her wealth, pre-eminence and location. He stipulated that the designs should be of the highest architectural character with conscious thought given to artistic effect and presence. As a result, paradoxically, Britain's finest heritage of High Victorian

Elphinstone Circle: an early photograph taken from the Town Hall steps in about 1870. Note the conspicuous absence of people in the European quarter, a characteristic conveyed in many early photographs. The delicate cast-iron balconies and attic verandahs were imported from England.

This splendid Venetian Gothic palazzo standing on the western edge of Elphinstone Circle was damaged by fire in 1982.

Gothic architecture lies in Bombay. Here in a great phalanx lie the Secretariat, University Library, Convocation Hall, Law Courts, Public Works Office, the Post Office and Telegraph Department, a truly Imperial vision, resembling a line of massive stone warships, monolithic, awe-inspiring and supremely self-confident. Once they faced out across the sea in silent tribute to the naval power which built them, but subsequent land reclamation has changed their relative location in the city. As a group they coalesce to form an impressively romantic skyline and they bequeathed an identity and style which was taken up and used all over the city for the remainder of the century.

The architectural prototypes for the public buildings of Bombay are not hard to find: they are the great Gothic buildings then in process of erection in London, which were readily available to the Public Works Department (PWD) in the pages of professional journals such as *The Builder*. Scott's competition design for the Foreign Office is a clear source for many with its central tower, symmetrical façade and Venetian inspiration.

The old Secretariat was the first government building planned by Frere and it was designed by Colonel (then Captain) Henry St Clair Wilkins, Royal Engineers. Wilkins is an elusive yet eminent figure in the architectural history of Anglo-India. Born in 1828 at Beelsby, Lincolnshire, he was educated privately and at Addiscombe College. In common with other officers in the Bombay Department of Public Works he was trained in civil architecture, and he worked in Aden, as well as Bombay. He commanded the Royal Engineers in the Abyssinia campaign of 1869 for which he was mentioned in despatches and made ADC to the Queen. He died in bed in London in 1896. The Secretariat was built between 1867 and 1874 and it coincided with the erection of Scott's St Pancras Station in London. Designed in a similar Venetian Gothic, the most Oriental of all Italian styles, it is an immense symmetrical pile comprising an arcaded central range with a lofty tower over the central staircase. The entire front elevation of this range is made up of arcaded verandahs enriched with structural polychromy,

The Secretariat: designed by Colonel Henry St Clair Wilkins and erected between 1867–1874.

and the central axis is further accentuated by a huge gable which breaks forward beneath the tower. This accommodates the staircase window in a single ninety-foot arch, recalling Scott's sheer west wall at St Pancras. The wings are terminated by chamfered end bays which are broken on the flanks by canted secondary staircase compartments. Besides the usual expedient of setting the rooms behind deep arcaded verandahs, the most obvious concessions to the climate are the huge projecting canopies which run in continuous bands over the first- and second-floor windows on the wings, affording protection from both sun and monsoon rains. These are covered in red tiles and carried on cast-iron brackets. The main roof, which is similarly treated, rises from behind a machicolated parapet, which is sufficiently robust to unify the entire composition. The whole is topped by crested ridges of ironwork and ventilating dormers. It is a magnificent structure faced in buff-coloured stone from Porebundar, enriched with blue and red basalt, with capitals and cornices by native artists in white Hemnagar stone. The quality of the carving is excellent.

Wilkins also designed the Public Works Office, which has a close affinity to the Secretariat. This is hardly surprising as it was commenced in May 1869 and was under construction at the same time. Its centrepiece is curious – a wide staircase tower with twin pyramidal roofs linked across the middle and crowned with finials. Beneath the tower the staircase block breaks forward to provide verandahs, and at ground level it breaks out again to form an umbrageous *porte-cochère*

158

with a terrace over. The wings are terminated by end bays which are the finest elements in the whole composition – pure Venetian Gothic with arcaded storeys enriched with structural polychromy. The Venetian inspiration, iron-crested, tiled roofs, common use of local stones, ventilating dormers, shutters and machicolated parapets are common themes which illustrate Wilkins's individual conception of tropical Gothic architecture.

The Public Works Office, a magnificent essay in Venetian Gothic, photographed shortly after its completion in 1872 and now obscured by the mature trees.

The Post Office was designed by James Trubshawe of the Ramparts Removal Committee who had been brought over to prepare an overall plan of civic improvements for Frere. He was assisted by W. Paris, who designed the adjacent Telegraph Office (1871–1874). Both buildings are faced in buff-coloured sandstone from Coorla in Salsette, with columns of blue basalt. The Post Office is mediaeval Italian Gothic in origin with bracketed eaves and shallow pitched roofs punctuated by two centrally placed towers with pyramidal roofs, between which projects an enormously deep two-storey carriage porch, the upper level constituting an outdoor tiffin room for clerks. Interestingly the staircases are not in the towers, but tucked away on the flanks. Today the original effect is impaired by the forest of aerials and masts which cluster on the roof, but the presence of the modern equipment bears witness to the original functional convenience of the building and its successful adaptation to the climate.

In 1869 when Wilkins was appointed as Chief Engineer for the campaign in Abyssinia, his absence enabled Lieutenant-Colonel James

Augustus Fuller (1828–1902) to step from the penumbra of his superior. Fuller had supervised the erection of all these major buildings and he was able to assume the commission for the new Law Courts with some confidence. They were started in 1871 and completed in 1879 in Early English Gothic with Venetian overtones; entirely appropriate for one of the principal groups of courts in the Raj, evoking all the historical associations of the rise of English liberty and the rule of law, but adapted to reflect the by now established style of their neighbours.

The building is colossal, 562 feet long and 187 feet broad, dominated by a large central tower on either side of which are octagonal towers 120 feet high, surmounted with spirelets of Porebundar stone and crowned by figures of Justice and Mercy. These towers accommodate private staircases for the judges, the main staircase lying on the eastern side and approached by a groin-vaulted corridor in Porebundar stone with a floor of Minton tiles. The courts embody all the august solemnity of their antecedents in England. The internal design and layout are clearly influenced by Street's successful designs for the Law Courts in the Strand. These had been exhibited in *The Builder* and *Building News* and were under construction at the same time as Fuller's in Bombay. The building embodied the latest fire precautions with four-inch hosetaps provided on each floor. Unlike the adjoining public offices the Law Courts have a more gaunt aspect, being faced in roughly dressed blue basalt enriched with dressings of chunam, and Porebundar, Coorla and Sewri stones, capped by roofs of Taylor's patent red tiles.

However, the most distinguished buildings in the group stand between the Secretariat and Law Courts and they were designed not by an enthusiastic military engineer, but by one of the most gifted architects of the 19th century – Sir George Gilbert Scott. The Convocation Hall and Library of the University, the latter with its enormous Rajabai Tower, is one of Scott's most outstanding designs, yet strangely it is little known in England.

The University Hall was funded by Sir Cowasjee Jehangir Readymoney, one of a number of Parsee benefactors whose generosity provided the resources to implement Frere's vision. The Hall is designed in the decorated early French style of the 15th century with an ecclesiastical air. The south end is apsidal and separated from the main body of the Hall by a grand arch. A handsome carved timber gallery passes round three sides of the Hall, carried on elegant cast-iron brackets, and the interior is enhanced by the light from a large rose window suffused with the colours from its stained glass. Externally the most distinctive elements are the open spiral staircases flanking the entrances, which provide access to the side verandahs, and which recall the mediaeval staircases of the French Renaissance at Blois and Chambord, but the glory of the University is the Library and Clock Tower completed in 1878. This, too, owes its existence to private munificence. It was endowed by Premchand Roychand, the most famous Hindu banker and broker of his day, a quiet, unassuming man whose modest manner concealed the brain of a financial wizard.

The choice of Scott, as architect, was inspired, for although he never visited India, he was able to indulge his knowledge and love of Italian

The Post Office, designed in a mediaeval Italianate style. The area over the porte-cochère *was an outdoor tiffin room for clerks.*

The Law Courts. This vast pile built by Lieutenant-Colonel James Fuller recalls the romantic Gothic fantasies of the competition for the London Law Courts.

The University Convocation Hall by George Gilbert Scott in the decorated French style of the 15th century.

and French Gothic detailing to an unprecedented degree, unconstrained by the cold, wet English weather. The Library has arcaded galleries taken straight from Venice crowned by a pierced parapet of finely detailed stonework, creating a feeling of airiness, delicacy and cool repose. The open spiral staircases placed in each corner are developed from those on the Hall and rise full height surmounted by stone spires, but the most remarkable feature of the whole complex is the soaring Rajabai clock tower, a paean of controlled exuberance celebrating the Gothic Revival and the memory of Roychand's mother, after whom it is named. The design is Scott's interpretation of Giotto's campanile in Florence, but it is highly individual and related to its context. Around the octagonal corona stand sculptured figures eight feet high representing the castes of Western India, and above these, forming finials flanking each face, stand another set of caste figures all modelled by the Assistant Engineer, Rao Bahadur Makund Ramchandra. There are twenty-four in all on the building. Although the location and figures may be Indian, and the inspiration Italian, the building exudes all the ecclesiastical fervour of mid-19th-century Oxbridge. From the chimes of this monumental landmark emanate the sounds of 'Home Sweet Home', 'God Save the Queen' and popular hymn tunes.

162

University Library. The corner spiral staircases are an eclectic blend of the Mediaeval and the French Renaissance.

Why was it that in a comparatively short space of time Bombay acquired a legacy of some of the finest Gothic Revival buildings in the world? Clearly the city's new-found wealth, enlightened patronage and enthusiastic government created an atmosphere for innovation and change, but the availability of good building stone was crucial, releasing the Bombay sappers and PWD architects from reliance on the brick and chunam which prevailed elsewhere. Moreover the process generated its own momentum. In the early years there were hardly any native sculptors capable of executing European carving, but in 1865 the appointment of John Lockwood Kipling to the Bombay School of Art marked the first stage in a rapid revival of native craftwork, and the growth of a local workforce well-versed in stone masonry became a factor in the continuation of the style. Kipling was the father of Indian Arts and Crafts and more than any one person he was responsible for a renaissance of native craft skills and pride in the quality of local workmanship. Now his reputation is eclipsed permanently by the meteoric career of his son, Rudyard, the Imperial muse. A revival in Indian crafts was sorely needed if there was ever to be any real fusion of styles between east and west. The Frere Fountain designed by Richard Norman Shaw and sculpted by James Forsyth demonstrates how even

163

The colossal Rajabai Tower over the University Library is one of Scott's finest and least-known works.

the most gifted architect and distinguished sculptor could go wrong when substituting frenetic European eclecticism for authentic native styles.

It is ironic that a style associated so closely in England with a revolution in ecclesiastical design should have given birth in Bombay to a revolution in secular works. The Afghan Memorial Church at Colaba was an important precursor of the revolution that was to follow, but in Bombay it had relatively little impact on church building. This was more by accident than design. An ambitious scheme for the complete reconstruction of St Thomas's Cathedral was put forward by James Trubshawe, but it became one of the first casualties of the financial collapse in 1865 with only the apsed chancel built. It survives as a curiously incongruous remnant tacked on to the original Cathedral. This and a vigorous little memorial fountain by Scott outside the west door are the only hints of an alternative vision for the Cathedral that never came to fruition. Elsewhere the only other ecclesiastical building worth mentioning is a small church built by William Emerson at Girgaum (1870–73), a quirky little French Gothic building of no great distinction but full of insouciant charm, designed by the future President of the Royal Institute of British Architects, and one of the most interesting architects at work in British India.

William Emerson (1843–1924) trained with W. G. Habershon and A. R. Pite, and became a pupil of the renowned William Burges in 1865. Burges had been commissioned to design a new home for the Bombay School of Art on the understanding that virtually unlimited money was available, and he produced a characteristic 13th-century French Gothic design infused with Oriental motifs and a flamboyant open staircase as an architectural centrepiece. Emerson worked on the design. It is difficult to know how much can be attributed to him, but it gave him an immediate focus for his not inconsiderable talents and launched him on a career in India. At the age of 23 he was dispatched to Bombay with Burges's drawings. The scheme was never executed, as the available funds were not nearly as extensive as Burges had been led to believe. The city is poorer for it, but for William Emerson new opportunities arose. For similar reasons designs for a new custom house by Cuthbert Brodrick, architect of the exotic Turkish Baths in Leeds, were stillborn.

Soon after Emerson's arrival he was commissioned to design the Arthur Crawford Markets, another facet of Frere's scheme for the city, brought to realisation by the eponymous Municipal Commissioner at a cost of £160,000. The building is supposedly 12th-century Gothic in origin, and the biographer of William Burges, Joseph Mordaunt Crook, has discerned echoes of Burges's stable block at Cardiff Castle. It stands on a corner site, and like some English country market buildings it has a prominent clock tower crowned by a cupola, with a gable to each frontage and open timber galleries beneath (now infilled). The main entrance is through three semi-circular polychrome arches above which are bas-reliefs by John Lockwood Kipling, depicting the

The Crawford Markets by William Emerson with panels of bas-reliefs carved by John Lockwood Kipling.

Imperial ideal — strong-limbed Indian peasants thriving under a beneficent Imperial sun. The human reality is beneath, an endless drama of survival played out on a stage of Caithness stone. Inside the market lies a drinking fountain designed by Emerson, but simplified when executed by Kipling, and paid for by the aptly-named Sir Cowasjee Jehangir Readymoney. Today it is almost overwhelmed by stalls.

A visit to the markets is one of the most compelling experiences in India. The noise is deafening, the crowd suffocating and the senses are assaulted by such an array of sights and smells that the unprepared visitor fresh from the order and calm of a European city emerges reeling. The main halls are carried on iron columns with corrugated-iron roofs designed by Mr Russel-Aitken and the walls are lined with elegant iron lamp brackets cast in the form of intertwined reptiles. Beneath these roofs one can obtain almost anything — brilliant fresh flowers, betel nuts, oranges, grapes, bananas, onions, mangoes, cat fish, sword fish, wildfowl, ducks, caged birds, all the exotic produce of the east concentrated into one enormous pageant. The market lies on the edge of the European quarter of the city. Beyond lie the bazaars of the native quarter. Sir Edwin Arnold wrote:

> A tide of Asiatic humanity ebbs and flows up and down the Bhendi bazaar, and through the chief mercantile thoroughfares. Nowhere could be seen a play of livelier hues, a busier and brighter city life. Besides the endless crowds of Hindu, Gujarati and Mahratta people coming and going between rows of grotesquely painted houses and temples, there are to be studied here specimens of every race and nation of the East.

Bombay resembles Victorian London not just in its civic architecture, but in its exuberance, colour and sheer dynamism. Both grew up with the same *laissez-faire* ethos, and both underwent similar attempts at civic improvement by well-meaning philanthropists and officials, but the difference is that in London the process continued. Gradually order was imposed on chaos and the congeries of uses and activities were unwound one by one. In Bombay this never happened, and it retains all the characteristics of the Victorian city, good and bad. As the wealth of the city increased, social problems of overcrowding, poor sanitation and epidemic disease rose in direct proportion. In 1864–65 there was a serious cholera outbreak, but the average annual death rate remained below that of London for many years, until improving environmental standards at home tipped the balance of figures against Bombay. As the programme of civic improvement gathered momentum Western innovations, such as gas lighting, were introduced. A portion of the town was lit in October 1866 and, as the lamplighters went from lamp to lamp, 'they were followed by crowds of inquisitive natives who gazed in mute astonishment at the new western wonder that had appeared in their midst.'

The munificence of the great Parsee and Hindu philanthropists was boundless. Sir Jamsetjee Jeejeebhoy endowed a Benevolent Institution for Parsees, Sir Cowasjee Jehangir Readymoney donated no less than forty drinking fountains to the city (and two in London), and David Sassoon, a Baghdadi Jew and patriarch of one of the wealthiest families in the world, was equally prolific.

The Mechanics or Sassoon Institute stands on Esplanade (now Mahatma Gandhi) Road, a delightful little building of immense charm and character sandwiched between the stately pile of Elphinstone College and the old headquarters of the Army and Navy Stores, one-time purveyors of tropical provisions to the newly-landed Indian civil servant. The Institute was founded to provide a library and lecture facilities for mechanics and engineers and includes a public reading room and a small museum of artifacts and drawings. The street frontage is faced in coursed rubble, arcaded on both storeys with an open verandah at first-floor level and a central entrance porch with a bust of Sassoon in *alto rilievo* by Kipling, all executed in Venetian Gothic like a miniature of Scott's rejected Foreign Office design. The centre bay rises another storey with corner spirelets and a little gable and clock. Inside there is a large entrance hall with a statue of Sassoon by Woolner, but the real surprise is at the rear where there is an octagonal lecture theatre beneath a ribbed roof ventilated by a central lantern, all finished in a complementary style.

The Mechanics Institute was designed by Colonel Fuller in conjunction with Scott, McClelland & Co, a firm of architect/builders who practised widely in the city. Precisely what relationship existed between the military authorities and the civil firm is unclear, but they were influential. In 1868 D. E. Gostling of the firm produced an unusual scheme for a group of four semi-detached bungalows, which unfortunately remained unexecuted. The firm also produced a design for an ice house for Messrs Tudor & Co, ice importers, which combined functional utility and Venetian Gothic apparel, complete with polychromy, crenellations and stepped gables.

Elsewhere the craze for Gothic buildings raged unabated. To the north of the city at Byculla, opposite the Victoria Memorial Gardens, James Trubshawe erected new premises for the Elphinstone College, an institution for the dissemination of Western education endowed by Sir Cowasjee Jehangir Readymoney. It opened in 1871, distinguished by a lofty central tower with a projecting canopied balcony. This appears to have been extended at a later date into an elaborate two-storey affair, reminiscent more of the ornately carved galleried façades of local Gujarati houses, than the architectural spirit of mediaeval Italy. Lalla Rookh would have been at home here rather than Romeo's Juliet. The building is now a hospital and has suffered from unsympathetic infilling of the first-floor arcade and painting of the stonework, but the red corrugated-iron roofs are probably original.

In 1865 Major Medley, RE wrote in *Professional Papers on Indian Engineering* 'Will somebody invent a new material for roofs in India?' Unfortunately they did. By the 1870s the use of corrugated and cast iron was increasing. The invention of corrugated iron and its export to the east in enormous quantities is one of the more dubious advantages conferred by the British Empire. It was mass produced in such

167

The former Mechanics' Institute, now the David Sassoon Library. Venetian Gothic on an intimate scale. (Below) Section through the octagonal lecture hall showing the internal ornament.

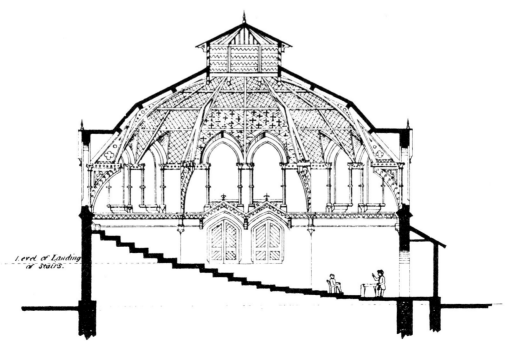

Level of Landing of Stairs.

Elphinstone College with its carved balcony and galleried bell-tower.

quantities and was so cheap that in the space of a few years it displaced traditional roofing materials and the skills that went with them. Graded shingles, ornamental tiles and other traditional materials were swept away causing irreparable damage not just to local industries, but to the visual appearance of countless Indian temples and monuments.

Cast iron had been used in India in small quantities for decades. In the 18th century bar iron was one of the recurrent imports from Europe and in 1815 an entire cast-iron bridge had been exported to Lucknow after designs by the eminent Sir John Rennie, although it was not mounted until 1844. By 1865 prefabrication reached more sophisticated levels and a railway bridge was designed for immediate use outside Bombay without abutments or intermediate columnar support. By the 1880s, Macfarlanes of Glasgow offered a wide range of prefabricated structures ranging from hotels to drinking fountains designed for colonial use. An entire Durbar Hall was exported from their Saracen Foundry to Madras, thoroughly Indian in inspiration, but the great masterpiece of prefabrication was a colossal cast-iron kiosk designed by Owen Jones and R. M. Ordish, the engineer, for use in Bombay. It was made by Handyside of Derby in 1866 and it was widely regarded as one of the most remarkable specimens of ornamental ironwork of its time. Before its despatch to India it was exhibited on land adjoining the Royal Horticultural Society Gardens in South Kensington. Its ultimate fate remains unknown. As depicted in *The Builder* for 1866, it may have been intended for the newly opened Victoria Gardens and Museum, but if it was, it does not appear to have arrived there.

The Victoria Museum, opposite Elphinstone College, is exceptional for it is the only significant Bombay building of the period designed in a classical style. Quite why this should be is puzzling. It may be that it was felt to be a more appropriate style for a public museum, but this is unlikely: the first significant 'correct' secular Gothic building in England was the University Museum, Oxford, finished in 1860. It is more likely that it was the personal whim of its founder, Dr George Birdwood. In any event in 1862 Sir Bartle Frere laid the corner-stone to a highly creditable Palladian building by William Tracey. At its inauguration the Museum was eulogised as 'one of the greatest boons which England could have conferred on India'. Today it is as popular as ever and a Sunday afternoon stroll in Victoria Gardens is as much a part of Bombay routine as is a post-prandial walk in Regent's Park in London. The Museum has acted as a magnet for discarded British artifacts – and in its gardens lie unloved statues and odd items of street furniture including a splendid brachiated cast-iron lamp column. Tracey died before he could supervise the layout of the remaining buildings in the gardens, and Scott, McClelland & Co stepped in to finish the job. The Italianate Sassoon Clock Tower is their work, in Porebundar stone inlaid with Minton tiles and panels, keystones, arches and dressings of Blashfield's terracotta imported from Lincolnshire. The four faces portray morning, evening, noon and night. At the entrance to the gardens is their classical screen enriched with medallions of the Prince and Princess of Wales sculpted by James Forsyth, who also carved the cupids in Portland stone. The capitals are copied from the Temple of Jupiter in Rome.

Inside the gardens stands a bust of Lady Frere by Noble under a circular rotunda designed by Tracey and closely based on the Choragic Monument of Lysicrates in Athens, a pure Greek temple with a cresting of acroteria. The greatest delight is a large tropical planthouse in the style of Decimus Burton's Palm House at Kew – a cast-iron curvilinear frame covered with dark green open latticework embracing all sorts of exotic foliage. Who was responsible for this extraordinary structure, I do not know, but it is a wonderfully inventive piece of design perfectly suited to the climate.

Victoria Gardens was a classical aberration and Bombay remained a city founded in the tradition of Ruskinian Gothic, but it was a tradition which had not yet reached its climax. Over the next twenty years enthusiasm for Gothic as the official style for public and private buildings remained unswayed by vitriolic attacks in the press and journals. In 1867 the *Bombay Builder* complained: 'Here in Bombay where lacs upon lacs have been spent within a few years, and within so small a radius, there is hardly a building that is not positively ugly to look at, not one that is in the least degree instructive.' *The Builder* at home in England commented: 'The fearful overdone Gothic architecture in our Bombay buildings should be a warning to all architects.'

Feelings between civil architects and the military engineers of the Public Works Department remained strained for the duration of the Raj, and often the unresolved professional relationship was exacerbated by social condescension on the part of the military. A report in

The cast-iron kiosk designed by Owen Jones and R. M. Ordish, and made by Handyside of Derby. Its fate remains a mystery.

Victoria Museum and Gardens shortly after its opening with the Sassoon Clock Tower in the foreground. The classical style was unusual in Bombay at a time when Gothic prevailed.

The Builder of 1869 called for reform and lamented: 'The few civil engineers are snubbed and made to eat humble pie to military engineers, who really do nothing but sit at office and write minutes and reports, and carry out a system of scarlet tape unknown even in red-tape England.' Even in 1920 the lowly status of the architect was noted by the Consulting Architect to the Government of India, John Begg: 'The opinion of a civilian of over twelve years' standing or, say, of a Lieutenant-Colonel, will outweigh that of any architect even on an architectural point. A full Colonel's or a Collector's, will make or mar the success of a cathedral.'

In spite of the constant rumble of criticism both in England and India and repeated allegations of incompetence, the PWD continued undeterred in its own complacent fashion. Throughout the 70s and 80s further additions were made to the city's stock of Gothic buildings. Many were concentrated in a triangle of land bounded by Cruickshank Road, Carnac Road and Hornby Road and they all follow the same unregenerated Ruskinian Gothic style of the 1860s. The Goculdas Tejpall Native General Hospital in Carnac Road is by Colonel Fuller in Early English Gothic, and boasts imported cast-iron staircases from Macfarlanes in Glasgow. It follows the common theme of a central tower and projecting bay over the *porte-cochère*, but the arches to the centre bay are slightly cusped, hinting at the greater concessions to Moorish and Saracenic architecture which were to follow. Even more surprisingly, the operating theatre is sited over the entrance porch.

In Cruickshank Road the Cama Albless Obstetric Hospital follows the same form, but the tower is embellished with corner turrets and, interestingly, the windows are shaded by conical iron hoods tucked into the window reveals. At the junction of Carnac Road and Cruickshank Road stands the Elphinstone High School, a more spirited interpretation of Ruskinian ideals, and it is no coincidence that it is by G. T. Molecey, colleague of W. Paris and assistant to James Trubshawe. It stands on a high platform screened by trees. A fine flight of steps leads to three semi-circular headed entrances enriched with clustered columns, radiating bands of red Bassein stone and elaborate wrought iron gates. St Xavier's College and the Police Court complete the group, the latter by John Adams, Architectural Executive Engineer and Surveyor to the Government. Completed in 1889 it has a slender flèche spire and exceptionally fine carved stonework, an indication of how far native craftsmen had developed under Kipling's tutelage in just over twenty years.

Throughout this period a most distinguished local architect was at work in Bombay using the established derivative Gothic style, but also developing a synthesis with indigenous styles that was to blossom at the end of the century. He was Frederick William Stevens (1848–1900). Stevens was trained as an architect in Bath and first went to India as a lowly assistant engineer in the PWD in 1867 under the capable Colonel Fuller. An early drawing of Poona Law Courts is in his name (although they were designed by Major G. J. Melliss), but his first significant work in Bombay was the Royal Alfred Sailors' Home (1872–76), superseding an earlier design in cast iron by J. Macvicar Anderson.

The Sailors' Home is interesting as it is an early attempt to infuse Gothic architecture with Muslim nuances. There is a faintly Saracenic influence to the arches, although the pediment has all the arcane qualities of a South Indian temple. It portrays Neptune, nymphs, seahorses and sealions, but it is English in origin, carved by Mr Boulton of Cheltenham in Bath stone. The capitals and cornices are by Kipling and the ironwork by Macfarlanes. It is not a happy composition and lacks cohesion, the pediment in particular appearing incongruous. In 1880 an editorial in *The Builder* remarked that 'the building in question looks handsome,' but that the pediment 'needs to be something more than what an ornamental sugar top is to a bride cake.'

Whatever its failings the Sailors' Home was sufficient to establish Stevens's reputation and two years after its completion, he received one of the most prestigious commissions ever offered in India – a new terminus for the Great Indian Peninsula Railway, at that time the largest and most extensive architectural work in India.

The Victoria Terminus station is the finest Victorian Gothic building in India. Inspired by Scott's St Pancras Station, it was erected between 1878 and 1887. It is a highly original work albeit one rooted firmly in the tradition of Ruskin, Scott and Burges. The building epitomises the spirit of the age in which it was built, and it is a paean of praise to the railway, which more than any other factor fostered the rise of Bombay. It is the supreme example of tropical Gothic architecture, with only a subtle hint of Saracenic motifs; a riotous extravaganza of polychromatic stone, decorated tile, marble and stained glass. Unlike St Pancras, VT is symmetrical and is surmounted by a colossal masonry dome, ostensibly 'the first applied to a Gothic building on scientific principles', and this claim is probably true. Beneath the dome the staircase rises in magisterial sweeps to each floor. The booking hall is spanned longitudinally and transversely by pointed arches with wooden groin-vaulted ceilings decorated with gold stars on an azure ground and reminiscent of Scott's interiors at St Pancras. The dado is · clad in Maw's glazed tiles of rich foliated designs. The windows are filled with stained glass or with ornamental wrought iron grille-work to

Victoria Terminus: an ambitious exercise in architectural exuberance. The riotous ornament and romantic skyline invoke comparisons with Scott's St Pancras Station.

The Victoria Terminus: (Below), *the dome crowned by Thomas Earp's statue of Progress;* (Above) *richly-carved detail on the* porte-cochère.

reduce the glare of the sun. The fittings of local woods are finished with brass railings. Small wonder that it cost over £250,000.

In the entrance corridor leading to the main hall the groin-vaulting has richly carved and decorated diagonal ribs springing from the backs of grotesque animals. The central bosses are formed into heads of the lion and tiger from the mouths of which the original gas lanterns were suspended. The Imperial Lion and the Indian Tiger to designs executed by Thomas Earp recur full size on the monumental gate piers flanking the main entrance. Most of the surface ornament, foliated sculpture and ironwork was designed by the Bombay School of Art in conjunction with Stevens, who conceded that it was quite the equal of anything to be found in Europe, but the enormous fourteen-foot-high figure of Progress crowning the dome is Earp's, as are the stone medallions of Imperial worthies (including Frere), which enrich the front elevation.

Victoria Terminus is an architectural sensation both in perspective and in detail, where the excellent use of local stones and fine native carving is a tribute to the School of Art. If it has a fault, it is perhaps in the ratio of its length to its height. Victorian Gothic buildings enjoy a natural verticality, which should be accentuated and enhanced, but the enormous foreground and the endless flank elevation of the train shed beyond, impart a horizontal emphasis. To those used to Scott's soaring clock tower at St Pancras or the Rajabai tower at the University, the towers to the end wings seem at least a storey too short, but swept along as one of the two million passengers who pass through the building every day such architectural delicacies seem rather academic. Bombay VT is one of the architectural treasures of India – long may it so remain.

However, Stevens hadn't finished by any means. On the success of Victoria Terminus, he resigned from government service in 1884 and set up his own practice, receiving the commission for the new Municipal Buildings in 1888 by invitation from the Bombay Corporation. He was joined by B.G. Triggs and T. S. Gregson and later by his son, Charles Frederick, in 1896. The buildings were finished in 1893: a vast office complex standing at the apex of two roads opposite the Victoria Terminus. The Municipal Buildings are Stevens's masterpiece in which he gave free reign to his creative impulses, combining Venetian Gothic and Indo-Saracenic architecture in an architectural symbiosis of exotic forms and details. For sheer ebullience it is unsurpassed in British India, and more than any other building, it exudes the twin qualities of Imperial and civic pride, self-confidently symbolised in the crowning figure on the central gable – 'Urbs Prima in Indis'. The stylistic experiments of Fuller and Wilkins, Trubshawe and Emerson to find a form of High Victorian Gothic architecture adapted to the climatic extremes of Bombay, here find their resolution in a supreme expression of controlled composition. The window arches are cusped, the corner towers elaborately domed, but the *tour de force* is the vast domed staircase tower triumphantly proclaiming British supremacy to the world at the zenith of the Empire. It is Xanadu conceived through very English eyes from the Bath office of a High Victorian Goth, for Stevens returned to England to prepare his drawings.

(Left) *Municipal Buildings on completion in 1893: a wonderful combination of Venetian Gothic and Indo-Saracenic forms. The winged figure crowning the gable is 'Urbs Prima in Indis'. Note the horse-drawn tram in the foreground.*

(Right) *Oriental Buildings, remodelled and romanticised from the existing Cathedral High School in a conscious attempt at civic improvement.*

History should know more of this man, for he was one of the most inventive, resourceful and romantic of all the practitioners of Victorian Gothic architecture, yet he is virtually unknown in England. Doubtless this has much to do with sheer distance. If he had practised in Bradford or Manchester, he would be venerated as an equal of Scott, Burges or Butterfield. It has more to do with subsequent attitudes to Victorian Gothic architecture and the hysterical denunciation of the period by the architectural historians of the succeeding generation. In 1931 the illustrious critic Robert Byron, referred to Bombay as 'that architectural Sodom' and wrote: 'The nineteenth century devised nothing lower than the municipal buildings of British India. Their ugliness is positive, daemonic.' Aldous Huxley thought Bombay 'one of the most appalling cities of either hemisphere' all 'lavatory bricks and Gothic spires,' and, sharing the prejudices of his generation, concluded that 'it had the misfortune to develop during what was, perhaps, the darkest period of all architectural history.' Not all showed such fanatical intolerance, mostly just those vociferous intellectuals mesmerised by the Modern movement. The journalist G. W. Steevens considered that Bombay had the richest and stateliest buildings in India 'challenging comparison with almost any city in the world,' and I agree with him. 'The Briton feels himself a greater man for his first sight of Bombay.' The Indians, of course, used to assimilating different races, cultures and conquerors, have never ceased to admire it all, and quite right too, for it is possible to love both Bombay and New Delhi simply for what they are

176

Churchgate Terminus by Frederick William Stevens. Cricket matches are still played on the Maidan, seen in the foreground, today.

— opposites, just as it is possible to appreciate St Pancras and King's Cross. The heart may belong to one, but the mind may enjoy both.

Stevens's romantic inclinations may have achieved apotheosis in the Municipal Buildings, but he went on to design a second great rival terminus for the Bombay, Baroda and Central India Railway at Churchgate in 1894–96. Oriental Buildings, opposite the Flora Fountain, was remodelled substantially at this time by Stevens from premises occupied by the Cathedral High School. It shares with Churchgate a common use of grey facings with bands of white stone dressings. It is an evocative affair with a spiky silhouette of spirelets, turrets and gables looking like a setting from some tropical *Gotterdämmerung*. It goes unmentioned in *Murray's Guide*, overshadowed by the reputation of the great termini and Municipal Buildings along the road, but it is an excellent climax in the townscape.

The Churchgate terminus is based on the plan and form of its rival. There is a similar gabled centrepiece and *porte-cochère*, projecting wings flanked by square towers, and the whole is surmounted by a large domed lantern which reduces in stages; but the differences are self-evident. The square towers to the wings and central gable are capped by Oriental domes and subsidiary domelets, and the whole mass of the building is different, more compact with a greater vertical emphasis accentuated by the huge west window which lights the central hall. The most obvious difference is in the external facings which at Churchgate are rough-hewn in blue basalt inlaid with bands of

177

Churchgate Terminus: (Left) *the receding stages of the tower and dome inlaid with structural polychromy:* (Right) *The spirit of Progress surmounting the gable on the west front.*

brilliant white counterpointed with red Bassein sandstone creating a Byzantine quality. The dome is Stevens's least successful, lacking the majestic qualities of both VT and Municipal Buildings, but it is an interesting feature punctuated with corner pavilions, the domes on which repeat on the buttresses to the upper stages. Monumental statuary plays an important role, the gable over the entrance being crowned by a statue of progress complete with locomotive.

Stevens died in 1900 in the city he did so much to improve. His obituary records that his buildings 'carried out in them with conspicuous success that blending of Venetian Gothic with Indian Saracenic by which he created a style of architecture so excellently adapted to the climate and environment of Bombay.' In this respect his works were outstanding, but while others elsewhere developed Indo-Saracenic themes based on a scholarly study of Moghul architecture and other precedents, in Bombay the vigour and originality which characterised Stevens's work was not replaced.

In 1909 a vast new General Post Office was raised in Indo-Saracenic style by John Begg, who had worked with Alfred Waterhouse and Colonel Edis before going to India via South Africa. It is a rambling building with corner domes and pierced balustrades to the window arches and with a central dome formed, unusually, in brick. However, the final manifestation of the impulse of civic improvement which had been triggered by Frere in the 1860s rippled in and around the Apollo Bunder overlooking the beautiful harbour of Bombay in the early 20th century.

The Taj Mahal Hotel was built in 1903 on the basin of the adjacent Bombay Yacht Club and its inception was due to Jamshetji Nusserwanji Tata, one of the wealthiest Parsees in the city, a man of enormous power and influence with diverse interests in iron and steel, hydro-electricity, shipping and banking. The hotel, designed by W. Chambers, who worked for a local practice, was one of the great hotels of the British Empire, on a par with Shepheards in Cairo and Raffles in Singapore. Its site is quite magnificent, facing out over the Arabian Sea to greet new arrivals as they steamed in on the great P. & O. liners. The building is reputed to have several allusions to Gujarati architecture, but it is really an eclectic confection calculated to whet the appetite of the incoming visitor. Predictably it is symmetrical and over its centre rises a huge red dome crowned by a belvedere. Each corner boasts a domed circular tower. The second to fourth floors have a rhythm of six projecting canopied balconies and the ground floor boasts a cool arcade which provides an outdoor bedroom for many of the beggars who haunt the hotel entrances in search of baksheesh.

Next door to the Taj stands the old Bombay Yacht Club now taken over by the Indian Atomic Energy Commission, a captivating pile, described by Jan Morris as 'a mixture of the Swiss and Hindu styles', but it is really nothing of the sort. It is a rather restrained affair by Bombay standards, symmetrical with corner towers crowned with conical roofs and bargeboarded gables, recalling the romantic juxtaposition of gables and spires which characterises the work of Norman Shaw and the Queen Anne Revival, although the lower stages betray its Gothic origins with square casement windows set in pointed arches.

Just round the corner near Stevens's Sailors' Home stands the Prince of Wales Museum – a stately pleasure dome, if ever there was one, with a foundation stone laid by the future George V, on his Indian visit of

The Taj Mahal Hotel: one of the great hotels of the British Empire overlooking the Arabian Sea.

179

The former Yacht Club, now the offices of the Indian Atomic Energy Commission.

(Right) *The Prince of Wales Museum in the course of erection using fragile bamboo scaffolding.* (Below) *George Wittet, seated on the left, the architect.*

1905. It is a vast complex of buildings given cohesion and character by a monumental tiled concrete dome and the scholarly interpretation of local Indian architecture of the 15th and 16th centuries, all finished in blue basalt and yellow sandstone from Coorla and set in luxuriant gardens where palms throw dappled light onto the textured coloured stone. The architect was George Wittet (1880–1926), Begg's successor as Consulting Architect to the Government of Bombay, and a committed Orientalist for public buildings.

Wittet was the designer of the last great building in the group, the Gateway of India, intended as a triumphal arch to commemorate the visit of George V and Queen Mary in 1911, en route to the Delhi Durbar. Today it is portrayed more often as the point of exit through which the last British regiment marched in 1948. These emotive associations have hindered its fair assessment as a work of architecture: it would be fanciful to read into it a subtle loss of confidence, as some have done. Wittet indulged his knowledge of local 16th-century architecture and produced a monument firmly in the Indo-Saracenic tradition, in honey-coloured basalt, complete with side chambers to accommodate civic receptions. Today it looks rather isolated and it remains unaligned with the axis of the former Yacht Club, but this was intentional for the arch was only part of a much wider scheme which Wittet intended for the area, but which never came to fruition. Since Independence this dislocation has been atoned for by the pleasant garden around the site, and the casual visitor, rummaging through the market stalls, pays little heed to such architectural improprieties – except perhaps the Englishman. To him this remains the spot where almost three hundred years of rule ended, and where the last British troops, like well-mannered guests who knew that the party was over, departed, not with animosity and bitterness, but in warmth and friendship. Never has a nation given up an Empire in such a way.

As the 1st Battalion of the Somerset Light Infantry marched through the streets on the morning of 28th February 1948 thousands packed the roads leading to the quayside, many an eye dimmed with tears. Spontaneous cheers of 'England Zindabad' and 'Jai England' greeted the troops as hundreds reached out to pat 'the boys' goodbye. 'I would think today of the finest act in the long and historic connection between the United Kingdom and India – the grant of freedom to our country, an act of courage and vision which will stand the test of time ... I wish you well, my friends, it is my earnest hope that friendly relations will continue to exist between Great Britain and India and that the two countries will play their part in the preservation of the peace of the world, which is so essential for the welfare and progress of mankind. Godspeed and every good wish for the future.' As the Governor's words faded there was a rush after the men as they embarked on the launches, farewells echoing across the water until they were far out to sea, and as the ships steamed from the bay the strains of 'Auld Lang Syne' floated from the quayside and out into the Arabian Sea.

The Gateway of India. Modelled on the Gujarati architecture of the 16th century and built to commemorate the visit of George V and Queen Mary in 1911.

CHAPTER 8

SARACENIC DREAMS

High on the table-land of the Deccan plateau, 120 miles east of Bombay, lies Poona. Once it was the capital of the fierce Maratha Confederacy which dominated Western India for over one hundred years until its final defeat by the British at Kirkee in 1817. With the establishment of British paramountcy it was transformed into a major military cantonment and hot-weather resort for Bombay. Even with the growth of the hill station of Mahabaleshwar, Poona retained its popularity and acquired a social cachet of international renown.

As a satellite of the greatest commercial city in India, it is no surprise to discover buildings of a similar form and style to those in Bombay. Christ Church, Kirkee was designed by Paris and Molecey, assistant architects to the Bombay Ramparts Removal Committee, after earlier designs by an amateur archaeologist and clergyman called Gell, ran into severe problems. It is an unpretentious affair which would go largely unnoticed in an English village, other than that its western face is protected from the monsoon by a cavernous wooden verandah. A far more eloquent essay in the tropical Gothic style is the Poona Law Courts, designed by Major G. J. Melliss, the local executive engineer, a vigorous and disciplined composition on which F. W. Stevens worked as assistant engineer, although it is pure, unregenerated Gothic and betrays none of the Indo-Saracenic nuances which were to develop so spectacularly in Stevens's later works in Bombay. Other prominent public buildings are consanguineous expressions of Bombay architecture – the Poona Engineering College, the Sassoon Hospital (by Wilkins and Melliss) and, in Eastern Kirkee, the Deccan College, an august institution founded by the first Parsee baronet, Sir Jamsetjee Jeejeebhoy, well executed in grey trap-stone.

However, the ambience of the town was set when Sir Bartle Frere decided to vacate the old government house at Dapuri, and to build a new edifice at Poona, or more precisely near a pass or 'Khind' dedicated to the elephant-god Ganesh, which gave the house its name: Ganesh Khind. Located just outside the city the house is approached through dense dry thicket. It was designed by James Trubshawe.

Architecturally it is most unusual, defying any obvious classification, but its spiritual antecedents are Italianate and the tall, eighty-foot high flag tower has been described accurately as a 'Victorian rendering of an Italian campanile'. Like the Lawrence Asylum at Ootacamund, the building is inspired by Prince Albert's ambitious Osborne House on the Isle of Wight, the progenitor of many Anglo-Indian Italianate compositions. It is crowned by a brightly painted open metal cupola carrying a flagstaff, but in fact the tower only

183

Government House, Ganesh Khind, Poona.

provides elegant accommodation for the water tanks. The building is a rambling affair lacking in cohesion, executed in grey stone with pink granite dressings, but the garden frontage is a sheer delight for the loggia opens out into a *cortile*, or recessed courtyard, with a marble pavement, providing a cool retreat large enough for formal entertainment. Quite why the Italian concept of the cortile should not have been taken up more widely in India remains a mystery, as it provides an ideal solution to the problem of climate and a charming variation from the ubiquitous peripheral verandah. Internally the principal rooms are the drawing room, complete with minstrels' gallery, and the ballroom with a clerestory at first-floor level lighting the bedroom passage behind it. Today the whole complex houses Poona University, an ideal use for the building. Contemplative students rather than dyspeptic majors and ADCs stroll past the stone medallions of former Governors, but the gardens replete with canna lilies, palms and bougainvillaea are as brilliant and colourful as ever.

Ganesh Khind was influential, at least in Poona, for it set an architectural as well as social fashion. As its popularity as a resort grew, the rich Parsee magnates built their country retreats in Poona, and the finest was closely modelled on Ganesh Khind. Garden Reach was commenced in 1862 by Colonel St Clair Wilkins for the Parsee, Mr Rustamjee Jamsetjee Jeejeebhoy, but he lost a fortune in the cotton boom, and it was completed for the Jew, Sir Albert Sassoon. The two houses are fruits of the same architectural inspiration. Garden Reach has a high flagstaff tower carrying water tanks surmounted by a similar open metal cupola, and the drawing room ceiling, executed by local hands, is an imitation of that in the ballroom of Ganesh Khind. The finishings to Garden Reach are a testimony to the opulence of Poona society. The rooms are floored with Carrara and Chinese marble and the dining room is connected to the main house by a long, open gallery with verandahs either side. Beside it lies an open room with carved wooden sides where the Sassoon family celebrated the Feast of Tabernacles. The interior is furnished sumptuously with a stained glass window carrying the arms of Rustamjee Jeejeebhoy, marble copies of the best Italian statuary and a bust of Garibaldi, the hero of the day. The gardens, washed by the river Mula, are enclosed by a high wall. Elaborate English cast-iron railings of a Regency Gothick pattern mark the road frontage, all overlaid with cascades of brilliantly-coloured foliage. Today the house belongs to the Readymoney family, but the days when Poona was on the social map of the world have passed. Over the river the Aga Khan's former mansion is known now more widely as the spot where once Gandhi was kept under house arrest.

'If used with freedom and taste, no style might be better adapted for Indian use than Gothic; but in order to apply it there ... various changes in arrangement must be made which unfortunately the purist can not tolerate', wrote James Fergusson in 1862. He considered 'the most correct Gothic building yet erected in India is the College at Benares, designed by the late Captain [afterwards Major] Markham Kittoe.' Kittoe was not educated as an architect, but he was an enthusiast who devoted much of his life to architectural study. He was an urbane, artistic individual, not averse to personal gestures; it was he who donated the font to St Paul's Cathedral, Calcutta. Queen's College, Benares was built between 1847 and 1852 and it is one of the earliest secular public buildings in the 'correct' Gothic style in India. Designed in a Perpendicular manner in Chunar stone it has a lofty central tower with corner towers joined by open arcades. It is an unusual building with all the vigorous assumptions of a prototype. Fergusson complained that Kittoe 'had not sufficient command of the details of the style to adapt them to the new circumstances, and his college is from this cause a failure, both as an artistic design and as a utilitarian building.' As a result of this lack of refinement it has been altered subsequently.

If Kittoe's early exercise in secular Gothic was a poorly digested piece of historicism, elsewhere a whole series of buildings were raised which took tropical Gothic architecture beyond its European antecedents and infused its forms and massing with Indo-Saracenic motifs and elements, in the same way that pure Gothic architecture was being adapted in Bombay by a process of hybridisation.

William Emerson, future President of the Royal Institute of British Architects, was active in Allahabad in the 1870s following the success of the Crawford Market buildings in Bombay. It was he who designed the Cathedral and Muir College, and also, I suspect, had a major influence in the design of two other public buildings which exude those French Gothic details so beloved of Burges and his pupil. The Thornhill and Mayne Memorial stands on the edge of Alfred Park, where, in 1858, Queen Victoria's proclamation announcing the transfer of the government of India from the East India Company to the Crown was read by Lord Canning. In 1906 a vast memorial statue of Victoria by George Wade was raised over the spot. This was removed in 1957 and its Italian limestone canopy now stands looking rather forlorn, bereft of a centrepiece.

Cuthbert Bensey Thornhill and Francis Otway Mayne were close

Sir William Emerson by Sir James Jebusa Shannon, RA, with the plans of the Victoria Memorial, Calcutta.

friends in the Bengal Civil Service. Thornhill died at sea in 1868 and lies buried in Aden. Mayne died four years later in Allahabad. Two stained glass windows in their memory can be seen in St John's Church, Naini Tal, one of the most invigorating hill stations in India, but their real memorial is the public library, museum and reading rooms which they endowed in the city which they served so well. The building was completed in 1878, a wonderfully accomplished piece of French Gothic designed by Roskell Bayne of Calcutta, but it has such a distinctive Burgesian touch that Emerson may well have been involved in some capacity. Faced in a creamy sandstone from Shankergarh, enriched with red stone dressings, it is designed as three loosely connected parts – a substantial *porte-cochère* over which rises a low octagonal spire, a massive central tower, and a separate reading room flanked by an arcaded Gothic cloister. The cloister acts as a verandah and is carried on slender paired stone columns linked by curious pierced cast-iron panels. The circular openings over the arcade are filled with pierced stonework, whilst the main reading room is lit by four gabled bays which each contain pairs of narrow lancet windows beneath rose windows. However, the *coup de finesse* is the tower, which has strongly modelled lower stages, crowning gabled bargeboards to each face and small paired arches at the base, each divided by a massive squat foliated column taken straight from Burges. It is the most inventive piece of Victorian Gothic architecture in the city – robust, disciplined, innovative and well-adapted to the climate, apt attributes for a memorial dedicated to two enlightened public servants.

The Mayo Memorial Hall nearby was completed in 1879 for public meetings, balls and receptions in commemoration of the assassinated Viceroy. It is an extraordinary pile with a tower over 180 feet high taken directly from the Thornhill and Mayne Memorial, to which it is so closely related, but it is a much less disciplined composition and it approaches the ham-fisted in its detailing, particularly around the corona to the tower. The main hall is far less inspiring than its prototype, a shallow semi-circular vault with half-hearted crocketed corner finials. Bayne was responsible for this as well, but it shows none of the mastery of the Gothic canons which is evident on the Thornhill and Mayne Memorial. Indeed when it was opened by Lord Lytton he remarked that the building was not the ideal of aesthetic beauty. 'It has', said his Lordship, 'certain incongruous peculiarities', and its general effect is hardly one of repose, although he was slightly less acerbic about the interior which he thought 'thoroughly comfortable and practicable'. The singular disparity between the quality of the two buildings, which were being built concurrently, does suggest that Emerson may have been involved in Thornhill and Mayne and we know he was in Allahabad at the time.

Emerson has been called a 'licentious eclectic' in his later work, a pejorative reference to his free combination of tropical Gothic and Saracenic styles of which the Muir College in Allahabad is a splendid example, yet he was the first to admit it: 'Indeed are not many of the most lovely flowers and plants hybrids, and has not the intermingling of different families of the human race produced some of the noblest

Thornhill and Mayne Memorial, Allahabad, by Roskell Bayne. (Above left): *View.* (Above right): *the tower and* porte-cochère. (Left): *the arcaded Gothic cloister with cast-iron panels between stone shafts.* (Below): *the massive squat column at the base of the tower and vigorous carved capitals are typical Burgesian details.*

types of men?' And he did it all so well that the romantic conception always overcomes the vulgarity inherent in its expression. To Emerson exuberance was the guiding light and when, in the course of designing the Muir College, he discovered that there were no minarets in Indian Muslim architecture, he went Egyptian.

> I determined not to follow too closely Indian art, but to avail myself of an Egyptian phase of Moslem architecture and work it up with the Saracenic style of Beejapore and the North West, combining the whole in a Western Gothic design. The beautiful lines of the Taj Mahal influenced me in my dome over the hall, and the Indian four centred arch suggested itself as convenient for my purpose, as well as working well with the general Gothic feeling. The details show how the Gothic tracery is blended with the Cairean Moucharabyeh wood-work; Gothic shafts and caps are united with Indian arches; and the domes stand on Gothicised Mohammedan pendentives and semi-circular arches; the open staircase is also a Gothic feature.

The college is dominated by the 200-foot-high minaret tower. With its emphasis on silhouette, romantic massing of the skyline and soaring vertical lines, the building illustrates Burges's influence on Emerson's designs. The whole composition is finished in cream-coloured sandstone from Mirzapur, with marble and mosaic floors. The domes are clad in Multan glazed tiles. The college forms a quadrangle comprising the convocation hall, lecture rooms, library and professors' room linked by arcaded verandahs which break into traceried Gothic at the base of the tower. It is a wonderfully romantic and evocative image of the East as it ought to be, and when illustrated in *The Architect* for 1873 it was depicted with an idealised foreground, all the multitudes of India brought together in easy harmony outside the new repository of learning.

Emerson's ambitious exercises in architectural miscegenation continued at Bhavanagar where he designed the Takhtsingi Hospital between 1879 and 1883 and a vast new palace for the Maharajah between 1894 and 1895. The hospital is clothed in a loose admixture of Hindu and Saracenic motifs, but these fail to disguise a classical conception in the Grand Manner – the form, symmetry and massing are wholly European with a domed centrepiece over a vestigial pediment, domed corner pavilions and a bowed staircase on the garden frontage. The carved ornament is vigorous enough, but there is no real fusion between East and West, just a superficial imposition of one over the other – Imperial camouflage. The palace is the most thoroughly Hindu-Saracenic of all Emerson's buildings, a development of the Muir College in a more Eastern guise, eschewing any trace of European Gothic in favour of engrailed arches infilled with carved *moucharabya* work, serrated parapets, roof pavilions and the dominating effect of a huge minaret tower punctuated at the corners with little *chattris*.

The Cathedral Church of All Saints, Allahabad makes few concessions to the Indian context and demonstrates Emerson's ability to

The Quadrangle, Muir College, Allahabad by William Emerson.

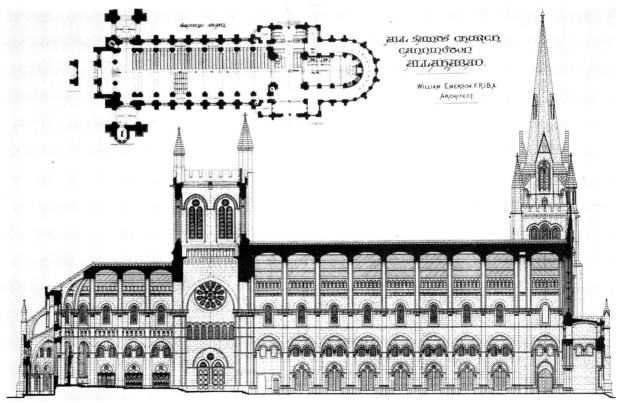

ALL SAINTS' CHURCH
CANNINGTON
ALLAHABAD.

WILLIAM EMERSON. F.R.I.B.A.
ARCHITECT.

design as easily in a straightforward Gothic style as in a boldly eclectic manner. The choir, transepts and a 'temporary' nave were finished in 1877, but the cathedral was not consecrated until 1887. Following a gift of £20,000 from an American as a memorial to his wife, six bays of the nave were completed by 1891, but the western towers never got built. Burges's influence can be discerned quite clearly in the choice of 13th-century Gothic, inspired by the choir at Canterbury, but adapted to the climate. The church is faced in white stone from Surajpur with red stone dressings and the five lower openings of the apse are enclosed by geometrical patterns copied from examples at Fatehpur Sikri. The pavement to the choir and sanctuary is pure Jaipur marble dappled with light coming through English stained glass, but the effect is reminiscent of Burges's Cork Cathedral.

Garrison churches were provided in every station in India for spiritual solace and guidance. Each old India hand will have his favourite, but the cantonment church at Peshawar is the last that many ever saw. Here situated amongst the trim lawns and bungalows on the edge of one of the most exciting cities in Asia, lay the last spiritual oasis for those en route for the Khyber and frontier duty. Many would not return, their only memorial one of the regimental insignia carved into the side of the Khyber by generations of British servicemen.

> A scrimmage in a border station –
> A canter down some dark defile –
> Two thousand pounds of education
> Drops to a ten-rupee jezail –
> The Crammer's boast, the Squadron's pride,
> Shot like a rabbit in a ride!

If Peshawar Church is imbued with a sombre, elegiac mood, it is for this reason, for architecturally it is a jolly piece of English Gothic imported straight from home. Nine hundred miles away in the centre of India, All Saints, Nagpur was also a conventional piece of Gothic, executed by Lieutenant (later Sir) Richard Sankey of the Madras Engineers in 1851, until it was transformed in 1879 into the Cathedral church by one of the leading English architects of the day, G. F. Bodley (1827–1907). Bodley's remodelling of the church was ambitious involving lengthening the nave, deepening the transepts, and providing a chancel, two vestries and an organ chamber. Above all else, Gothic prevailed – St John's, Ambala in 14th-century brick by Captain Atkinson was a notable addition to the ranks of cathedral churches in India after its consecration in 1857. Even Calcutta succumbed to the blandishments of the Gothic propagandists. St James, Calcutta was designed in 1860 by C. G. Wray and Walter Granville, in an Early English manner with Norman detailing. The interior is handsome, embellished with elaborately carved roof trusses in geometric style and a groined vault over the crossing. Granville supervised its erection and was responsible for substantial departures from the original design. However, it was at Lahore in the Punjab that one of the great cathedrals of India arose between 1883 and 1914 and to the designs not of a PWD engineer but of

(Above) *Cathedral Church of All Saints, Allahabad by William Emerson.* (Below) *Plan and section showing the uncompleted western towers and spires.*

191

John Oldrid Scott (1841–1913), second son of the great Sir George Gilbert Scott, architect of the University buildings in Bombay. A late 13th-century style was chosen in a local medium of pink brick and sandstone in common use in the city. Internally it is groin vaulted throughout, carried on clustered shafts with an apsidal choir and ambulatory, the apse being distinguished by enormous stone columns with highly foliated capitals. The stained glass to the choir is by Clayton and Bell, and one haunting opalescent memorial window is by Leonard Walker, a long way from his studio in N.W.3.

Lahore is pure Kipling. It was immortalised in *Kim*, who sits 'astride the gun Zam-Zammah on her brick platform opposite the old Ajaib-Gher – the Wonder House, as natives call the Lahore Museum' in the opening lines of the novel. Zam-Zammah (lion's roar) has a Persian inscription around its muzzle which concludes 'What a cannon! Its face, like a monstrous serpent, vomits fire.' However it was Rudyard's father John Lockwood Kipling who, as Curator, did as much to foster a renaissance of Indian arts and crafts in Lahore as he had at the School of Art in Bombay. The Museum collections are wide-ranging, a testament to his zealous conservation of Indian artefacts, and the interior has been described wonderfully by Jan Morris as 'rather dim-lit, almost opaque in fact, as though wood-smoke is perpetually drifting through it'. Many of the buildings in the city owe their form and spirit to John Lockwood Kipling for it was he who enthusiastically advocated the use of native styles and craftsmanship. The High Court, for instance, in the late Pathan style of the 14th century is by J. W. Brassington, who was involved in the Madras Law Courts. There is pure Gothic here too. The Government College was completed in 1877 to the designs of W. Purdon, the local executive engineer, an excellent complex of Gothic buildings with a central octagonal tower and spire in five stages. The main hall has a splendid hammer beam roof with a gallery at first-floor level, and when the building was extended in 1937 a sympathetic matching style was used.

The search to achieve a truly Imperial style appropriate to the country over which they ruled occupied the British for the duration of the Raj. There were two main schools of thought – the aesthetic imperialists and the native revivalists. The former argued that the British should seek to emulate the Romans and impose British architecture with confidence, along with British law, order, justice and culture, not just out of duty but for the glory of the Empire. Civic architecture should embody an expression of all these things to the Indian people. They deprecated all attempts at revivalist architecture and argued that public buildings should stand as a true memorial to the selfless work of the Raj. The great advantage of Gothic architecture was that it was felt to be a Christian, 'national' style, even though, in practice, its actual expression owed far more to Venice and Italy than to English mediaevalism. Later proponents of the argument favoured the style of Wren and the English Renaissance, as the quintessence of English values. They were opposed by the revivalist school who taught that an uninterrupted living tradition existed in architecture, connecting the present and past. The

Lahore Cathedral by John Oldrid Scott built in stages between 1883–1914.

true policy should be to shun all imported forms and ideas, and to foster this living tradition by sustaining the Indian master craftsman or *mistri*, whose craft skills and expertise were in danger of dying out from lack of patronage. From time to time the tension between both schools of thought erupted into outright hostility. The conventional aesthetic imperialists who ran the PWD as an élite club looked aghast upon the interfering civilian architects who wanted to go native and adopt indigenous architectural apparel. It was as if the inner, trousered sanctum of the Raj were under attack from men advocating the use of loin cloths – and not natives, but Englishmen. It was unheard of, dangerously seditious and damned un-English. The revivalists, on the other hand, were exasperated at the obstructive nature of the PWD and as late as 1920 John Begg, Consulting Architect to the Government of India complained that 'the architect in India is handicapped at the outset by a universal ignorance of his functions.'

James Fergusson, the great architectural historian, argued the middle ground. Although he thought 'copying the Indian styles a crime' he maintained that 'there are principles underlying them which cannot be too deeply studied.' John Begg agreed and sixty years later urged, 'Let the architect take to India all his real principles, all of his technical skill both in design and in execution, all the essence of his training, but nothing more – there let him absorb indigenous forms and expressions into his consciousness.'

People like Fergusson and John Lockwood Kipling were responsible for inculcating in India the ideals which William Morris was advocating in England, a return to quality craftsmanship and tried and established methods. This was both a reaction against the mass production of the new industrial age and a vision of an art and

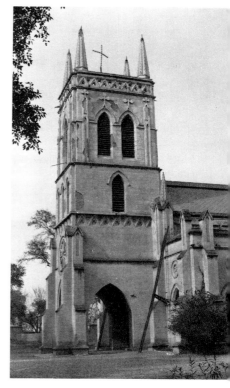

Peshawar: typical garrison church, peeling stucco showing the brick core.

Government College, Lahore: the tower and spire.

architecture based on principles of simple structural integrity. Lockwood Kipling's enthusiasm for craftsmanship had been fired by the Great Exhibition of 1851. He had studied art and sculpture under Sir Philip Cunliffe-Owen at South Kensington and worked as a stone mason on the new Victoria and Albert Museum. He was brother-in-law to Edward Burne-Jones.

The search for Imperial identity rumbled on into the 20th century. E. B. Havell, one-time head of the Madras School of Art, remonstrated against the official mind in his polemic *Indian Architecture*:

> The official architect sits in his office at Simla, Calcutta or Bombay surrounded by pattern-books of styles — Renaissance, Gothic, Indo-Saracenic and the like — and, having calculated precisely the dimensions and arrangement of a building suited to the departmental requirements, offers for approval a choice of the 'styles' ... for clothing the structure with architectural garments in varying degrees of smartness ... The European dilettanti who rule India do not generally know that any other system than this is possible or desirable.

The PWD simply retorted that the unsupervised work of the *'mistri'* was decadent and undisciplined, to which Havell replied that it was all part of a process of hybridisation which had recurred in Europe when a new style was being evolved. And so it all went on.

One notable victim of the struggle was the revivalist, F. S. Growse, an Oxford antiquarian, who supervised the erection of numerous buildings in the Bulandshahar District between 1878 and 1884. He wrote a number of scholarly monographs on local Indian architecture in Mathura and a self-publicising polemic called 'Indian Architecture of Today as Exemplified by Buildings in the Bulandshahar District', i.e. his own work. A Goth by training he was seduced by the principles of Kipling and Havell and gave the native builders their head. The result was such an extraordinary spontaneous regeneration of exuberant Indian craftsmanship that the traders in the principal bazaar 'were vying with one another in the excellence of the curved wood arcades with which they are ornamenting their shopfronts'. Richly carved doors with brass wire inlay (Mynpuri) work were made for the new town hall and the whole district buzzed with exchanges between Growse and the PWD. 'Mr Growse cries out against the strangling effect of Government red-tape, and also against the tyranny of the Public Works Department', wrote one reviewer of his book. The PWD, appalled that he had gone native, promptly posted him elsewhere out of harm's way. However, one of the great benefits arising from serious study of Indian architecture and the resurgence of traditional arts and crafts was the conservation of many of India's finest buildings.

English antiquaries had been interested in the restoration and repair of Indian monuments since the early 19th century. James Prinsep in Benares was a pioneer. But the results were not always to be admired. The reinstatement of the Ashoka Pillar at Allahabad by Captain Edward Smith in 1838 was a dismal failure. Prinsep thought 'the animal on the top is small and recumbent, and altogether the design is insignificant. Indeed it looks not unlike a stuffed poodle stuck on the top of an inverted flower-pot.' In the early years the PWD did much insensitive work. The beautiful red sandstone palace of Akbar's son at Allahabad was simply whitewashed all over by the PWD in one of those supreme acts of philistine ignorance which were the hallmark of the lower echelons of the service. Techniques did not improve until the foundation of the Archaeological Survey of India in 1861 and the pioneering work of Lord Curzon in the early 20th century (see Chapter 10).

The most prolific practitioner of the Indian revival was one of the most gifted architects in India, Robert Fellowes Chisholm (1840–1915). His principal works are to be found in Madras, where he was the first head of the School of Industrial Art founded in 1855. He set up the Drawing and Painting Academy after complaining bitterly of 'the injurious influence which the large importations of European manufactures of the worst possible designs have had on native handicrafts.' Chisholm was nothing if not versatile for it was he who designed the Lawrence Asylum at Ootacamund (1865) in an Italianate style, after the manner of Osborne House, and who later turned out an equally eloquent essay in Victorian Gothic for the Post and Telegraph Office in Madras (1875–1884), but it was as a practitioner of Indo-Saracenic styles that he excelled. In 1864 the Government of Madras advertised a competition for two new buildings – a Presidency College and Senate House for the University. Chisholm won and was appointed Consulting Architect to the Government. The Presidency College is essentially a cross-fertilisation of Italianate and Saracenic styles designed to sympathise with the nearby Chepauk Palace, which until 1865 had been the home of the Nawabs of Arcot. It was then taken over as government offices. The Senate House is a more ambitious Saracenic exercise. Conceived symmetrically in a Byzantine manner, it has four corner towers crowned by onion domes, each face of each of the towers

Senate House, University of Madras, on the left of the picture, by Robert Fellowes Chisholm. A fusion of Oriental and Byzantine styles.

bursting into arcuated fans of polychrome brick and stonework with carved voussoirs, tiled domes and pendentives. Outside the south entrance stands a statue of Queen Victoria seated in Imperial majesty under a magnificent pavilion of intricate cast-iron work supplied by Macfarlanes of Glasgow.

In 1870 the Government of Madras resolved to develop and extend the Chepauk Palace into a complex of offices for the Revenue Board, and Chisholm was instructed by Lord Napier to prepare designs that would harmonise with the original palace buildings. Napier was an enthusiastic advocate of native styles and his influence was instrumental in transforming Madras from a classical city into a magnificent Indo-British metropolis. In a lecture on modern architecture in India he asserted that 'the Government of India might ... do well to consider whether the Mussulman forms might not be adopted generally as the official style of architecture.' He considered it 'far superior with reference to shade, coolness, ventilation, convenience and beauty to all we see around us.' The original palace buildings were probably designed by Paul Benfield in the 1760s, a Company engineer of dubious repute who later acquired notoriety as the chief money-lender to the Nawab, but in Chisholm's substantial extensions purer details and superior materials were used, rationalising the confused jumble of native elements employed by Benfield over one hundred years earlier. The result is a happy commingling of new and old work dominated by a central tower which has domed corner spirelets, a massive machicolated parapet and a crowning onion dome. The project was sufficiently

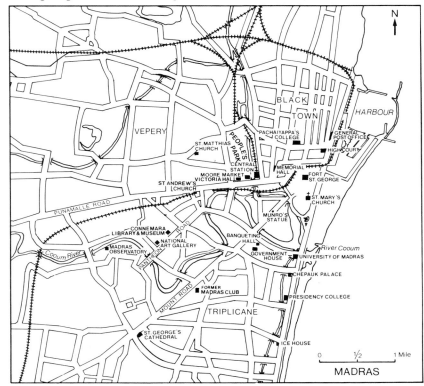

controversial for Napier to defend it at length in *The Builder* for 1870. 'The Government had endeavoured, with the advice of an accomplished architect, to exhibit in the improvements at the Revenue Board an example of the adoption of a Mussulman style to contemporaneous use ... He has paid the first tribute to the genius of the past; he has set the first example of a revival in native art, which I hope will not remain unappreciated and unfruitful.'

Chisholm recognised the importance of the craftsman, 'the men who will actually leave the impress of their hands on the materials'. He maintained that 'those men have an art-language of their own, a language which you can recognise, but cannot thoroughly understand. For this reason an architect practising in India should unhesitatingly elect to practise in the native styles of art – indeed, the natural art-expression of these men is the only art to be obtained in the country.'

As the complex of public buildings began to grow along the waterfront of Madras, they mutually complemented each other to create a magnificent townscape vista of Indo-Oriental architecture. The government tacitly acknowledged this when the Governor Grant-Duff (1881–1886) enhanced this nascent composition by constructing the Marina, one of the most beautiful seafront promenades in the world, a wide sweep of broad carriageway running for three miles down the Coromandel coast to San Thomé Cathedral, punctuated with palms and all the exotic vegetation of Southern India. In spite of Chisholm's extensive work all over the city the focus of the composition was created by other hands. The construction of the Law Courts between

Board of Revenue Offices, Madras, formerly Chepauk palace. A happy commingling of new and old work. The central tower to the right of the picture is part of the original palace.

197

1888 and 1892 represented the high point of Indo-Saracenic architecture in India – a romantic confection of multi-coloured Moghul domes, Buddhist stupas, canopied balconies, arcaded verandahs, and soaring high over the whole vast red brick pile, a bulbous domed minaret with its upper stage forming a lighthouse equipped with the latest dioptic light. The lighthouse became such a landmark that shortly after the outbreak of the First World War it received some unwelcome attentions from the German Cruiser *Emden*, which astonished Madras in an audacious attack on the city, an incident commemorated by a plaque on the building. The designs and estimates were prepared by Chisholm's successor as Consulting Architect, J. W. Brassington, but he died before work commenced and the scheme was revised by his successor Henry Irwin, and the assistant engineer J. H. Stephens. The materials – brick and terracotta – were local and all the details were executed by students from the School of Art. However, for all its unrestrained Romanticism the building remains firmly in the European tradition, an ingenious and spirited attempt to disguise a Gothic building in Indo-Saracenic clothing. It reflects the same concern with internal circulation, Romantic massing, skyline and silhouette that were the hallmark of the grandiloquent Gothic fantasies that had appeared in the competition for the London Law Courts twenty years earlier. The Law College next door was completed in the same year in a complementary style, but disregard the Moghul domes, and the building is as Gothic as the Bombay Law Courts. Internally the circulation areas, cascading external staircases and arcaded verandahs occupy an enormous part of the volume of the building, limiting the actual usable floorspace.

The Madras Marina offers a valuable lesson in civic design which has long been forgotten in England – that the unity of the whole should transcend the sum of the constituent parts. In Madras, without eschewing individuality, flair or integrity a whole series of public buildings were designed over a period of seventy years which shared several unifying attributes – the common use of available local materials, red brick and terracotta, a delight in quality craftsmanship, an intuitive awareness of the site in its context on the horizon and a controlled enthusiasm for traditional or hybrid styles which were well-adapted to the climate.

If Irwin failed to achieve a real synthesis of East and West in the planning and design of the Madras Law Courts, he was able to explore the way forward in a series of public buildings in the Museum complex in Pantheon Road. Irwin was as versatile as his predecessor Chisholm. He designed the sinister grey Viceregal Lodge in Simla in a gaunt Elizabethan style, just prior to the Law Courts, but it is evident that his real predilections lay in revivalism. Notwithstanding the Victoria Public Hall (1883–1885), a charming Romanesque affair for which probably he was responsible, his purest building is the former Victoria Memorial Hall and Technical Institute (1909), now the National Art Gallery. It is an absolute gem. Executed in the warm pink sandstone which was associated with the best Moghul architecture it is a very accomplished work with the centrepiece based on the principal gateway of Akbar's abandoned city of Fatehpur Sikri. It is compact,

Law Courts, Madras, 1888–1892: the culmination of Indo-Saracenic architecture, imbued with all the gorgeous exoticism of the East. The minaret on the right of the picture is crowned by a lighthouse.

198

coherent and timeless, quite as good as the Moghul prototypes on which it is based.

Some of the most sophisticated essays in native styles lay in the princely states, where sympathetic architects could work unfettered by the opposition of the local PWD. At Hyderabad, the ancient commercial cross-roads of the Deccan, Vincent Esch was active in the 1920s, adorning the city with a number of public buildings in an Indo-Saracenic style which, whilst they failed to demonstrate any real fusion of the two architectural traditions, nonetheless provided some fine new townscape entirely appropriate to such an ethnic melting-pot. In many ways these buildings and those by British architects in other native states are quite sophisticated political symbols of the Imperial presence. The external camouflage may be Indian, and an Indian workforce may have been used, but the designs, plans and overall control remain British, in the same way that in the political arena the British lay as the power behind the princely native thrones.

This symbolism was not lost on the Nizam who presided over a state in which the Muslim élite were outnumbered by Hindus and where conciliation was essential if sectarian strife was to be averted. In a similar manner to Kirkpatrick's Residency nearby, architecture was used for political ends. In his address at the opening of the Osmania University the Nizam pronounced:

> The architecture of this building represents a blending of the Hindu and Muslim styles, and the art and culture of both these races are reflected in the pillars and traceries and carvings on the doors and walls. Thus the building symbolises the close contacts and friendly relations subsisting for centuries between the various classes of my subjects, as a result of which the people of my state have always in the past lived in harmony with each other.

The central tower and domes of the dazzling white Osmania General Hospital owe much to Churchgate Railway Terminus in Bombay, but Esch's buildings, including the High Court and Town Hall, are wonderful evocations of Eastern magnificence, albeit seen through a very Western eye.

Elsewhere in the native states British architects were active, patronised by native princes eager for the approbation accorded by the Viceroy to social improvers, particularly for the more tangible manifestation of a CSI or KCSI.

> Rustum Beg of Kolazai – slightly backward Native State –
> Lusted for a C.S.I. – so began to sanitate.
> Built a Gaol and Hospital – nearby built a City drain –
> Till his faithful subjects all thought their ruler was insane . . .
> . . . Then the Birthday Honours came. Sad to state and sad to see,
> Stood against the Rajah's name nothing more than C.I.E.

Chisholm moved to Baroda after his departure from Madras, working

National Art Gallery, Madras, formerly the Victoria Memorial Hall and Technical Institute, designed by Henry Irwin and modelled on the principal gateway at Fatehpur Sikri.

on the completion of a new palace for the Gaekwar, which had been commenced by Major Mant (1840–1881) of the Bombay Engineers. Mant was one of the most fascinating and ingenious of all the English Sappers to work in India, yet he remains rather an enigma. He arrived in 1859, fresh from Addiscombe, and worked in the prevailing Venetian Gothic style on the High School at Surat, but soon he acquired a scholarly interest in local architecture and began 'to unite the usefulness of the scientific European designs together with the beauty, taste, grandeur and sublimity of the native'. His greatest opportunities came in 1875, a year after his promotion to Major, when he produced designs for four palaces, virtually simultaneously, at Cooch Behar, Darbhanga, Baroda and Kolhapur. The designs for Cooch Behar were still-born owing to cost, but the others were all implemented.

To the European purist it would be easy to dismiss these extraordinary designs as ostentatious expressions of a decadent ruling class, unrestrained by any semblance of architectural propriety, but by Indian standards they were merely the latest manifestations of a

The High Court, Hyderabad by Vincent Esch.

constant process of cultural miscegenation, whereby India acknowledges, adapts and then assimilates the cultural attributes of its latest rulers: in this case, the British. Indubitably many of these riotously eclectic buildings, such as those at Junagadh, were little more than 'orgiastic shopping sprees in the bargain basement of architecture', in the words of the Maharajah of Baroda, but Mant's designs showed an intelligent appreciation of local styles. At Kolhapur he designed a conventional Venetian Gothic town hall, and later an Indo-Saracenic memorial for Florence to commemorate the Maharajah's son who died there in 1870. However, his real *tour de force* is the palace, which has a skyline based on the multiple, clustered domes of the Jain temples at Ahmedabad, and other elements drawn from local examples at Bharatpur, Deeg and Mathura, centres of Maratha culture relatively uninfluenced by the Moghul tradition. Thus the palace is not Indo-Saracenic at all, but a more precise commingling of locally based styles with details drawn by native draughtsmen. Mant became convinced that his palaces would collapse due to his own structural inaccuracies, and he died in 1881 from insanity induced by overwork; hardly surprising, some have thought rather unkindly, given the febrile eclecticism of his later work.

Laxhmi Vilas Palace, Baroda, reputedly the most expensive building erected by a private individual in the 19th century, was designed by Major Charles Mant and completed by Robert Fellowes Chisholm, after Mant died insane.

202

At Baroda Chisholm was brought in to finish Mant's earlier designs. The Laxhmi Vilas Palace is reputed to be the most expensive building constructed by a private individual in the 19th century. It is colossal, so large in fact that the building transmutes itself from Hindu martial architecture, through various Moghul nuances via a flurry of domes taken from Jain sources, towards Gothic and classical references. The materials, craftsmanship and accommodation represent a blending of Eastern and Western cultures appropriate to the dualistic role adopted by the Indian princes at this time, with one foot rooted firmly in the glories of the Indian past and another planted in British and European society. Chisholm remained in Baroda where he designed the new College for the Gaekwar, which has a close affinity to the Madras Senate House and other local buildings, before he retired to London where he designed and prepared a scheme for an Indian Museum and also the Church of Christ Scientist, Wilbraham Place, Sloane Street.

Another great Madras architect, Henry Irwin also moved on to design in the native states after his successful work in the city. The Amba Vilas Palace at Mysore is one of the most extravagant and lavish in the whole of India. Twenty of its rooms accommodated nothing more than the accumulated hunting trophies of generations of the family. Built in 1898 for the Maharajah of Mysore it is the most astonishing juxtaposition of Hindu, Saracenic and Hoysala elements conceivable, wilfully plundered from examples all over India and capped by a minaret and an onion dome strikingly similar to that on the High Court in Madras. As architecture it may be ill-mannered and vulgar, but it is enormous fun and beautifully transcribed by the local temple stonemasons. On certain nights the gates of the palace are thrown open to the whole city and the building is illuminated by fifty thousand individual light bulbs in a display of dazzling luminescence.

The most accomplished of all the exponents of the Indo-Saracenic style was Colonel Sir Samuel Swinton Jacob (1841–1917), close relative of Brigadier-General John Jacob, the legendary hero of Sind after whom Jacobabad is named. He was a contemporary of Mant's at Addiscombe and entered the Bombay Artillery in 1858. Initially he served in the PWD, in Rajputana and later, in 1865–66, in Aden with the Field Force, but on his return in 1867 he was appointed to Jaipur State where he spent most of his working life. As a leading exponent of hybridisation he received an enormous number of commissions from all over India. He was responsible for the Secretariat at Simla (grim Scottish baronial), as well as more lively affairs such as the Victoria Memorial Hall, Peshawar; St Stephen's College, Delhi; the State Bank of Madras; St John's College, Agra and numerous buildings in Jaipur. However, his great love was Rajput architecture and whilst in Jaipur he prepared an enormous portfolio of architectural details of the city's buildings, which became a pattern book for many architects practising in the field. His most lavish design in the princely states was at Bikaner where the Lallgarh palace was designed with exquisitely carved arcaded screens and friezes culled from Rajput examples in the old fort.

One of his most ardent disciples was Major-General Sir Sydney Crookshank, who worked as executive engineer in Lucknow between

Amba Vilas Palace, Mysore designed by Henry Irwin; ostentatious, ill-mannered, and vulgar, but enormous fun. Compare the domed minaret with that on the Madras Law Courts.

Sir Samuel Swinton Jacob as a young cadet at Addiscombe College.

1908 and 1910. Earlier he had supervised the erection of Government House, Naini Tal to the designs of F. W. Stevens, and also the Imperial Bacteriological Institute at Maktesar. At Lucknow Crookshank planned and constructed King George's Medical School and Hospital, the Canning College and Technical School, the Arabic College, School of Design, Post Office and Balrampur Hospital, after submitting the designs to Jacob for his approval. Crookshank moved to Delhi where he oversaw the erection of the Indo-Saracenic pavilions for the Durbar of 1911. After the Great War he played a crucial role on the Imperial Delhi Committee, liaising between the government engineers and Lutyens and Baker.

The wealth of the Indian maharajahs was legendary as was their reputation for extravagance and eccentricity, but under the British Raj these reached the most outrageous extremes. It was probably one of the greatest strengths of the Raj that the Indians were as dotty as the British themselves, yet each society was too polite to point it out to the other. The Maharajah of Junagadh, who commissioned some of the most decadent buildings of the period, was keen on dogs. His favourite animals were set up in their own quarters with telephones, electricity and domestic servants, and when finally they left this vale of tears their little canine souls were carried aloft to the doleful strains of Chopin's funeral march. At Kapurthala the Maharajah took his francophilia to exceptional lengths, importing M. Marcel, a French architect, and an army of French craftsmen to create a French chateau in the style of Louis XIV, before himself assuming the role of Sun King and insisting on the use of French at his court. Once a year until 1900 the Maharajah of Patiala appeared before his subjects, in a state of full sexual arousal, wearing a brilliant breast plate studded with over one thousand diamonds, and precious little else. Standing erect, but with considerable sang-froid, he responded nonchalantly to the roars of approval from his subjects who equated his potency with that of Lord Shiva and the fertility of the land. Fortunately the family were used to public exposure and there were no linked cases of crop failure. The Maharajah of Gwalior ordered a new Palace to commemorate the visit of the Prince of Wales in 1874. He asked his chief adviser, Lieutenant-Colonel Sir Michael Filose, to design it for him in an Italianate style and, as a centrepiece for the royal visit, the Durbar Hall was embellished with two of the world's largest chandeliers, each weighing over three tons. In order to ensure the structural stability of the ceiling three of his largest elephants were hoisted on to the roof by a special crane before the two Venetian chandeliers were installed. The palace was sumptuously finished to provide a fairy-tale setting with glass fountains, glass balusters to the staircase, glass furniture and glass fringes and decorations – all it lacked was the odd glass slipper. It became even more bizarre under his successor, Madhav Rao Scindia, for he indulged his passion for trains by constructing a private narrow gauge railway in the grounds, which he himself drove, and another in the palace dining room, which circulated around the vast central dining table dispensing brandy, port and cigars. It enabled the Maharajah to bypass his more inebriated guests.

Ironically as fast as many British architects searched for an effective synthesis of styles between East and West, distilled from the diverse architectural heritage of India, many of the wealthiest Indian patrons cultivated British customs and manners and sought to emulate the finest European architecture. The Maharajah of Mysore's Bangalore

Maharajah of Mysore's Palace, Bangalore: echoes of Arthurian England.

Palace was modelled on Windsor Castle with battlemented parapets and fortified towers looming over the South Indian countryside, a bizarre vision of mediaeval England, distorted in transposition, for use by an Indian prince.

In contrast with the fanciful architectural creations of many of the native states, a number of towns remained well within the classical tradition, uninfluenced by the exotic experiments in hybridisation which occurred elsewhere. Bangalore, for instance, had grown up as the principal garrison town for Mysore state in the early 19th century following the defeat of Tipu Sultan at Seringapatam in 1799. At a level of 3,000 feet Bangalore was healthier and cooler than Seringapatam, and a large military station grew up on spacious lines with widely dispersed buildings. Under the Commissioner L. B. Bowring between 1862 and 1870 the cantonment area grew rapidly in size and importance, becoming an administrative centre for the whole region and something of a resort. Bowring was responsible for the erection of the handsome Public Offices, which now house the High Court, a vast classical range with Ionic porticos to the centre and end pavilions, linked by extensive arcaded wings, all finished in deep Pompeian red stone. The building was designed by Colonel (later Sir) Richard Sankey between 1864 and 1868 and it set a prevailing classical tone which has been perpetuated to this day, for the new Post Office building, currently under construction, is a splendid dressed-granite classical composition with beautifully carved detailing. The development of classical public buildings such as the Government Arts College, Mayo Hall and Public Library was part of a conscious policy of civic improvement, as a result of which Bangalore acquired the air of a 'garden city' and this was accentuated as peripheral areas such as Cleveland Town, Richmond Town and Benson Town were developed along 'garden city' lines. Today Bangalore seems strikingly familiar to the English visitor for it resembles Welwyn Garden City or Bournemouth with its beautifully maintained parks and open spaces at the centre of the city, its bandstand, its tree-lined vistas and its jealously guarded statues of Queen Victoria and Edward VII. When proposals were mooted to remove these anachronistic monuments to Imperial rule the citizens of Bangalore firmly resisted such a civic outrage. Quite how much the later Garden City movement in England owed to the dispersed cantonments of the military and civil stations of British India is a question which deserves greater investigation, but Ebenezer Howard and his followers must have been aware of the success of the Indian cantonments as a steady stream of retired India hands flowed home to the closest English equivalents in Cheltenham, Eastbourne and St John's Wood.

It seems apparent that once a particular style began to prevail in any one area there was little incentive to depart from it. Bombay remained dominated by its Ruskinian Gothic buildings, which were still being constructed well into the early 1900s, long after the style had gone out of fashion in England. Madras went native with exotic experiments in Indo-Saracenic architecture, Calcutta remained with its classical origins, other than one notable exception, the High Court. John Begg

206

considered, 'Bombay is energetic, exuberant, sparkling, breezy and has building stone of many kinds and colours. Calcutta is calm, respectable, orthodox and its leading materials are brick and plaster. A massive (apparently) type of Classic renaissance, by no means to be sneered at, early asserted itself there, and has retained its hold.'

Calcutta's leading Victorian architect was Walter L. B. Granville (1819–1874), a prolific designer who was responsible for many of the best public buildings of the later 19th century in the city. It was he who designed The Memorial Church, Cawnpore. From 1858 he worked for the Eastern Bengal Railway before being appointed as consulting architect to the government of India from 1863 to 1868 for the express purpose of designing public buildings in Calcutta. One of his earliest briefs was for the construction of a large new complex of buildings to house the University between 1866 and 1872. These were a fine group, dispersed around Granville's Ionic Senate House, and their demolition in 1961 was a civic tragedy, perpetrated by an institution which ought to have known better. Perhaps it would be unreasonable to expect the University authorities in Calcutta to have behaved any more responsibly than their counterparts at the University of London, who demolished acres of Bloomsbury in the pursuit of learning. Granville's monumental Post Office in Dalhousie Square stands on the site of the Black Hole and it was raised between 1864 and 1868. It is a noble, even stately, structure of considerable sophistication dominated by a corner dome and punctuated by huge rusticated pylons which are linked by Corinthian colonnades. The main chamber rises full height through the building and provides a grand setting for the tide of humanity that ebbs and flows beneath the dome. This is Granville's best classical composition, although the Indian Museum is also worthy of note for its massive simplicity with a central quadrangle enclosed by galleries of Ionic columns.

The only significant secular Gothic building in the city is the High Court, also by Granville, but this lacks the confident mastery of style which characterises his work in the classical idiom. Nonetheless it is a handsome and impressive edifice taken straight from Gilbert Scott's

Public Offices, now the High Court, Bangalore by Colonel Richard Sankey; monumental civic classicism inspiring a spirit which continues to this day.

207

Post Office, Calcutta by Walter Granville, on the site of the Black Hole.

project for the Hamburg Rathaus of 1854–1856. The plan, elevations, composition and much of the detail are Scott's, who in turn used the great mediaeval prototype of the Cloth Hall at Ypres for his model. Subsequently it has been extended into a wider complex of court buildings linked at a high level by arcaded Gothic bridges. It is faced in red brick with stucco dressings. The ground floor is an elegant vaulted cloister of Barakur sandstone with capitals of Caen stone. Like Garstin's Town Hall immediately next door, Granville's High Court suffered from the semi-liquid subsoil and underwent such subsidence that the tower was never completed to its original designs, accounting for its most obvious difference from Scott's prototype in that it is far too low for such a long frontage. The high-pitched iron-plated roof was intended to act as a furnace, drawing up the heated air from the courts below through orifices made in the ceilings. The buildings are grouped around a quadrangle which is landscaped with pleasant gardens and fountains. Gowned advocates with Oxbridge accents stroll along the groin-vaulted cloisters in earnest discussion with their clients, a living monument to the durability of English law, which ironically has far firmer foundations in India than the building in which it is practised.

The Court of Small Causes stands nearby. It is a wholly classical composition designed in 1878 by William H. White, who spent thirteen months in India attached to the PWD. Unfortunately the curious Ionic capitals to the exterior are woefully inadequate attempts by Indian craftsmen to copy those on the Senate House, which had been sent out to India in Ransome's patent stone, and the copies more closely resemble intertwined serpents and dolphins. Its style is French Palladian seen through Victorian eyes, but it is a bold, imaginative and functional building of considerable merit and it is unfortunate that White left the PWD and returned to England after completing just one building.

The High Court, Calcutta is closely based on Gilbert Scott's design for the Hamburg Rathaus but the tower was modified owing to subsidence.

The High Court, Calcutta. (Left): *the iron-crested tower and pierced parapet.* (Above): *echoes of Renaissance Italy in a distant land.*

High Court: carved stone capital to the arcade.

Granville's Gothic High Court was very much an aberration in the 'city of palaces'. Other principal public buildings of the period were firmly classical or Italianate in origin. The Telegraph Office (now demolished) was an Italianate composition with a campanile commenced to original designs by Barnfather and Clark, assistant engineers, but completed in 1873 to revised designs by Mr Vivian. It was interesting not only for its Italianate conception, but for the use of terracotta made from local red Barrackpore clay for the caps, columns and strings, a material which was used later in the uninspiring refacing of Writer's Buildings (1877–1882). Perhaps the most unusual composition is the East Indian Railway Offices by Roskell Bayne, a marvellous Italian palazzo. It has wide projecting eaves for protection against the elements and the principal cornice is taken directly from the Farnese Palace in Rome. Structurally it is quite extraordinary, pioneering a combination of iron and concrete. The floor trusses and columns are made from worn-out rails, the floors from brick carried on concrete arches and the doors and windows are all pivoted on stone cills and architraves to create a structure both cheap and fireproof. The building covers an

209

East India Railway Offices, Calcutta, by Roskell Bayne. The principal cornice is copied from the Palazzo Farnese in Rome.

entire street block, and the two principal corner pavilions are decorated in Italian *sgraffito* work. The four main panels depict Architecture, Sculpture, Music and Commerce, and the lower stages are inscribed with names of the principal stations served by the railway. To complete the Italian effect the main floors are tessellated marble pavements.

Bayne is an interesting architect, for it was he who designed the Thornhill and Mayne Memorial Library and Mayo Memorial in Allahabad, as well as the Indo-Gothic Husainabad clocktower in Lucknow, but he remains rather elusive, a Calcutta-based man who practised widely elsewhere. On Granville's death he assumed the mantle of the city's leading architect.

As late as 1916 public buildings were being erected in a classical style faced in chunam. The Royal Exchange by T. S. Gregson, once a partner of F. W. Stevens in Bombay, is remarkable for its date, for it could easily have been erected sixty or seventy years earlier. With its eloquent use of paired Corinthian columns in antis, modillioned cornice and chastely detailed attic storey it looks more like a mid-19th-century London club or bank. Not all of Calcutta's new buildings were so traditionally conceived for the great new station at Howrah, rebuilt between 1900 and 1908, was designed by the imaginative English Arts and Crafts architect, Halsey Ricardo (1854–1928). Articulated by eight square towers it is an unusual, if slightly incoherent, red brick design infused with Oriental and Romanesque references. However, by this date all civic architecture in Calcutta had been eclipsed by the most potent symbol of Empire erected anywhere in the world – the Victoria Memorial.

The Victoria Memorial, Calcutta is an enduring testimony to the Imperial connection, a connection which bound India and Britain for almost 300 years, and one which lay at the very heart of Britain's claim to be a world power. Conceived at the very climax of Empire, it is itself the architectural climax of a city which owed its existence to the

210

Victoria Memorial, Calcutta: the most potent symbol of Empire in the world, dominating the centre of the city.

Imperial ideal. The building dominates the whole of Calcutta and, without doubt, it is one of the most important to be erected in the 20th century, not because it is an architectural masterpiece but because it stands as an historical symbol, a monument to a Queen-Empress, completed at the very moment that the Imperial impulse was dying, its chivalric ideals lying shattered on the fields of Flanders and its self-confident vigour drained by the exertions of the Great War.

The Victoria Memorial owes its inception to Lord Curzon and it was paid for by contributions from the princes and peoples of India, a largely spontaneous outburst of generosity doubtless assisted by the fact that few wished to be seen not to contribute. It was Curzon who envisaged a repository of Anglo-Indian art and relics, a sort of Imperial valhalla, in which all the widely dispersed monuments, sculpture, paintings and documents relating to the history of British India could be concentrated and displayed. 'How little anyone seemed to care about, or even to remember, the mighty deeds that had been wrought on Indian soil, or to inculcate their lessons for the sake of posterity', he wrote. 'I felt that the lack of this historical sense – the surest spring of national self-respect – was injurious in its effect both upon English and Indian interests.'

A magnificent building was envisaged, the central feature of which was to be a marble statue of Queen Victoria beneath a central dome. Close by would be halls consecrated to personal memorials of the Queen and her reign. The remainder of the building would be given over to artefacts, prints, drawings and models illustrating the entire period since the end of Moghul rule and the start of the British connection with India. 'The test of admission was to be not artistic, or even merely historical interest; but, in the case of objects or events, exceptional importance, in the case of persons, exceptional distinction or service, irrespective of race or creed.' For the crucial choice of architect, Curzon approached Lord Esher, Secretary to the Office of Works, who recommended William Emerson, then President of the RIBA and an old

India hand. The style was specified by Curzon who expounded on the subject with conviction:

> In Calcutta – a city of European origin and construction – where all the main buildings had been erected in a quasi-classical or Palladian style, and which possessed no indigenous architectural type of its own – it was impossible to erect a building in any native style. A Moghul building, however appropriate for the mosques and tombs of the Moslem Kings, or even for the modern Palace of an Indian Prince in his own State, would have been quite unsuited for the Memorial of a British Sovereign. A Hindu fabric would have been profoundly ill-adapted for the purposes of an exhibition. It was evident that a structure in some variety of the classical or Renaissance style was essential, and that a European architect must be employed.

It was Curzon too who insisted on the use of Indian marble and in this he was inspired, for it came from the Makrana quarries, the same which had supplied material for the Taj Mahal, the spiritual antecedent of the Victoria Memorial Hall. It produces an exquisite effect, the blueish veins in the stone reducing glare and conferring a restful tone. Given the unstable nature of the Calcutta ground, the use of marble posed considerable problems, so the foundations of the entire structure were raised above ground on a low marble terrace, elevating the building above the flat Maidan and enhancing its dignity. So important was Curzon to the impetus of the whole project that when he left India, late in 1905, it ran into severe difficulties and only his continuing interest and indefatigable lobbying ensured its completion. The Great War halted building works with the cupolas to the corner towers incomplete, but finally in December 1921 the entire monument was finished and opened by the Prince of Wales.

Architecturally the Victoria Memorial Hall may lack the essential spark of genius and the discipline which creates the masterpiece, but for sheer impact and presence it has a certain sublime quality which transcends the loose amalgam of its constituent parts. Its form and massing are wholly European in conception and these are loosely based on Emerson's earlier design approach for the Takhtsingi Hospital at Bhawanagar, but at the Victoria Memorial Emerson introduced more subtle concessions to India. The corner domes are faintly Moghul in origin, the window arches are carved with Indian filigree or *moucharabya* work, whilst over the windows on the corner towers flow the great rivers of India, in stone – symbolising the life-giving work of the British Raj. Many of the Saracenic details were designed by Vincent Esch, who supervised the erection of the building on the strength of his work in Hyderabad. The crowning dome, the fifth largest in the world when erected, is surmounted by a huge bronze revolving angel of Victory – sixteen feet high and weighing three tons – and directly beneath the dome, in one vast central chamber, stands a solitary marble statue of Victoria as a young girl. Executed by Sir Thomas Brock RA, it is taken from Chantrey's bust of the Queen at Windsor. Surrounding

Victoria Memorial, Calcutta: Lord Curzon's statue stands beneath an arch inscribed with the royal coat of arms and ciphers. The bronze statue of Victory crowning the dome slowly revolves, proclaiming British dominion in India to all.

the statue are marble friezes and panels by Frank Salisbury depicting scenes from her reign – from the timorous, white-robed young girl on the morning of her accession to the triumphant Imperial climax of the Diamond Jubilee. The central panels are inscribed with the great Imperial attributes – Dominion, Power, Loyalty and Freedom. Yet ironically it was the fundamental conflict between the concepts of Dominion and Freedom, expressed in the continuing tension between the high Imperial mission and the English liberal tradition, that led to the end of the Raj. Empires tend to have the weaknesses of their strengths and all it needed was for the subjects of the Empire to appeal to the innate sense of freedom for which the Empire stood, and the whole edifice came tumbling down.

Pax Britannica: bronze statuary outside the Victoria Memorial.

CHAPTER 9

NEW DELHI : THE ROME OF HINDOSTAN

An empire can nurse no finer ideal than the cohesion of its dominions in cities erected in one style of architecture recognised throughout the world as the expression of its own imperial ideals. The encouragement of such an empire-pervading style through-out colonies, dependencies, and protectorates will tend to annihil-ate distance and conduce to an imperial liberty, equality and fraternity.

In 1912, when this resounding Imperial polemic appeared in *The Builder*, attempts to impose an artificial unity of any sort whether political, economic or architectural were doomed to failure. The Empire was united only in its diversity. It never assumed an identifiable pattern for it was constantly changing like a global kaleidoscope. The elusive search for architectural unity was important as a way of expressing national vigour, virility, and Imperial resolve; if the British faltered others would seize pre-eminence. *The Builder* continued: 'When Great Britain is incapable of setting an example of architectural achievement to her dependencies other nations more virile will slowly but surely take advantage of her relapse – step into the breach, undermine her prestige, and bring about an imperial disaffection more effectual in its consequences than the ravages of internal feuds.' It remains the supreme irony that when at New Delhi Britain did make an architectural statement which symbolised to the world her Imperial mission and artistic genius, it was all to no avail.

The combative climate of international rivalry that characterised the New Imperialism of the 1880s is clearly discernible in the patriotic prolixity of *The Builder*. It also added impetus to the martial impulse, present from the earliest days of the old East India Company. Military power was not just a tool for commercial ends, but an instrument in the burgeoning struggle for global supremacy. In India this was the Great Game, the often illusory secret struggle with Russia at one remove away across the frozen wastes of the Hindu Kush and the barren deserts of Afghanistan. The focus for this confrontation was the North-West Frontier and the Tribal Territory on the Afghan border.

Here the architecture reflected the chronic insecurity of the whole region. At Lahore, the great crossroads of the Punjab, situated on the main railway line from Upper India to the Frontier, the railway station, like that in Delhi, was designed as a fortress by the local engineer, William Brunton, with colossal crenellated corner towers, and cavernous trainsheds which could be sealed in an emergency, crowned by a romantic bevy of bartizans and turrets. Further towards the

Frontier the landscape changes to an undulating, unyielding wasteland of sand, rock and scrub. The mud villages and houses are designed to repel attack with loopholed walls, corner towers, crenellated parapets and steel shutters to the windows. They still carry guns here, but the old jezails were traded in long ago for Kalashnikovs and M 13s. Perhaps the Great Game was not so illusory after all, for the Russians have played it as a waiting game and won the first round. The Victorians thought it real enough: after years of deliberation as to the respective merits of tunnel or bridge, when they came to drive the railway up to Peshawar and the Frontier itself, they straddled the mighty Indus gorge at Attock with a spectacular double-decker bridge guarded by iron gates and battlemented towers. This astonishing feat of Imperial engineering was designed by Sir Francis O'Callaghan and Mr Johnson. The ironwork with girders twenty-six feet deep was sent out by Westwood Baillie & Co. Opened in 1883, and later remodelled in 1926, it soars across the river in a series of six spans carried on five vast stone piers. Almost 1,700 feet long the upper deck carries the railway across the chasm 100 feet beneath, whilst the lower deck accommodates the road traffic, which is swept across the river in full view of Akbar's imposing fort on the opposite bank, and past a chillingly apt Frontier war memorial – a huge inverted stone bullet standing on an isolated ridge beside the railway line. The railway remains the main strategic route to the Frontier and when, in 1971, I tried to photograph it from inside the Khyber Mail, a passenger pressed his gun to my head, convinced that my enthusiasm exceeded the merely historical.

The Khyber Pass is part of the very myth of Empire, and rightly so, for it is one of the most evocative and spectacular places on earth. The twisting road climbs over 3,500 feet through a series of defiles, valleys and reverse curves guarded every hundred yards or so by a crouching soldier of the Khyber Rifles. At the entrance to the pass stands Fort Jamrud, a mud-brick fort built in 1823, looking like something straight out of *Beau Geste*. Nearby lies a memorial plaque inscribed with lines from Kipling's 'Arithmetic on the Frontier':

> The flying bullet down the Pass,
> That whistles clear: 'All flesh is grass'

together with a fulsome tribute to the mutual respect which existed between the British and Pathans. Every knoll and outcrop of the pass is fortified with blockhouses, bunkers, wire and watchtowers and, sprawling across the foreground at Landi Kotal lies a colossal fort. But most haunting of all are the stone plaques set straight into the barren hillsides carrying the insignia of the British regiments who lived, fought and died here. It is fitting that the railway, that hallmark of British dominion, reached this most hallowed spot. Between 1920 and 1925 a railway was built through the Pass twenty-six and a half miles long, a seemingly impossible undertaking, which cost over £2 million sterling, but it enabled the British cohorts to be brought up speedily from Peshawar in times of emergency through thirty-four tunnels aggregating over three miles in length and across ninety-two bridges.

This was the high point of Imperial engineering in every sense of the word; British power and prestige lapping the very borders of the Indian sub-continent yet at the very moment when the tide was turning at the centre.

If the mood could be expansive and martial, it could also be domestic, even homely, in contrast to the display of strength on the Frontier or the grandiloquent expressions of civic and Imperial pride which arose in the great cities. The work of the two Consulting Architects to the Government of India, James Ransome (1865–1944) and John Begg (1866–1937) between 1902 and 1921 was varied enough to accommodate most expressions of the Imperial mood. Both held clear views about style. Ransome affirmed: 'It is . . . by no means easy, to a designer of Indian buildings, to steer an even course between a natural and healthy predilection for style and the necessity for the employment of that which is not strictly in keeping with that style.' He went on to highlight the fundamental problem facing all architects in India:

> The chief difficulty with which I have had to contend . . . has been that of expressing a sufficient sense of solidity in verandahs, admitting the maximum amount of light at so low a level as to preclude the sun's rays from striking the main walls of the building, and pierced at ceiling level with shaded clerestories for purpose of ventilation and for the admission of sufficient light to compensate for the loss entailed by the restricted height of the lower openings.

He pleaded against the dictates of purity and in favour of ingenuity when using the principal available styles, concluding that even though native styles were rich in useful suggestions, 'the peculiarities of their construction and their extravagant ornament and elaborate features render their faithful interpretation inexpedient.'

A competent architect as well as an advocate of bastardisation, Ransome's designs are intelligent and sophisticated essays. It was he, more than any other practitioner, who came closest to using an Arts and Crafts style in India, reflecting the domestic, nostalgic mood which pervaded the hill stations. At Simla he produced an elegant little

217

building on the Mall for use as a library and offices in local Kalka stone with half-timbered gables, red brick chimneys and rough grey slates, in the subdued style of Norman Shaw, and without the ornamental bargeboards which were Simla's hallmark. Later the open rear verandahs were glazed, detracting from the original concept. His second design for the Kennedy House Secretariat, also in Simla, was developed from an earlier French Renaissance concept, and most closely resembles a large Edwardian block of flats with a rhythm of canted bays rising to a frieze of *sgraffito* work beneath wide projecting eaves. The roof has a central tower crowned by an open belvedere for use by the Meteorological Department. Both wings are approached by enormous sweeping stone staircases. The buildings for the Imperial Cadet Corps at Dehra Dun are just as homely. Intended to resemble half-timbered two-storey English cottages, the upper windows act as clerestories to large single internal spaces. The roof lighting is adeptly handled with the windows recessed in projecting dormers which are carried on timber posts. Similar Arts and Crafts influences pervade Government House in Chittagong, which has battered side entrances and a projecting half-timbered porch, the Secretariat at Nagpur, and the Burma Chief Court at Rangoon. The latter two major civic buildings both enjoy alternating stone banding, shallow cupolas and gables with long tapering finials. However, Ransome was versatile and turned out competent designs in a variety of styles for the PWD Secretariat in Lahore, Renaissance conceptions for the Agricultural College, Pusa, and pure classicism of an Ionic order for buildings in Wellesley Place, Calcutta, orchestrating two parallel blocks of official residences and stables into a grand civic composition. He was well-versed in architectural history too for his designs for the Ludhiana Clock Tower were suggested by the Campanile of the Palazzo Scaglieri in Verona.

Ransome's successor John Begg was born at Bo'ness, Scotland and educated at Edinburgh Academy and the Royal Academy Schools. He was articled to Hippolyte Blanc and later worked with Alfred Waterhouse, R. W. Edis, and Young and Hall, the hospital specialists, before going to South Africa in 1898. In 1901 he was appointed Consulting Architect to the Government of Bombay where his principal work was the huge domed Indo-Saracenic General Post Office. Seven years later he succeeded Ransome in the post he was to hold for twelve years. Like Ransome, he was proficient in a variety of styles and he too felt his way towards the evolution of an Anglo-Indian style suited to the conditions of the country. Perhaps his finest work is the Lady Hardinge Medical College and Hospital for women in Delhi (1915–1916), where he hit upon an original treatment and style. Its accentuated horizontality and severity of line and form reflected the work of his great rival, Lutyens. Begg had enormous energy and made significant progress towards a greater harmony between design and function. He acted as consultant to the Indian railway, designed housing and barracks for the new cantonment at Delhi and evolved a standardised design for the Post and Telegraph Departments. The Nagpur and Agra Post Offices and Simla and Rangoon Telegraph Offices are good examples. It was Begg too who complemented Ransome's elegant little Municipal Library and offices at Simla with a group of charming half-timbered and cream plaster structures with overhanging upper storeys and eaves. He produced over twenty churches including the delightful cantonment church at Maymyo outside Mandalay, Burma. His new wing at Craigdhu, Simla was regarded simply as 'the best thing in residential hotel construction for the hills that we have yet seen', complete with quaint and cosy suites of rooms with big brown beams, white plaster, wood block floors and brick fireplaces. However Begg was most at ease when designing in the monumental classical style. The Robertson Arts College, Jubbulpore, and Benares High Court are both well executed, but the Agricultural College at Poona is most inventive with a first-floor arcaded verandah of alternating paired and single columns terminated by vast domed aedicular pavilions to each end bay. Begg also developed Ransome's earlier designs for the Council House Secretariat, Calcutta into a finely proportioned brick and stucco edifice which provided some of the most comfortable government offices in India.

With the growing popularity of Beaux Arts classicism in England great Imperial thoroughfares were planned at the heart of London. Kingsway was opened in 1912. In the West End Regent Street and Piccadilly were reconstructed on suitably Imperial lines. Whole streets in the City of London were recast in a magnificent display of Imperial self-confidence. Even Buckingham Palace received a new façade from Aston Webb to complement the Victoria Memorial and its circumjacent *rond-point* of Imperial statuary. In India this was reflected in a move towards a new interest in Renaissance and Baroque styles and a revival of the quest for a synthesis between classicism and indigenous forms.

Frank Lishman was consulting architect to the United Provinces and his High Court at Allahabad (1916) is one of the most distinctive expressions of the new enthusiasm for Baroque architecture and civic classicism under Indian skies. The superintending engineer was F. O. Oertel, an enthusiastic exponent of a revival of Indian arts and crafts. 'What we want for India is not a Greek and Roman Renaissance, but a renaissance of Indian art and architecture', he cried, but in the High Court Building he presided over the erection of a structure which comprised a very effective synthesis between East and West. Conceived in the Grand Manner, it is a monumental Baroque statement with a pedimented domed centrepiece. Wings and covered ways link this with separate blocks of chambers dispersed around a central courtyard. It appears to be a conventional piece of European design, but the arcaded wings are treated with pierced stone balustrades, screens and engrailed arches set between austere stone columns, imparting a wonderfully cool and mannered appearance to the ensemble. Still, this is a British building and a Court of Law at that, so the cartouche to the central pediment carries a crisply executed royal cipher, a perpetual reminder of the 'Pax Britannica'.

In other hands the same theme of grand civic classicism assumed a more self-important pomposity which tended to accentuate the alien nature of the British rather than to stress the close affinity between the rulers and the ruled. Henry V. Lanchester (1863–1953) was one of the most enthusiastic and inventive advocates of Baroque civic classicism in England, with buildings such as Cardiff City Hall and Law Courts (1897–1906) and Central Hall, Westminster (1905–1911) to his credit. However Lanchester was the planner and engineer and his partner Edwin Rickards, the draughtsman, was the real creative force. Lanchester was involved in India only after Rickards's death in 1920, and his buildings for all their assumed confidence are disappointing and lack the creative spark which Rickards might have imparted. The Council Chamber in Lucknow (1928) resembles Central Hall Westminster in its conception. Lanchester was assisted by Rodeck, and they went on to design the nearby Post and Telegraph Office with its lofty square central tower in 1931–2, but Lanchester's real *tour de force* was the Umaid Bhawan Palace at Jodhpur erected between 1929 and 1944.

The Indian princes had a penchant for European styles and in 1923 the Maharajah of Jodhpur planned a colossal new palace as a famine relief exercise to provide employment for his starving population. Lanchester was chosen as architect and he created a huge domed building which bears the firm imprint of his English civic training. It is a vast monolithic pile, essentially classical in its form and configuration, but with a traditionally Indian layout of centrally placed reception rooms, with staff quarters in one wing and zenana in the other. Hindu details and devices were used because Jodhpur had little Muslim or Saracenic tradition.

The classical tradition was a potent force. Far to the south in Mysore, the Lalitha Mahal Palace of the Maharajah of Mysore was nothing less than a bold attempt to transpose St Paul's Cathedral to a South Indian setting. It was designed by E. W. Fritchley in 1930 in the manner of an Edwardian hotel. Its domed two-storey pedimented centrepiece is openly derived from St Paul's but with additional attenuated wings carrying long colonnades of paired Corinthian columns culminating in secondary domed pavilions. Rising like some evanescent dream palace from the heat haze of the South Indian plain, it is an extraordinary edifice, which has been converted into a hotel for well-heeled Western visitors, eager to sample the delights of a Maharajah's palace. It is an ideal use, for the interiors remain unspoiled with a magnificent suite of principal rooms, complete with stained glass lanterns, ornate plaster-work and finely-chased metalwork.

Lalitha Mahal Palace, Mysore, designed by E. W. Fritchley in 1930, is a loose essay on St Paul's Cathedral. The palace is now a hotel.

However, the political and architectural future lay not in the Native States or in the self-indulgent whims of the ancient princely families of Hindustan. Neither did it lie in the exploitation of the new styles of the 20th century. Art Nouveau styles by their very origin and nature were too avant-garde to be identified with the Imperial ideal and they found little fulfilment in India, although Sir George Frampton's statue of Queen Victoria outside the Memorial Hall, Calcutta, does have a marked Art Nouveau influence with panels of intertwined vine trees on the plinth and some delightfully spiky bronze work. Similarly the style popularised by the Paris Exposition of 1926, Art Deco, found little official favour, although it did prove influential amongst certain wealthy sectors of the native population who were keen to identify with the latest in Western art and culture. Where it occurs it is often wonderfully inventive. The Maharajah of Morvi built a large Art Deco palace with all the sumptuous fittings and finishings of a Hollywood cinema. Most towns in India have a sprinkling of Art Deco houses of the period, the flat roofs, banded fenestration and concrete construction proving remarkably well-suited to the climate.

It is a curious fact of history that empires in decline often undergo a resurgence of cultural vigour before the end, and the British Empire, like those of Spain, Rome or Austria-Hungary, was no exception. The genesis of an Anglo-Indian architectural renaissance lay in the momentous decision to move the capital of India from Calcutta to Delhi. This idea had been current for fifty or sixty years, but cost, inertia and strategic considerations had prevailed against it. By 1910 perceptions were changing. The decision to move the capital formed part of a wider political expedient to defuse the mounting tension and violence in Upper India and Bengal. In 1905 Lord Curzon had partitioned Bengal in the interests of administrative convenience. It was a monumental mistake for the division accentuated communal strife provoking sustained resistance and violence from Bengali nationalists. By 1910 the unrest was so serious that even the new King-Emperor George V was alarmed for the stability of Upper India. When the opportunity arose for a major demonstration of Imperial unity at the Coronation Durbar of 1911, it was seen as a real chance to renew the bonds of Anglo-Indian unity at the very moment when they were in greatest danger of being torn asunder. The Viceroy, Lord Hardinge, a man of common qualities possessed to a rare degree, hid an astute brain behind a mask of shyness and austerity. With some of his closest advisers and with the sanction of George V, a secret plan was prepared of consummate political dexterity to mitigate Curzon's *faux pas* of 1905. The intention was to unite Bihar and Orissa into a new Lieutenant-Governorship with a Legislative Council and a new capital at Patna, to reinstate a Chief Commissioner in Assam, to create a unified Bengal as a Presidency and, most important of all, to create a wholly new Imperial capital at Delhi directly administered by the Government of India. When the decision was announced at the Delhi Durbar on 12th December 1911 the assembly was astonished and there was a spontaneous outburst of joy from the Delhi crowd that moved the King to tears.

The transfer of the capital made profound sense for more than just political reasons. For a start it was much closer to Simla, the summer capital, and the climate was infinitely more salubrious than that of Calcutta. It was a major route centre for road and rail and lay close to the Punjab and United Provinces, but most importantly, Delhi was a symbol with deep-rooted historical associations. It had been the Imperial capital for centuries and was the centre of the Moghul Court. It was to here that the mutineers streamed in 1857, to the symbolic rallying point of Bahadur Shah, the last of the Moghul Emperors. By identifying with Delhi the British were placing themselves in a direct historical continuum for traditionally the whole of India looked to the city as the focus of suzerain power in the sub-continent. Lord Crewe, Secretary of State for India considered 'the ancient walls of Delhi enshrine an Imperial tradition comparable with that of Constantinople, or with that of Rome itself.' In spite of the vociferous offensive launched by vested Calcutta interests, and the virulent opposition of Lord Curzon who envisaged his great Victoria Memorial Hall, then in the course of erection in Calcutta, as the spiritual sanctum of an Imperial capital, the move went ahead.

Before embarking on the story of New Delhi proper we can make a telling comparison with the new capital of the United Provinces of Bihar and Orissa at Patna, another part of Hardinge's emollient plan for India. Admittedly one is a provincial and the other a national capital but even so, the originality of Lutyens's creation is shown up at once.

Patna was laid out by the consulting architect, Joseph Fearis Munnings. In spite of its eclipse by New Delhi, it is an interesting piece of Edwardian classicism. Government House, a subdued Italianate block with projecting eaves and arcaded bridge links to separate wings, is set at the end of a long vista, King George V Avenue, which forms the principal axis of the town. This axis forms a visual link between the Secretariat block and Government House, which are separated by a serpentine lake. The capital was complete by 1918 and the buildings share a common muted form of classicism.

Early in 1912 a tripartite Town Planning Committee was formed with a limited brief to assess the task of laying out the new Imperial city, the eighth which Delhi had seen in its long and ancient history. The City Engineer of Liverpool, John Brodie, was nominated by the Local Government Board and Captain George Swinton, Chairman of the London County Council was appointed to head the Committee, but for the post of architectural adviser, the most frantic lobbying took place. S. D. Adshead was in serious contention until rejected as too academic, and amongst those advanced by interested parties were the cream of the British architectural profession – Leonard Stokes, Reginald Blomfield and Sir Robert Lorimer – as well as those with Indian experience – George Wittet and John Begg. With characteristic modesty Professor Patrick Geddes suggested himself, and interestingly, Raymond Unwin, the percipient and enlightened planner of Hampstead Garden Suburb, was favoured by none other than Lord Crewe. Eventually the decision narrowed to a choice between Edwin Lutyens, nominated by the RIBA, and Henry Lanchester. Hardinge chose Lutyens with Lanchester employed as a temporary consultant. The composition of the Committee put quite a few architectural noses out of joint, not least that of John Begg who, as Consulting Architect to the Government of India, remained ignored and unconsulted.

The Committee set to work energetically and examined all the possible sites for the new city. The arguments against the northern site, where the foundation stones had been laid by King George and Queen Mary at the Durbar of 1911, were strong, but the decision whether to choose the northern site on the historic Ridge or a more open site to the south vacillated alarmingly, long after detailed planning had com-

New Delhi from the air showing the complex geometric plan dominated by the huge central axis which leads past the Secretariats and on to the great climax at Viceroy's House. The circular Council Chamber may be seen to the left of the Secretariats.

menced on the latter. Apparently the southern site for Government House was settled by the Viceroy himself.

> The moment I saw the selected site I realised its objections. It would be hot; it had no views; and it had no room for expansion ... [We] then mounted and galloped over the plain to a hill some distance away. From the top of the hill there was a magnificent view embracing Old Delhi and all the principal monuments situated outside the town, with the river Jumna winding its way like a silver streak in the foreground at a little distance. I said at once ... 'This is the site for Government House'.

The geometrical plan form of the new city was the product of the complex discussions of the Committee and Lanchester with the Viceroy and his advisers, but the concept of a huge central axis remained a constant throughout. The basic ideas of axial symmetry and kinetics, whereby a fresh series of views and aspects revealed themselves as one moved through the city, were fundamental to the whole conception of ceremonial function, but the Committee's reports also revealed an awareness of the complexity of city planning. Extensive thought was given to the problems of communications, recreation, water supply, drainage and housing for all classes, as well as to the finer points of three-dimensional civic design. The actual plan itself changed even in the process of construction, but Lutyens confessed that Hardinge's dictum that one principal avenue should lead to the Purana Qila and another to the Jumma Masjid, major focal points of the old city, was 'the father of the equilateral and hexagonal plan'.

Lutyens was well-versed in the grand traditions of town planning on a city scale and in the precepts and ideals of the Garden City movement. Before departing for India he had been consulting architect to the Hampstead Garden Suburb Trust with specific responsibility for the design of the Central Square and the general layout of the estate. The concept of a central place with radiating vistas, *rond-points*, *pattes-d'oie* and accentuated axes, the idea of capturing the horizon and grouping individual buildings into a corporate whole were printed firmly in his mind, so that when he arrived in Delhi the challenge of designing an entire community was not intimidating; nor was the prospect of working closely with the Viceroy of India for he had just left an equally imperious client in Henrietta Barnett. In Hampstead Garden Suburb Lutyens had been designing within a framework which reflected the specific social ideals of its creator; in Delhi the new city would reflect the concept of Imperial supremacy, but in a subtle English way. The plan of New Delhi reflects other influences too: L'Enfant's plan of Washington, Haussmann's plan of Paris and the contemporaneous erection of a new Federal capital at Canberra in Australia, where the Australian Government had appointed an American as supervisory architect, Walter Burley Griffin. More significantly it reflects the rigid social hierarchy of the British Raj.

In New Delhi the social structure of Edwardian India was petrified for future generations to see. The socio-spatial layout of the city reflected the cultural values and relationships of a colonial society which had changed little for sixty or seventy years. The relative status and privileges attached to each rank were guarded jealously and set out in official publications such as the *Warrant of Precedence*. For instance, in the forty-fourth grade of the Warrant the Civilian Superintendent of Clothing Factories ranked a cut above the Deputy Director-General Indian Medical Services, but beneath the Director-General of Public Information, and all three were inferior to the Financial Adviser, Post and Telegraphs. This tortuous and arcane official hierarchy was underscored by social deference and the general presumption that the 'heaven-born' civil servant, and indeed any government official, was superior to a military officer of the same rank. Wives assumed the rank of their husbands, unless they held a post in their own right, which was rare. It was against this deferential social hierarchy that the physical and spatial forms of the city emerged. The disposition of the residences was the work of the Secretary of the Imperial Delhi Committee, Geoffrey de Montmorency, and the engineer Thomas Ward. Within the hexagonal grid pattern five areas were allocated according to race, occupational rank and social status – one, for gazetted officers (fat whites), another for European clerks, a third for indigenous clerks and lower ranking officials, a fourth for Indian princes and nobility and finally a discrete area for non-persons of the lowest ranks. Land plots were allotted according to status. Ruling princes received between four and eight acres, gazetted officers between two and three-and-a-half acres, and Members of the Legislature, one-quarter acre. The relationship between size and status was reflected in price, a bungalow for gazetted officers fetching between 40,000 and 44,000 rupees compared with Class I Married European Clerks' Quarters at 8,600 rupees. So rigid and inflexible was this hierarchy that it is possible to assess the relative social status of each individual road. King George's Avenue, for example, held those in ranks 42 to 43, Deputy Secretaries and Brigadiers; Hastings Road held Major-Generals and above in social ranks 8 to 26. Thus a clear pattern of social and racial segregation was established and as Anthony King has noted: 'Symbolically, the Anglo-Indians caught between two strongly hierarchical cultures and looked down upon by both were located outside the walls of the indigenous city and on the perimeter of the imperial capital.'

The passionate pursuit of system and symmetry in the new city represented a final attempt by the British to impose order on the chaos of Indian society. Based on a complex combination of radial axes and polygons, it not only overcame visual monotony, but provided suitable civic foci for the great institutions of state. The Garden City layout with vast ceremonial avenues and open spaces may have been based on the prevailing antipathy for urban values, but Lutyens's use of monumental classicism as a basis for a unified architectural style more than reconciled both town and country in one glorious composition. The magnitude of the task and its symbolic importance affected most observers. To Lord Curzon it symbolised the moral supremacy of the British Empire, 'Our work is righteous and . . . it shall endure'; to the architectural critic Robert Byron, New Delhi was 'The Rome of

Hindostan'; above all it represented the apotheosis of the Imperial ideal itself.

Vested with such metaphysical, political and social meaning, the question of style achieved paramount importance. What would encapsulate the Imperial ideal but still represent the concept of Britain in India? Advice poured in from all quarters. Stanley Adshead, a disappointed aspirant for Lutyens's job, thought 'New Delhi should be Greek, not Hellenic Greek, but Hellenistic Greek — The Greek of the Alexandrian period, with its rich ornament borrowed more than 2,000 years ago from India herself.' John Begg, desperate to participate, advocated a competition for the principal buildings. The Viceroy insisted that 'the architecture . . . should harmonise externally with the monuments of Old Delhi and with the traditions of Indian art', and the aged Sir Swinton Jacob was brought in to advise on appropriate Indian materials and detailing, much to Lutyens's chagrin, who derided his buildings as a mish-mash of historical motifs. Lutyens had little time for Indian architecture in general. He was disparaging and dismissive of those fervent advocates of Indo-Saracenic architecture, who assailed him on all sides. Few were reticent in advancing their views, but the official decision expressed by the Viceroy was a compromise solution: 'Western architecture with an Oriental motif'. A petition signed by eminent public figures including Thomas Hardy and George Bernard Shaw pressed for the use of the Indian master builder and an Indian style. The battle of the styles raged for months. The influential E. B. Havell enquired, 'How will New Delhi be built? Will it be the starting point of a real Anglo-Indian architecture, or only the opportunity of a lifetime for the modern Western stylist?' Lutyens's old friend, Herbert Baker, whom he invited to join him in the great venture, held clear views, which impressed the authorities and won him the appointment as Lutyens's collaborator and partner. 'First and foremost it is the spirit of British sovereignty which must be imprisoned in its stone and bronze . . . To realise this ideal the architecture of the Roman Empire, as embodying "the more elemental and universal forms", should be used as the basis of the style, while Eastern "features" must be woven into the fabric as a concession to Indian sentiment.'

The city which arose under the transcendent influence of Lutyens and Baker represents the culmination of over two hundred years of persistent endeavour to achieve a true architectural synthesis of Eastern and Western styles. In Lutyens's magisterial Viceroy's House the architectural experiments which began in the 18th century to create an Anglo-Indian architecture in its own right reach a triumphant culmination. A building of supreme serenity, it stands on the highest point, Raisina Hill, sharing a platform with the twin Secretariat buildings designed by Baker, a concession which Lutyens later bitterly regretted, and one which seemed to compromise symbolically the supreme authority of the Viceroy. To others it merely confirmed their suspicions that India was run by the vast unchecked bureaucracy contained within them. New Delhi combines 20th-century architecture and town planning on a 17th-century scale, a pure expression of political power. Every single building and vista reflects the hierarchy

of the society which built it and at its centre stands the focus of the entire city, Viceroy's House, the supreme fount of political, cultural and social patronage. The pattern of avenues and waterways of the city converges inexorably on a romantic mass of domes and towers. Robert Byron wrote:

> The beauty of this building transcends the merely panoramic. The coloured and theatrical facade of Islam has been annexed to a more intellectual, three-dimensional tradition of solid form and exact proportion – the tradition of Europe. The result has been to create one of the great palaces of the world, and the only one erected within the last hundred years. Its architecture combines the grandeur of Bernini and the subtlety of Palladio with the colour, shade, and water of Mohammedan Asia.

Twenty years after his arrival in India George Swinton, head of the original Committee, stood before Viceroy's House and remarked, 'It is very rarely that one sees a great building, indeed anything, which is so thoroughly satisfactory that all criticism ceases . . . The Viceroy's House would seem to express the perfect architecture which takes its stand on proportions alone.'

Viceroy's House is a masterpiece: like all great works of architecture the house has a total unity and does not rely on one decorated façade for effect. It was conceived as a three-dimensional composition and it exhales the inspiration of its creator right down to the witty and playful treatment of its finest details. The house is larger than Versailles and it

Viceroy's House, New Delhi: one of the great masterpieces of 20th-century architecture and the culmination of an architectural quest to find a unique Anglo-Indian Imperial style. The Jaipur column and Great Screen may be seen in the foreground.

227

Viceroy's House: pavilion with full-size caparisoned elephant ornament.

dominates the entire city. It straddles Raisina Hill, so that the north and south façades rise from the surrounding plain, whereas the east and west fronts stand on an elevated platform, the top twenty feet of the hill having been blasted away with explosives. The difference in level is an essential component of the overall functional configuration of the building, providing a highly ingenious system of access for state occasions. Guests drive into the South Court, on through arches at the base of the main east front and then turn right under the house itself through two long arched carriageways, seventy-four yards long, to arrive outside the main cloakroom area and guest staircase, thereby eliminating at a stroke the usual undignified pandemonium when two thousand guests and cars arrive at a single entrance.

Externally the principal building is dominated by a monumental dome, which rises majestically over the entire composition. In time it came to be regarded as an architectural metaphor for the British Empire itself, as Imperial in spirit as the solar topee which it vaguely resembles, but the dome is unique for it unites the traditions of East and West in a wholly original form. The copper hemisphere rises from a white stone drum incised in the manner of the Buddhist railings at Sanchi, whilst beneath the drum stand sentinel four octagonal corner turrets linked by a gallery set in deep shade, a reminder of the perpetual vigilance which was the cornerstone of Imperial security. Beneath the dome the monumental colonnades of the principal east front almost form a continuous band. In the centre is a gigantic dodecastyle portico, thirty feet high, with irregular intercolumniation, slightly accentuated in front of the doors, which stand deep in shade. The columns are five times the height of the entablature, the correct proportion for the Corinthian order, except that Lutyens eschewed the architectural canons in favour of a wholly original Delhi order based on fusion of acanthus leaves and four pendant Indian bells. Legend asserted that as long as the bells were silent, so long would the dynasty reign, so the Delhi order recurs throughout the house, as if their very presence would stem the tide of history.

Beneath the dome and over the colonnade the house is given cohesion and unity by the use of a Moghul device, the *chujja*, a crisply finished blade of stone which projects eight feet from the face of the building and throws a band of deep shadow around the entire perimeter. Lutyens understood the essential qualities of traditional native architecture and the crucial importance of the interplay of light and shade. The loggias which run right round the external faces of the building mask the actual window and door openings and provide a common repetitive theme. Thus there is not a window or opening out of place, nothing which does not contribute to the balance of solid to void or to the proportion of the whole. This imposition of a strict conceptual discipline on the outside achieves a transcendental harmonious simplicity, 'architecture in excelsis'. The importance of silhouette has been grasped and integrated into the design, for in the shimmering haze of the city, to have relied on intricacy of detail for external effect would have been fatal. The distinctive brooding profile of the dome imbued with all its Imperial associations is complemented by the use of other

228

Indian devices – the *chujja* wrapping round the whole exterior, little *chattris*, which punctuate the skyline of the attic, and plain circular stone basins set on instepped plinths at the outer and inner ends of the wings and flanking the east portico, in which cascades of water flow from the upper to lower saucers. Most important of all Lutyens acknowledged the vital role of colour and texture under the violent Indian sun, so he used the same red sandstone that the Moghuls had used at Fatehpur Sikri interspersed with cream stone from Dholpur, Bharatpur and Agra, in brilliant horizontal bands of colour accentuating the horizontal emphasis of the whole edifice. In a country where space seems boundless and the horizon everlasting the setting of the house needed to be in proportion to the space around it, so the entire forecourt area is annexed to the design and becomes an integral part of the building enhancing the ceremonial and processional function. This is achieved by an ornate iron entrance screen 224 yards long broken by stone aedicules and piers carrying elephants and wreathed urns, behind which stretches an immense courtyard of crushed red sandstone. At the centre of this courtyard and on the crossing point of the principal axes stands the Jaipur Column, a thin needle of red sandstone carrying a white egg and bronze lotus, from the calyx of which arises the six-pointed glass star of India.

Viceroy's House: Corridors of power. (Below) *an entrance to the Durbar Hall.*

Symmetry, discipline, silhouette, colour and harmony are all elements which one might expect to find in a palace of this scale and magnitude, but the real genius lies in the interior, for this is not merely a piece of gorgeous façadism in which Eastern and Western motifs and forms are commingled, it is a complete marriage of Eastern and Western lifestyles. 'The fusion between East and West is only incidentally one of architectural motives,' wrote Robert Byron. 'It is a fusion also of tastes, comforts, and conceptions of beauty, in different climates . . . Lutyens has combined the gorgeous facade, coloured and dramatic, of Asia, with the solid habit, cubic and intellectual, of European building. Taking the best of East and West, bests which are complementary, he has made of them a double magnificence.' The interior is brilliantly suited to its purpose as a Viceregal palace. The real achievement of the architect lies in the superbly functional layout of the interior which has been intellectually conceived as a totality, a totality which is expressed externally in the cohesion and unity of the façades, each of which has a different function – the east, for state occasions; the south, for domestic affairs and tradesmen; the north, for officials on administrative matters; and the west for recreation and leisure.

Internally the principal floor is given over to a magnificent series of state apartments at the centre of which, beneath the great dome, lies the circular Durbar Hall. This is the innermost sanctum of the Indian Empire, a space of supreme majesty and serenity approached through thirteen-feet-high entrance doors, and it relies for its effect primarily on proportion and materials. Soaring to a height of almost eighty feet this immense circular pantheon is clearly derived from that in Rome, for inset into the walls are four huge apses whose vaulted roofs are enriched with coffered squares up into the main dome. Around the base of the dome are square windows carved into lyre-pattern screens like

Indian *jaalis*, which give light to upper parts of the hall. Beneath this runs a continuous cornice and entablature carried right across the apses on pairs of marble columns. The eye of the dome is open to allow sunshine to flood the chamber, bathing the Viceregal thrones in a glow of divine approbation. A dazzling array of Indian marbles complete the effect – white from Makrana, green from Baroda, pink from Alwar, black from Bhaislana, grey from Marwar, and most splendid of all, yellow marble from Jaisalmer carried by camel across the burning deserts of Rajasthan.

Beyond the Durbar Hall lie the north and south drawing rooms and between them the large drawing room; and beyond these again lies the famous open staircase. This descends in two great sweeps beneath a coved plaster ceiling with a central field of blue, but look again, for the ceiling is not a ceiling, it is open to the azure sky. This is the sort of gleeful, but totally practical, joke which Lutyens loved to employ. Lutyens excelled at the adaptation of corridors and staircases to form vital spatial elements in the compositional whole. The feeling of spatial compression and release and his unerring sense of proportion create surprise, movement and a pervasive sense of ordered repose, drawing the visitor on through the house via a series of beautifully related cubic spaces. Nothing is repeated. Each room is treated differently, but with the same inventive architectural vocabulary intermingling the classical language of the West with the historical expressions of the Moghul and Asokan Empires. Indeed much of the floorspace is out-of-doors in the manner of a Moghul house with a series of small and large internal courtyards overlooked by shaded verandahs, allowing a cool flow of air to pass through the house to the innermost chambers. From the Moghuls too, he borrowed the idea of water which recurs throughout the house, cascading from the saucers on the parapets, jetting from the mouths of Imperial lions and motionless in the garden pools in the Viceregal garden – a symbol of purity of spirit and purpose.

The ornament within the house is remarkably restrained, even austere. The great barrel-vaulted State Drawing Room is plainly treated with domestic fireplaces and an absence of painted decoration. Similarly the State Dining Room is sober with teak panelling enriched with the Star of India, another recurrent theme, beneath a deeply coffered coved ceiling. 'An individual and peculiarly English splendour pervades the rooms and corridors, a splendour, which far from continuing the immemorial traditions of Royal vulgarity, expresses, perhaps for the last time, the spirit of humanist aristocracy in the language of a dwelling', wrote one critic. This English ambience extends to the State Ballroom, which is enriched with Old English mirror glass. The State Library too is quintessentially English, yet unique in conception. Based on the form of Wren's St Stephen's, Walbrook, the central dome is carried on eight vaulted arches and the room is nearly as tall as it is wide. Yet it is in the Viceroy's own personal quarters that Lutyens's wit and playful sense of the ridiculous were given greatest vent. In the nursery the light fittings are designed as four hens and chicks with broken eggs spilling out yolk in the form of light bulbs. Elsewhere the door handles are brass Britannic lions.

The concept of Imperial order and hierarchy permeates not just the city, but also the Viceroy's House itself, and the two should coalesce into a single composition. The great east front faces the principal axis, King's Way, the architectural climax of the entire city approached along a vast triumphal route almost two miles long and embellished with Imperial monuments, but it is here at this critical point, that the masterpiece is flawed by a conceptual error. Lutyens had always intended the house to occupy the highest point on the site, and only reluctantly agreed to move it westward to allow the flanking Secretariats to stand on the same level. He envisaged the great processional route dividing the two buildings as a gentle slope carefully designed to ensure that the immense vista was closed by the east colonnade and dome of the main house, but the task of supervising the design of the Secretariats and the gradient was allotted to Herbert Baker. It was built too steep. The result was disastrous for at the very point of climax in the Great Place the House disappears behind a huge expanse of asphalt, leaving only a remnant of the dome visible from the triumphal axis before the Secretariats. Ever after Lutyens referred to this as his 'Bakerloo'. Acrimonious recriminations soured relations between the two men for the rest of their lives. Mary Lutyens later wrote, 'We were brought up to look on Baker as a villain who had ruined Father's life's work.' For years after Lutyens lobbied vociferously to raise the necessary sum to rectify the mistake. Who was to blame? Probably both were at fault. Lutyens was difficult to work with and Baker was strong-minded enough to resist becoming a mere subordinate. Essentially it was a failure to collaborate closely enough in an area which fell between two stools. Both were absorbed in their own compositions and had different design philosophies. Also it is worth considering that if Lutyens had had his way the great courtyard area linking the two Secretariats on the crest of the hill would have been severed by the shallow gradient of the road.

Herbert Baker (1862–1946) was an immensely capable architect whose work has had the misfortune of being compared with that of a genius. In his earliest years he served as a pupil in the office of Sir Ernest George, where he became friendly with Lutyens, and when he joined him in New Delhi in 1912, he had an established reputation through his work in Pretoria, South Africa. There he designed the Union Buildings, the progenitors of the New Delhi Secretariats.

The flaw in the jewel in the crown. The steep gradient between the Secretariats conceals the facade of the Viceroy's House beyond.

The dome of the West Secretariat: the spirit of British sovereignty imprisoned in stone and bronze.

They are remarkably similar in conception – two ranges of classical buildings with projecting colonnades and large Baroque domes dominating the compositions. Both are derived from Wren's Royal Naval College at Greenwich. Baker appreciated the political significance of architecture and its use as an instrument of public policy, and when he arrived in New Delhi he considered that it should be built 'according to the great elemental qualities and traditions which have become classical, of the architecture of Greece and Rome', but they should 'graft thereon structural features of the architecture of India as well as decoration expressing the myths, symbols and history of its people.' And this is what his buildings essentially are – European in configuration, conception and form, but with Indian detailing applied as superficial ornament. There is no real assimilation of two cultures leading to the birth of a new Indo-British form of architecture which Lutyens achieved, yet ironically Baker's more conventional manner and patriotic fervour commended him to British officialdom. His connection with Rhodes in South Africa led to commissions for Government Houses in Mombasa and Pretoria, cathedrals at Capetown, Johannesburg, Pretoria and Salisbury and his appointment as architect to the Governments of South Africa and Kenya.

For all the absence of any real fusion of European and Indian forms, the Secretariats are wonderful pieces of civic design which have the same architectonic discipline as Lutyens's Viceroy's House – deeply recessed loggias, strictly controlled relationships of solid to void, the structural use of colour and the emphasis on mass, shadow, line and profile. As official buildings they embody the same hierarchical principles that pervade the whole city with space and ornament allocated on the basis of status and rank. The towers that flank the entrance from the Great Place were designed to be twice their present height to act as obelisks guarding the way to the inner Imperial sanctum, but they were reduced in scale and in the process lost some of their impact. The great domes which rise over each building are embellished with lotuses and elephants, and in axial view they frame Lutyens's great hemispherical dome beyond. On the north and south

Council House, by Herbert Baker: the circular plan was suggested by Lutyens.

elevations stand huge Moghul gateways centred on the horizontal axis between the domes, each inscribed with a resounding inscription. 'Liberty will not descend to a people: a people must raise themselves to liberty; it is a blessing which must be earned before it can be enjoyed.' Thus reads the condescending one on the North Secretariat. There were many in India who felt that the blessing was an inherent right which should not have to be earned from a paternalistic alien government. In the Government Court, lying between the Secretariat and before the Viceroy's House, stand the four Dominion columns donated by the governments of Canada, Australia, New Zealand and South Africa, each crowned by a bronze ship symbolising the maritime power which gave birth to the British Empire.

Baker's other great building is the Council House which was added to the plan of the city in 1919 to accommodate the fledgling Legislative Assembly. It was Lutyens who suggested the form which the new building should take – an enormous circular structure which broke the formal symmetry of the layout, but closed a rather unsatisfactory vista which ended unresolved on the north block of the Secretariat. Ominously its circular form came to be regarded as an architectural parody of the simple spinning wheel which was the symbol of Gandhiji and the nationalist movement. Originally it was to have a crowning dome, but this was dropped and, when an attic storey was added ten years later, a rather pathetic little cupola was provided which is visible only from afar. Internally the building is divided into a circular library block and three convex-shaped chambers for the Council of State, Chamber of the Princes and the Legislative Assembly, the latter adorned with the escutcheons and arms of the territories of the British Empire. Here Baker's love of heraldry and symbolism was used for political ends in an overt attempt to mould the emerging national consciousness into a form which could be accommodated within the aegis of the Empire, but the building owed its very existence to the gathering momentum of political change and the aspirations of the Indian people.

Lutyens's role in New Delhi was not just confined to the city plan and its spectacular centrepiece, the Viceroy's House, although this remains his *chef d'oeuvre*. He was responsible for two major palaces for the Indian princes of Hyderabad and Baroda and he supervised the erection of a number of others. Hyderabad and Baroda House both have a similar plan based on a butterfly-shape, but adapted in a highly original manner. Hyderabad House is capped by a large plain dome rising over a concave entrance portal which forms part of a continuous arcaded loggia round the ground storey. The first-floor bays are punctuated by obelisks and urns and the whole building is articulated by the subtle variation in the depth of the principal secondary and tertiary cornices. Baroda House has many similar attributes – concave entrance and crowning dome over a circular salon – but Lutyens's genius for three-dimensional design overcame the difficulties inherent in the plan which in less gifted hands might have generated awkward internal spaces.

Along the great processional axis of King's Way Lutyens was

233

Hyderabad House, New Delhi by Edwin Lutyens.

responsible for two major Imperial monuments which accentuated the formal symmetry of the street and provided a focus for state occasions. These were the All-India War Memorial Arch and the King George V Memorial. The Arch was not completed until 1931, but it was imbued with the same simple, elegiac grandeur as Lutyens's great war memorials in Flanders. It commemorates the 60,000 Indian losses in the First World War and the 13,516 British and Indian officers and men whose bones lay scattered across the mountains and defiles of the North-West Frontier. It is a colossal structure almost 140 feet high with sculptured panels of stonework relief and a dentilled cornice dividing the huge central arch from the massive masonry of the attic above, which is inscribed with the single word – INDIA. Crowning the attic is a shallow dome which quietly echoes that on the Viceroy's House almost one and a half miles distant, and from the eye at the top of the dome rises a column of sacred smoke. Five years later in the centre of a *rond-point* to the east of the Arch the King George V Memorial was raised, an elegant Indo-British *baldacchino* of cream and pink stone set in a rectangular pool adorned with symbols of kingship and rich in allegorical sculpture. Examples of architecture and public sculpture used for political ends, the Arch and the Memorial were intended to be emotive unifying symbols; one a testimony to the blood ties which linked Britain and India in perpetual fraternity, the other investing the concept of Imperial dominion with the mystical qualities of kingship. Today the radiating rays of the Imperial suns carved beneath the cornice of the Arch demonstrate that the stones which commemorate power are a more durable medium than power itself. Indeed from under Lutyens's great Moghul-Renaissance canopy the statue of George V has been removed, and it frames only thin air.

> Cities and Thrones and Powers
> Stand in Time's eye,

234

> Almost as long as flowers,
> Which daily die . . .

Lutyens was active in two other areas in the city: on the Viceregal estate itself, where he designed a complex of staff quarters, and at the intersection of King's Way and its main cross axis, Queen's Way, where a large complex of civic buildings was planned, but only a fragment was completed – a building now occupied by the National Archives of India. On the Viceregal estate the staff quarters and bodyguard lines reflect in miniature the complex interlocking geometrical relationships of the city as a whole and the preoccupation of colonial society with hierarchy, status and rank. All the buildings are faced in snow-white stucco relieved only by channelling, rustication and deeply recessed window openings. Some are delightfully inventive exercises in Baroque and Palladian design. The Band House makes several allusions to English buildings including Chiswick House and the Horse Guards, with a central clock tower and cupola rising from a platform adorned with four corner obelisks, whilst some of the smaller ranges of buildings are grouped together as single architectural compositions.

However, the greatest number of buildings in New Delhi were designed neither by Lutyens nor Baker but by a largely unknown Englishman, Robert Tor Russell (1888–1972), who succeeded John Begg as Consulting Architect to the Government of India in 1919. Russell

All-India War Memorial Arch completed in 1931. Beneath the cornice are radiating Imperial suns, emotive symbols of everlasting life.

came from a family of architects. He was educated at Bedford Modern School before joining his father at their Hitchin practice in 1906. In 1914 he joined Begg as his assistant in India and after distinguished war service, he assumed control for the design of all official housing, shopping centres, hospitals, bungalows, police stations and post offices in New Delhi. It was Russell who designed Connaught Place, a vast circular space around which were disposed the most important shops, restaurants, cafés and hotels in the new city. The circus comprises a series of two-storey stuccoed ranges with arcaded loggias at both levels. It is a determined exercise in classical civic design which provides a major centre of commercial activity mid-way between the old city and the formal avenues and boulevards of New Delhi. Architecturally it is impressive and creates a very distinct sense of place and purpose. Its muted classical detailing and cool arcaded loggias make a pleasant and relaxing environment in which to stroll and shop, the European antithesis to the native bazaar of Chandni Chauk in Old Delhi, where pandemonium reigns. Elsewhere in New Delhi elegant white stucco police stations and post offices arose and in Queen's Way Russell designed two parallel ranges of three-storey buildings – Eastern Court and Western Court – hostels for members of the newly-convened Legislative Assembly. Arcaded verandahs of a Tuscan order articulate the compositions which stand on massive raised basements. Russell's best work is Flagstaff House which was designed for the Commander-in-Chief, and which was occupied later by Prime Minister Nehru.

At Flagstaff House Russell's work comes closest to the style of Lutyens. It was finished in 1930, a long two-storey range executed in stucco with stone banding which accentuates its horizontality. The ground storey is faced in channelled stucco relieved by semi-circular headed openings, but on the south garden front the upper storey has a large recessed balcony. The entire house is sited on one of the main axial vistas from Viceroy's House, demonstrating the interdependent relationship between political and military power in India.

The careful disposition of buildings within the city and their relationship to the supreme symbol of authority, the Viceroy's House, applied equally to ecclesiastical buildings. God too knew his place. Lutyens had prepared sketches for a great new Anglican cathedral in the city, but the funds needed to realise such an ambitious scheme were never forthcoming, and in 1923 a competition was held to find an alternative design. Lutyens chose an entry submitted by Henry Medd (1892–1977), one of the numerous young aspiring acolytes who revered his work. Until recently Medd was forgotten, but pioneering research by the architectural historian Gavin Stamp, has placed Medd in his rightful place at the forefront of that imaginative and inventive school who carried the ideals and beliefs of Lutyens onto a further level of refinement. Medd's early design for the Cathedral was for a site south of King's Way, but in 1926 a more prominent one was found on the lateral axis of the Jaipur Column. This was due to the personal intervention of the new Viceroy, Lord Irwin, an ardent Anglo-Catholic of such high moral integrity that even the saintly Gandhi was impressed. Irwin's personal enthusiasm for the Cathedral attracted large subscriptions

Connaught Place, designed by Robert Tor Russell. The commercial hub of the new city.

Flagstaff House, New Delhi: residence of the Commander-in-Chief and later of Jawaharlal Nehru. Designed by Robert Tor Russell and completed in 1930.

from Britain and in 1928 Medd's building began to rise on the skyline of the new city. Its design is strikingly similar to Lutyens's Free Church at Hampstead Garden Suburb with its projecting vestries, large crowning dome and Baroque detailing, but interestingly, whilst Medd acknowledged the reference to Palladio's *Il Redentore* in Venice, he maintained that he made no conscious attempt to reflect the Free Church. However, Medd's Cathedral Church of the Redemption is a finer building than its Hampstead progenitor, a powerful fragmented mass exuding spiritual strength in a heathen land. It is cleverly conceived in a Baroque manner with a dome over the central tower and a cool, shaded interior perfectly adapted to the unrelenting climate. The mass of the building rises in stages to the crowning dome and cupola. Window openings are kept to a minimum in the large expanses of external masonry, but internally

Cathedral Church of the Redemption, New Delhi by Henry Medd. Infused with the spirit of Palladio and Lutyens.

the building is light and voluminous assisted by the small square openings around the base of the dome, which is clad in split red sandstone like the cascading roofs beneath. The east end is apsidal with a mahogany reredos and there are the ubiquitous tropical cane pews, but the overriding impression is one of cool repose and dignity created by the barrel-vaulted ceilings and intersecting lateral arches.

Medd's other great work in New Delhi is the Roman Catholic Church of the Sacred Heart, completed in 1934, in which the interior is manipulated in a similar manner to the Church of the Redemption with a system of proportion, based on Lutyens's famous Thiepval Arch, whereby arches are piled one against the other, each springing from the level of the keystone of another. Externally the main south front was conceived with a single open tower, but the Church authorities insisted

Catholic Church of the Sacred Heart, New Delhi by Henry Medd completed in 1934.

St Martin's Garrison Church 1928–1930 by Arthur Shoosmith, a gaunt, sculptured cenotaph of brickwork, timeless, immutable and forbidding.

upon twin towers, and then proceeded to acquire an oval mosaic cartouche of St Francis, which they demanded be incorporated into the scheme. The result was that the façade lost much of its original simplicity of line and understated classical dignity which characterises the best work of the Lutyens school in India. Instead it acquired an over-ornate Italianate character which seems very fussy under the harsh glare of the Indian sun, and in sharp contrast to the huge expanses of unbroken brickwork on the flanks.

In Lutyens's designs for the Viceroy's House and elsewhere in New Delhi the size, number and position of window openings is carefully controlled in relation to the whole, and in Medd's two great churches

240

this discipline was refined much further, so that the only breaks in the vast expanses of surface walling are small rectangular openings punched through the brickwork.

Three miles from Raisina Hill lies the Garrison Church of St Martin designed by Arthur Shoosmith (1888–1974), between 1928 and 1930. Shoosmith had worked on the Viceroy's House for Lutyens and later designed the elegant Lady Hardinge Serai, but St Martin's represents the ultimate expression of that form of 20th-century Anglo-Indian architecture promulgated by Lutyens and developed by his disciples. 'I have no hesitation in saying [this] is one of the great buildings of the 20th century,' wrote Gavin Stamp, and it is without question an extraordinarily original composition – a massive gaunt monolith of $3\frac{1}{2}$ million bricks looming straight out of the arid Indian plain. The walls are battered and rise in a series of setbacks; a huge sculptured cenotaph of brickwork pierced by small deeply shaded openings cut straight through the mass. If the exterior is timeless, immutable and forbidding, the interior is surprisingly light given the minute window areas, but it is entirely devoid of any human comfort. Many have contemplated its strange form and most acknowledge its symbolic importance. To Robert Grant Irving: 'The stripped classicism of the church interior seemed to underscore the severity of cantonment barracks and the rigors of military life as well as to embody the Imperial code of ascetic duty and that stern doctrine of Curzonian efficiency which discarded non-essentials.' To Robert Byron simply, 'It is superb.' St Martin's is a great lumbering dinosaur of a building – 'Lego in Indis' – yet like all great works of architecture it embodies and reflects the spirit of the age, and the effect it induces is not so much one of grandeur as one of melancholy – a forgotten example of a style of architecture cut off in its prime by the shifting sands of history. Its atmosphere is forbidding, even frightening, for it is redolent of the great war memorials of Flanders. At the same time it anticipated the holocaust yet to come, and the great Pyrrhic victory of 1945 which spelt the end of British Imperial power in India.

CHAPTER 10

ARCHITECTURAL REFLECTIONS

The architectural dialogue between Britain and India was not entirely one-sided. In order to complete the picture it is important to acknowledge the few instances where Indian styles were able to impress themselves on buildings in Britain, and also to assess the future prospects for conservation in India.

For thirty or forty years after the Battle of Plassey in 1757 the prospect of rich pickings in Bengal lured many eastward in search of wealth. For most it was a one-way journey which ended in South Park Street Cemetery or one of the many other burial grounds of Bengal and the Carnatic, but a few made vast individual fortunes and returned to England in search of the status and respect to which their new-found wealth entitled them. These were the Nabobs.

To the aristocratic élite who ruled England, the Nabobs were a bunch of uncouth, ruthless opportunists from the trading classes who had acquired wealth which in some instances exceeded their own, not by birth, blood or sheer hard work, but by speculation and double-dealing. Contrary to popular opinion, this capital did not finance the Industrial Revolution. Very little was reinvested in trade, commerce or manufacturing enterprises. Most went into land or government stock, which provided security and social standing.

There were few allusions to the origins of their wealth in the houses built by the Nabobs. When Clive returned to England in 1767 he devoted the last years of his life to the improvement of his newly-acquired estates, and when William Chambers built a great new house for him at Styche, it was an urbane English Palladian mansion that arose, the only allusions to India being in some of the paintings and furnishings. Few Nabobs had any desire to advertise their dubious past by indulging in architectural references to India, and few English architects were even aware of India's astonishing cultural heritage, let alone capable of expressing it.

In the last quarter of the 18th century this changed with the publication in England of the paintings and engravings of William Hodges and of Thomas and William Daniell. It was these which provided the inspiration for the handful of Indian-style buildings which were designed at this time and they constitute a limited, but unique chapter in the history of English taste. Between 1785 and 1788 Hodges's *Select Views of India* was published based on his travels in the sub-continent between 1781 and 1783. It had an immediate impact on certain circles of society and suggested new models of composition and form. The architect George Dance was an acquaintance and neighbour of Hodges, and when, in 1788, Dance was asked to design a new south front for the Guildhall in the City of London, he produced one with a strong Indian flavour, although few recognised it as such. Elsewhere Dance used Indian motifs and details such as scroll mouldings, but always within the discipline of a European composition. Warren Hastings's house at Daylesford by S. P. Cockerell was exceptional in reflecting its owner's Indian career. The garden was laid out in a similar manner to his house at Alipur, and Cockerell, also a friend of Hodges, designed an Eastern salon in the basement, which was adorned with Hodges's paintings. Two carved marble chimneypieces by Thomas Banks were installed in the first-floor drawing rooms, depicting Indian themes. Over the exterior rose a shallow dome crowned by an Indian finial.

Between 1795 and 1808 a whole series of wonderful aquatints by Thomas and William Daniell were published in *Oriental Scenery* based on their six years of travel in India. They provided a fresh source of inspiration for those interested in esoterica. On the basis of these illustrations Indian themes and details became popular and were mixed with other exotic styles from the Levant and Far East in idiosyncratic hybrid designs. Some tea merchants and dealers boasted elaborate Indian-style shopfronts. However, at Sezincote House in Gloucestershire there is the only Indian country house ever built in Europe. It owes its origins to the fortuitous combination of a wealthy Indian Nabob, Charles Cockerell, his brother the architect S. P. Cockerell, and their acquaintance with Thomas Daniell, whom Charles had met in India. The house is faced in a rich orange masonry, not dissimilar to the burnt umber colour of painted Indian stucco, and it is dominated by a single onion dome with four chimneys at its base. The central block has a large bracketed *chujja* to the parapet which is adorned with four corner *chattris*. To the west an orangery sweeps in an elegant curve to terminate in an hexagonal aviary capped by a domelet and finials. It is not merely the profile and general impact which is Indian, the detail is too, with cusped arches, radiating curved glazing bars and carved ornament. The garden is adorned with a Hindu temple, and two pairs of Brahmin bulls stand on the bridge which Daniell designed.

A creative imitation of Indian styles occurred virtually simultaneously at Brighton, and with little reference to Sezincote. Here the architect William Porden designed the great domed Royal Stables and Riding House which were completed in 1808, modelled on the Daniells' engraving of the Jumma Masjid (Great Mosque) in Delhi. In the Prince Regent's search for an exotic style for his sea-side Xanadu he consulted the most eminent designers of the day including Humphry Repton, James Wyatt and Henry Holland, but it was John Nash who finally recast the existing group of buildings into a wild extravaganza of Indian Regency Gothick, which dominated local architecture for seventy or eighty years. As late as 1880 Sir Albert Sassoon, the Jewish magnate, built himself a circular mausoleum in Brighton with scalloped arches and an ogival roof. Even the elegant West Pier reflected the prevailing Oriental ethos of the resort.

Splendid though Sezincote and the Royal Pavilion are, they were never more than eccentric aberrations. The fashionable vogue for

243

exotic Orientalism faded. Changing perceptions of India and the Empire and cultural superiority coloured European views towards the East. The fearful events of the Great Mutiny in 1857 merely confirmed Western suspicions of Indian culture. Thus when the Durbar Court of the new India Office was erected in London in 1867 to the designs of Matthew Digby Wyatt the building was thoroughly classical in conception, based on Italian Renaissance sources with *Della Robbia* majolica friezes. There was no suggestion of infusing Indian motifs or forms into the structure. Twenty-eight busts of British worthies from Admiral Watson to General Havelock commemorated the triumph of British arms in India together with four sculptured panels of high relief depicting scenes from Indian history.

In the later 19th century Victoria created the Durbar Room at Osborne House as a focus for her interest in Indian affairs. John Lockwood Kipling designed some of the *basso rilievo* plasterwork. At Elvedon Hall, Suffolk the exiled Maharajah Duleep Singh created an elaborate Indian interior for his own use between 1863 and 1870 to designs by the Goth, John Norton, but these odd exceptions remained the fanciful expressions of personal caprice and never suggested a wider cultural exchange with India. As late as 1914 Sir Herbert Baker's India House in Aldwych was designed in a thoroughly European manner superficially ornamented with Indian devices and allusions, but it never embodied the gorgeous exoticism of the Indian Empire. Language and social custom rather than architecture remained the areas of greatest cultural exchange.

Far more typical of England's connection with India are the commercial buildings and warehouses which once lined the river frontage and East India and London Docks. Today the great majority of these robust but elegant buildings are demolished or derelict. Few bonded tea warehouses remain, but here and there traces of the Indian connection survive. Free Trade Wharf – the riverside warehouse of the East India Company, was built in 1795 to the designs of Richard Jupp, Surveyor to the Company. It lingers on empty and derelict, the entrance still crowned by the Company arms. From here goods were brought up for later distribution throughout the country to the great complex of warehouses at Cutler Street on the edge of the City of London. Until 1980 Cutler Street remained one of the finest groups of early 19th-century warehouses in England, but their partial redevelopment and conversion destroyed much of their gaunt Piranesian grandeur. Not far from Free Trade Wharf stands the little church of St Matthias, Poplar, with its roof supported by the teak masts of old East Indiamen. Here crews and passengers put themselves in the hands of God before departing on the hazardous voyage east. Today the churchyard lies overgrown, and the tombs of old sea-captains are worn smooth with age and neglect. The church too is ruinous, though there are hopes it may be saved.

Contrary to Kipling's 'Recessional', much of Britain's architectural pomp is not at 'one with Nineveh and Tyre' for the Indian authorities have acknowledged the importance of their national legacy of British buildings. Some of the most prominent have statutory protection, including St Mary's, Madras, the Ochterlony Monument, and the Victoria Memorial in Calcutta. It would be impertinent to criticise the Indian government for not having done enough to conserve the best examples of Anglo-Indian architecture, when the British have taken relatively little interest in their own connection. The very limited resources devoted to architectural conservation in India need to be allocated to the care of many ancient monuments infinitely older and more fragile, from the Buddhist, Moghul and Hindu past. If 7th-century temples are crumbling then 19th-century churches cannot be regarded as a particularly high priority. However it would be Britain's loss as well as India's if any of the buildings mentioned in this book were to disappear.

Neglect is always the worst enemy. All buildings decay, and time, money and expertise are required to secure their long-term conservation. India is fortunate as it has a large reservoir of expertise in the conservation of ancient monuments which is the envy of most countries. This is based on generations of effort. As early as the late 18th century Company officers carefully noted and recorded Indian monuments in sketchbooks and drawings. In 1808 the Governor General, the Earl of Minto, set up a Taj committee, and government funds were set aside for repairs to monuments at Agra and Fatehpur Sikri, but a coherent policy towards ancient monuments and archaeological remains only came with the foundation of the Archaeological Survey of India in 1861. Unlike England, it was the Government which led the way. Conservation was delegated to the provincial Governments with advice from a centrally-appointed Curator of Ancient Monuments, although the post was abolished later in 1883. It was Lord Curzon who provided the present statutory framework for architectural conservation in India. In 1900 he noted 'I cannot conceive of any obligation more strictly appertaining to a Supreme Government than the Conservation of the most beautiful and perfect collection of monuments in the world.' As a result the Archaeological Survey was reorganised under Sir John Marshall, and in 1904 the Ancient Monuments Preservation Act was introduced, providing statutory protection for India's heritage for the first time.

Under Marshall the highest principles of architectural conservation were formulated and set out in the 'Conservation Manual', a document of profound significance, which became the working philosophy of the Survey. It set standards which are rarely attained even now in England. It exhorts conservation officers to:

Never forget that the reparation of any remnant of ancient architecture, however humble, is a work to be entered upon with totally different feelings from a new work or from repairs to a modern building. Although there are many ancient buildings whose state of disrepair suggests at first sight a renewal, it should never be forgotten that their historical value is gone when their authenticity is destroyed, and that our first duty is not to renew them but to preserve them.

245

Since Independence these principles have been developed and incorporated into the Ancient Monuments and Archaeological Sites and Remains Act 1958 and the Antiquities Act 1972. India has adopted a mature and sensitive policy to the architectural heritage of its Imperial past, regarding it as the most recent element of its richly diverse history, and one which gave birth to four of its greatest cities – Bombay, Madras, Calcutta and New Delhi, together with countless other settlements and buildings across the sub-continent. A start has been made on protecting individual buildings, but integrated policies designed to safeguard complete areas have yet to come. In the great cities whole neighbourhoods and streets retain their original period character. In Bombay the entire core of the Victorian city should be designated as a Conservation Area from Apollo Bunder through Horniman Circle, Mahatma Gandhi Road and the Esplanade and on to Victoria Terminus, including the triangle of buildings in Carnac Road, Cruickshank Road and Hornby Road. Conservation should not be regarded as a constraint against change, but rather as a discipline for change which must take place within a tighter physical and historical framework. The concept should be extended to other Indian 'heritage cities' such as Jaipur, Fatehpur Sikri, Benares and Allahabad.

Unthinking modernisation and redevelopment are threats to much of what remains. In Madras the Victoria Memorial Hall and the elegant Indo-Saracenic Moore Market by R. E. Ellis are at risk from proposals for railway expansion: the story of the Euston Arch all over again. Once we exhorted India to follow our example, and now perhaps it is not too late to warn against the chimera of rampant commercial development. Experience shows that the dreams of planners are often the nightmares of the people. Elsewhere in Madras Henry Irwin's South India Co-operative Insurance Building has been demolished, and many other commercial buildings have been lost to random redevelopment proposals. The scale and insensitivity of recent building and the adoption of aggressive international styles devoid of local character does not augur well for the future. At Fort St George and in the Pantheon complex, Madras, new multi-storey buildings have been erected which are entirely out of keeping with the character of their surroundings, and more are threatened. The Fort Museum, including the Old Exchange Hall, where factors and traders once met and dined, is threatened by proposals for an expanding secretariat. Elsewhere Wellesley House, where the future Duke of Wellington stayed when stationed in Madras, is in a state of partial collapse, and there have been no moves to restore it. The event went unreported in British newspapers, and not a single British voice has been raised to save it. How insular we have become. More promisingly Bentincks Building, which houses the Collectorate, and which has been threatened with demolition since 1974, has been saved through the personal intervention of the Prime Minister, Indira Gandhi, after a local newspaper campaign to preserve it.

In the grounds of the former Residency at Hyderabad Kirkpatrick's little model house lies smashed by a fallen branch, and few care. In Calcutta the tomb of its founder Job Charnock is affected by proposals to sell part of St John's Churchyard for redevelopment, and an unholy row continues in the columns of the Indian press about the obtrusive nature of the multi-storey block proposed for the site. Opponents of the scheme have brought in the West Bengal Government, and the Archaeological Survey of India have expressed deep reservations. Fortunately, in the absence of a sophisticated planning inquiry system the resolution of such disputes takes many years and the site remains intact. Nearby, Garstin's Town Hall remains threatened with demolition. It still stands, although no one seems clear what its future will be. Its demolition would be a major loss for the city's heritage of Georgian buildings. Equally destructive are new proposals to construct a bridge link between Granville's Gothic High Court and its nearby modern annexe.

In New Delhi international demand for multi-storey offices is beginning to have an adverse impact on the spacious character of the city. Originally built for a population of 60,000 the population reached 6 million in 1971. Land values have soared and the poorer classes have been pushed out from the centre. Indeed it is surprising that it still appears so unaffected, given such acute social and economic pressures. Here too there has been a civic response to the problem. In 1979 the People's Party called for a ban on all high-rise development and in 1980 there was a major public exhibition devoted to the history and architecture of the city, calling for stricter control over new development and statutory protection for the entire area between Connaught Place and the Safdarjang Tomb, including the Central Vista. In the garden city of Bangalore similar pressures and high-rise proposals threaten the symmetrical axis at the centre.

There is evidence of a growing awareness of the dangers. In Bombay the Save Bombay Committee has waged a successful battle against the State Government to stop further land reclamation in the Back Bay area. It has had considerable success in mobilising public opinion against unco-ordinated expansion of the city and in favour of the preservation of historic buildings. In conjunction with the Bombay Local History Society it has done much to stimulate interest in the early history of the city. The long and invaluable task of identifying and listing buildings for preservation has commenced. Elsewhere there are healthy signs of a grass-roots reaction to the sometimes reckless and haphazard development of historic areas. An Indian Heritage Society has been formed. Encouragingly there is growing interest in Britain. South Park Street Cemetery in Calcutta has been saved, and the British Association for Cemeteries in South Asia is now active throughout India recording and collating information on some of the oldest surviving European graves. Recently under the aegis of the British Council, the English specialist in architectural conservation, Donald Insall, assisted the Indian authorities in formulating ideas and policies for the future, whilst Angus Stirling, the Director of the National Trust, has advised on the creation of a National Trust for India, a device which would offer hope for a large number of outstanding, but neglected, historic buildings and ancient monuments. Other exchanges are in the offing, but until there is greater integration between the work of the Archaeological Survey

247

Senate House, Calcutta University by Walter Granville. Demolished in 1961.

and day-to-day planning control the prospect of planning policy paying due regard to historic buildings remains in doubt.

A coherent national strategy is needed with supreme control vested at a national, rather than local level. Existing conservation machinery needs to be overhauled with a national body responsible for the preparation of criteria for the listing of buildings and for the actual survey work. This body should also have the power to designate Conservation Areas where provincial or state authorities prove reluctant or recalcitrant. Protection needs to be extended to the setting of buildings and monuments, and aggressive commercial advertising must be curbed. The whole management of ancient monuments and sites for tourism remains in its infant stages, but if properly looked after and developed India's architectural heritage could prove one of its most valuable assets.

The purpose of this book is to draw attention to one relatively recent aspect of this heritage and to plead for its long-term conservation. It is a shared heritage, the physical expression of the special relationship that exists between the two countries. More than most nations, the people of India acknowledge that the past and present are part of a single continuum. In simple recognition of the patterns which bind the two countries, part of the proceeds of this book will go towards repairing the little model in the garden of the former Residency at Hyderabad. It is as much a symbol of love as the great Taj itself, the love of one nation for another, and with love comes understanding.

*Begum's garden in the former
residency, Hyderabad. The endearing
model house built by Major James
Achilles Kirkpatrick for his wife:
a unique heritage in ruins.*

GLOSSARY

abacus the flat slab on top of the capital of a column

acroteria ornaments placed at apex or ends of a pediment

aedicule framing of an opening with two columns carrying a gable, lintel or entablature

annular arch a vaulted roof over a space between two concentric walls

arcuated a building depending on structural use of the arch

atrium an inner court open to the sky

baksheesh alms

baldacchino a canopy over a throne, statue or altar

bania trader or money-lender

bargeboard projecting board on edge of gable, often decorated or carved

bartizan a small turret projecting from the top of a tower or parapet

batter the sloping face of a wall

begum Indian Muslim princess

belvedere summerhouse or small room on the roof of a house

boss ornamental knob covering intersecting ribs in a vault or ceiling

budgeroe river-boat

campanile Italian name for a bell-tower

cantonment a large planned estate or military station

caryatid a sculptured female figure used as a column

chattri an umbrella-shaped dome or pavilion

chujja a thin projection of stone resembling a cornice

chunam a form of stucco made from burnt seashells which can be polished to resemble marble

clerestory upper stage of main walls of a building pierced by windows

coffer ceiling decoration comprising sunken square or polygonal panels

cortile a courtyard usually internal and arcaded

crocket a decorative feature projecting from angles of a spire

cutcha built with sun-dried bricks, unreliable

decastyle with ten columns

dentil a small square block used as part of a cornice

divan smoking room

dodecastyle with twelve columns

durbar public audience of governor, prince or viceroy

embrasure splayed opening in wall or fortification

engrailed arch arch with serrated or indented edge

entablature the upper part of an order incorporating architrave, frieze and cornice

festoon carved ornament resembling a garland of fruit and flowers

finial a crowning ornament on a gable, spire or pinnacle

flèche a slender spire

foliated carved with leaf ornament

ghat landing place on riverside with steps

godown warehouse

gola conical-shaped storehouse

groin-vault formed by intersection of two tunnelvaults at right angles

hexastyle with six columns

hood mould a projecting moulding over arch or opening

howdah seat on elephant's back, sometimes canopied

hummum a Turkish bath

in antis a recessed portico

interlacing arches arches which overlap each other

jaali a pierced ornamental screen to a window opening

jalousies slatted shutters or blinds

jampan a rickshaw

jezail long-barrelled Afghan musket

jhilmil projecting canopies over window or door openings

khind pass

lakh (lac) a hundred thousand rupees

lunette fortification with two faces and two flanks

machicolation a projecting parapet carried on brackets

maidan large open space in town

metope the square space between triglyphs in a Doric order

modillion a small bracket or scrolled console

mofussil the country or hinterland, as distinct from the town

moucharabya carved elaborate latticework

musnud seat or throne of cushions used by an Indian prince

mutule a projecting square block above the triglyph in a Doric order

nabob wealthy person from India

octastyle with eight columns

palanquin covered litter for one carried by four or six men

palmette a fan-shaped ornament resembling a palm leaf

patera a small, flat circular or oval ornament

patte-d'oie radiating vistas resembling in plan the imprint of a bird's foot

pendentive a concave spandrel leading from the angle of two walls to the base of a circular dome

polychromy structural use of colour in building

porte-cochère a porch for vehicles to pass through

pukka solidly-built, reliable

punkah large suspended cloth fan worked by cord

purdah seclusion of women from public view

pylon a rectangular vertical structure terminating a composition

quatrefoil four leaf-shaped curves formed by the cusping of a circle

reredos a screen behind an altar

rond-point a circular space with radiating streets or vistas

rustication masonry or stucco cut in incised blocks

sgraffito plaster decoration of incised patterns revealing different coloured coat beneath

stela upright inscribed slab or pillar used as gravestone

stupa a domed or beehive-shaped Buddhist monument

stylobate a platform on which a colonnade stands

tatties cane or grass screen for shade

tetrastyle with four columns

tiffin lunch or light meal

trabeated a building constructed on post and lintel principles

triglyphs grooved blocks on a Doric frieze

tulwar a razor-sharp Indian sabre

tykhana an underground room in a house in Upper India for use in hot weather

tympanum the area enclosed by a pediment

Venetian arch a large central arched opening flanked by tall narrow square-headed openings

volute the spiral scroll on an Ionic capital

voussoir a brick or wedge-shaped stone in an arch

zenana secluded women's quarters

BIOGRAPHICAL DETAILS OF PRINCIPAL ARCHITECTS AND ENGINEERS

These selective biographical notes on some of the more important architects and military engineers were taken from individual service records, obituaries and sundry other sources. Dates and ultimate ranks are given where known, together with principal confirmed attributions.

Agg, Lieutenant James (c1758–1828) Designed St John's Calcutta 1784–1787. Born Cheltenham. Arrived in India November 1777. Assistant to Colonel Henry Watson, Chief Engineer. Retired with handsome fortune 1799. Declined post of Lieutenant-Governor of St Helena. Died in England.

Anbury, Major-General Sir Thomas (1760–1840) Designed Government House, Barrackpore and some lesser buildings in station. Superintendent of Buildings, Barrackpore 1815–1816. Superintendent Engineer, PWD N.W. Frontier 1829–1831. Chief Engineer 1830. CB, October 1818; Kt, August 1827; KCB, July 1838. Died at Saugor.

Baker, Sir Herbert (1862–1946) Designed Secretariats and Council House, New Delhi and worked with Lutyens on the new capital. Also worked in South Africa, Kenya, Belgium, Rhodesia. KCIE, RA, Hon DCL, Oxford and Johannesburg. FRIBA Gold Medallist. Outstanding Imperial architect.

Bayne, Roskell R. (fl.1875–1895) Designed East Indian Railway Office, Calcutta; Hoseinabad Clock Tower, Lucknow; Thornhill and Mayne Memorial and Mayo Hall, Allahabad. Widely regarded when architect under Chief Engineer, Calcutta, Sir Bradford Leslie.

Begg, John (1866–1937) Designed Lady Hardinge Medical College, New Delhi; General Post Office, Operating Theatres, Dock Custom House, Bombay; Council House Street Secretariat, Stationery Office, Medical College block, Calcutta; Benares Law Courts; Nagpur and Agra Post Offices; churches in Simla, Jubbulpore and Quetta; military buildings in Rangoon, Delhi and elsewhere. Born Bo'ness, Scotland, son of ironmaster. Educated Edinburgh and Royal Academy Schools. RIBA silver medal 1894. Articled to H. Blanc. Served with Waterhouse and Edis. 1898–1901 South Africa. Consulting Architect to Government of Bombay 1901–1908. Consulting Architect to Government of India 1908–1921. Private practice Edinburgh 1921–1937, FRIBA, FRIAS.

Blane, Captain George Rodney (1791–1821) Designed Temple of Fame, Barrackpore. Born London, third son of Sir Gilbert Blane, physician-in-ordinary to George III. Educated at Charterhouse. Arrived India 1808. Superintendent of Public Works, Diamond Harbour and Mayapore 1811; Surveyor at Saugor 1818. Nepal War 1814–1815. Superintendent of Buildings, Ludhiana 1819. Died Ludhiana.

Boileau, Major-General John Theophilus (1805–1886) Designed St George's, Agra; Christ Church, Simla; Observatory House, Simla and others. Born Calcutta. Educated Bury St Edmunds Grammar School. Arrived India 1822. Retired 1857. In charge of Observatory, Simla 1840–1857. Chief Engineer NWP, 1848–1857. Commandant Engineer 1855. Died at 31 Ladbroke Square, London. *Brother*: Alexander Henry Edmonstone Boileau (1807–1862), Superintendent Engineer NWP, 1854.

Brohier, Captain John Designed Fort William, Calcutta. Transferred from Madras to Bengal, 1757. Chief Engineer, Calcutta. Arrested for fraud, 1760. Absconded from parole, 29th July 1760 and fled to Ceylon.

Caldwell, General Sir James Lillyman (1770–1863) Designed St George's Cathedral (1816) and St Andrew's Kirk, Madras (1821) in conjunction with Thomas Fiott de Havilland. Senior Engineer, Mauritius 1810. Special Surveyor of Fortresses 1813. Acting Chief Engineer, Madras 1816. CB, 1815; KCB, 1837; GCB, 1848. Died Isle of Wight.

Chisholm, Robert Fellowes (1840–1915) Designed University buildings, Madras; Lawrence Asylum, Nilgiri Library, Ootacamund; Laxmi Vilas Palace, New College, Museum and Pavilion, Baroda. Consulting Architect to Government of Madras. Retired from India 1900. Resumed practice at John Street, Adelphi 1902. Designed Church of Christ Scientist, Wilbraham Place, Sloane Street, London SW1; also designs for Indian Museum, Belvedere Road, Southwark. Died Southsea.

Conybeare, Henry (fl.1847–1873) Designed Afghan Memorial Church of St John the Evangelist, Colaba, Bombay 1847. Son of Dean of Llandaff. Town Engineer of Bombay. Dismissed in August 1850. Church completed by Captain Tremenheere.

Cowper, Lieutenant-Colonel Thomas Alexander (1781–1825) Designed Town Hall, Bombay. Captain 1812. Lieutenant-Colonel 1824. Died Bombay.

Crookshank, Major-General Sir Sidney D'Aguilar (1870–1941) Planned and constructed King George's Medical College and Hospital, Canning College and Technical High School, School of Design, Arabic College, Post Office, Balrampur Hospital, two bridges over Gumti, Lucknow. Constructed Government House, Naini Tal, Imperial Bacteriological Institute at Maktesar. Executive Engineer, Lucknow 1908–1910. Chief Engineer Delhi, 1910–1912. Later on Imperial Delhi Committee. KCMG, CB, CIE, DSO, MVO. Consulting Engineer to Government of India, 1923.

De Havilland, Colonel Thomas Fiott (1775–1866) Designed St George's Cathedral and St Andrew's Kirk, Madras in conjunction with James Caldwell. Also ballroom extension to Government House, Mysore, and De Havilland Arch, Seringapatam. Elder son of Sir Peter de Havilland, Bailiff of Guernsey. Educated Queen Elizabeth College, Guernsey. Served Pondicherry 1793, Ceylon 1795–1796, Mysore 1799, Egypt 1801. Engineer to Nizam's Subsidiary Force, 1805. Surveyed Deccan, 1806. Superintendent of Tanks, Madras 1819. Prominent part in mutiny at Seringapatam, 1809; tried by Court Martial and reinstated. Died in Guernsey.

Emerson, Sir William (1843–1924) Designed Girgaum Church 1872–1873; Crawford Markets and fountain, Bombay 1865–1871; Cathedral of All Saints, Allahabad 1869–1893, Muir College, Allahabad 1872–1878; Takhtsingi Hospital 1879–1893 and palace 1894–1895, Bhavanagar; Victoria Memorial Hall, Calcutta 1905–1921. Trained with Habershon and Pite. Pupil of William Burges; PRIBA 1899–1902. Kt. 1902.

Esch, Vincent Jerome (1876–1950) Designed High Court, Osmania General Hospital, City High School and Railway Station, Hyderabad: Temple Chambers, Royal Calcutta Turf Club race stand and dining hall, Calcutta. CVO for work as superintending architect on Victoria Memorial Hall, Calcutta. Architect to Bengal Nagpur Railway Co.

Forbes, Major-General William Nairn (1796–1855) Designed The Mint, St Paul's Cathedral, Calcutta. Born Auchterless, Aberdeen. Educated Addiscombe College 1812–1813. Cadet 1815. Captain 1827. Colonel 1851. Major-General 1854. Wounded Bhurtpore. Mint Master and Superintendent of Government Machinery 1836–1855. Died on board *Oriental* off Aden. Buried St Paul's Cathedral, Calcutta.

Fuller, General James Augustus (1828–1902) Designed Law Courts, Sassoon Mechanics Institute, Bombay. Supervised erection of Public Works Office, Secretariat, Telegraph Office, Post Office, University Library and Clock Tower, Convocation Hall and Sailors Home, Bombay.

Eldest son of Robert Fuller of Lingfield Lodge, East Grinstead. Educated by tutors and at Addiscombe College 1845–1846. Arrived in India 1848. Severely wounded Punjab 1848–1849. Captain 1858. Colonel 1871. Lieutenant-Colonel 1882. CIE 1882. Retired 1883.

Garstin, Major-General John (1756–1820) Designed Town Hall, Calcutta; The Gola, Patna; bridge, Benares. Born Manchester Square, London. Cadet 1778. Captain 1781. Surveyor-General of Bengal. *Son*: Edward (1794–1871) became General, Field Engineers.

Goldingham, John (c1765/6–1849) Designed Government House and estate and Banqueting Hall, Madras. Company's astronomer, Madras Observatory 1796–1830.

Granville, Walter L. B. (1819–1874) Designed Memorial Church, Cawnpore; High Court, General Post Office, University Complex and Indian Museum, Calcutta. Architect to East Bengal Railway 1858–1863. Consulting Architect to Government of India 1863–1868.

Gregson, T. S. (fl.1890–1914) Designed Royal Exchange, Calcutta. Partner in Stevens & Co, Bombay.

Hawkins, Major John (1783–1831) Designed The Mint, Bombay. Born Kingsbridge, Devon.

Irwin, Henry (1841–1922) Designed Law Courts, Madras (with J. W. Brassington and J. H. Stephens); Victoria Public Hall, Victoria Memorial Hall and Technical Institute, Madras; Viceregal Lodge, Ripon Hospital, Simla; Amba Vilas Palace, Mysore. Influential and resourceful architect well-versed in a variety of styles.

Jacob, Colonel Sir Samuel Swinton (1841–1917) Designed Victoria Memorial Hall, Peshawar; St Stephen's College, Delhi; State Bank of Madras; Gorton Castle, Simla; Lallgarh Palace, Bikaner; and extensive works in Jaipur, Lucknow and Lahore. Born January 14th 1841. Educated Cheam & Addiscombe. Indian Staff Corps 1862. Served in PWD Rajputana; Aden 1865–1866. Chief Engineer, Jaipur 1867–1911.

CIE, 1890; KCIE, 1902; MRIBA; AICE. Scholarly exponent of Indian styles.

Kittoe, Major Markham (1808–1853) Designed Queen's College, Benares. Born Woolwich, Kent. Arrived India, October 1825. Died Coddenham, Suffolk, April 1853. Court-martialled December 1837. Reinstated January 1839.

Lanchester, Henry Vaughan (1863–1953) Designed Council Chamber, Post and Telegraph Offices, Lucknow; Umaid Bhawan Palace, Jodhpur 1922–1944. Exponent of monumental civic classicism. Temporary consultant to New Delhi Town Planning Committee.

Lishman, Frank (1869–1938) Designed High Court, Allahabad (1916). Consulting architect to United Provinces, 1912–1924. Worked for T. E. Collcutt and G. F. Bodley. Born Herrington, Co. Durham. Educated Uppingham School.

Lutyens, Sir Edwin (1869–1944) Designed Viceroy's House and estate, All India War Memorial Arch, King George V Memorial, Record Office, Hyderabad House and Baroda House and basic plan and layout of New Delhi. ARA, 1913; Kt, 1918; RA, 1920; KCIE, 1930; DCL Oxford, 1934; FSA, OM, 1942. Outstanding architect of his generation. Inspiration behind the concept, plan and form of New Delhi. Prolific designer of major public, commercial and domestic buildings in England, Europe and the Empire.

Lyon, Thomas Designed Writer's Buildings, Calcutta 1780. Sailed for Calcutta in March 1763 as one of three carpenters to supervise native workforce at Fort William.

Mant, Major Charles (1840–1881) Designed High School, Surat; Town Hall, Kolhapur; Court House and High School, Bhavanagar 1873–1874; churches at Balasore and Chapra 1876; Hospital and Library, Baroda 1876; Medical School, Patna 1877; Kolhapur Hospital 1878; palaces for Gaekwar of Baroda 1881 and Raja of Kolhapur 1881; also palaces at Darbhanga and Cooch Behar. Educated Cheltenham College 1853–1855 and Addiscombe 1856–1857. Lieutenant 1858. Major

1874. Superintendent of Antiquarian Remains 1877. FRIBA, 1881. Died insane 1881. Pioneer of Indian styles.

Martin, Major-General Claude (1735–1800) Designed Constantia and Farhad Bakhsh, Lucknow. Born Lyons, second son of Fleury Martin, cooper. Educated in Lyons. Arrived India 1752. Captured 1761. Joined EIC 1763. Surveyed Bihar and Bengal 1764–1766. Retired 1779 to Lucknow. 1789 Indigo farming. 1792 Mysore Campaign. Died Constantia, Lucknow. Eccentric dilettante.

Medd, Henry Alexander Nesbitt (1892–1977) Designed Cathedral Church of the Redemption and Church of the Sacred Heart, New Delhi; High Court, Nagpur; New Mint, Calcutta. Born 1892. Articled to F. C. Eden. Baker's representative in New Delhi, 1919.

Munnings, Joseph Fearis Designed new capital at Patna. Consulting Architect, Bihar and Orissa 1913–1918. Principal works include Secretariat, Government House and Council Chamber at Patna. Partner in Power, Adam and Munnings, Sydney, Australia.

Parker, J. P. Designed Ochterlony Monument, Calcutta 1828; column at Constantia, Lucknow; La Martinière Girls' School, Calcutta 1835 with Captain Hutchinson and R. H. Rattray.

Prinsep, James (1799–1840) Designed The Mint and Nandeswar Kothi, Benares. Scholar, architect and antiquary. Assay Master. Prinsep's Ghat, Calcutta named after him. Secretary, Asiatic Society, FRS.

Ransome, James (1865–1944) Designed government offices, Calcutta; Agricultural College, Pusa; High Court, Rangoon; Government Houses, Chittagong and Dacca; Secretariats, Simla and Nagpur; military buildings Dehra Dun; churches in Umballa, Lucknow; clock tower, Ludhiana; Simla bandstand. Consulting architect to Government of India, 1902–1908.

Ricardo, Halsey (1854–1928) Designed Howrah Station, Calcutta. Influential English architect in Arts and Crafts tradition.

Robison, C. K. (fl.1835–1850) Designed Metcalfe Hall, Calcutta; served on Building Committee of St Paul's Cathedral, Calcutta. Magistrate of Calcutta. Influential Calcutta figure and antiquary.

Russell, Robert Tor (1888–1972) Designed Connaught Place, bungalows, police stations, hospitals, post offices, Eastern and Western Courts, Queen's Way and Commander-in-Chief's House, New Delhi. Chief Architect to Government of India. Together with staff he designed public and domestic buildings throughout New Delhi. Capable and industrious architect.

Russell, Lieutenant Samuel (fl.1790–1810) Designed The Residency, Hyderabad. Son of Royal Academician, John Russell.

Sankey, Lieutenant-General Sir Richard Hieram (1829–1908) Designed All Saints, Nagpur (subsequently altered by G. F. Bodley); Public Offices and other civic buildings, Bangalore. Educated Addiscombe College. Madras Engineers 1846. Indian Mutiny 1857–1858. Afghanistan 1878–1879. Chief Engineer to PWD, Madras 1883.

Scott, Sir George Gilbert (1811–1878) Designed University Library, Convocation Hall and Rajabai Tower, Bombay; Lady Canning Memorial, Barrackpore; Memorial at St Thomas's Cathedral, Bombay. Leading exponent of Gothic Revival in England, providing prototypes for many Indian Gothic buildings. Kt, 1872. FRIBA, 1873.

Scott, John Oldrid (1841–1913) Designed Anglican Cathedral, Lahore. Educated Bradfield College. Succeeded to Scott practice, 1878. FSA, FRIBA. Specialised in ecclesiastical works.

Shoosmith, Arthur Gordon (1888–1974) Designed St Martin's Garrison Church and Lady Hardinge Serai, New Delhi. Born St Petersburg. Educated Russia, Finland, Haileybury, and Royal Academy Schools. Pupil of Goodhart–Rendel & Burnet. Lutyens's representative at New Delhi, 1920–1931.

Stevens, Frederick William (1848–1900) Designed Royal Alfred Sailors Home, Victoria Terminus, Churchgate Terminus, Municipal Buildings, Oriental Buildings, Chartered Bank Offices, Bombay; Government House, Naini Tal; Court House at Mehsana; Standard Life Offices, Calcutta; waterworks at Cawnpore, Agra and Benares; church at Igatpuri. Educated King Edward VI Grammar School, Bath. Articled to Charles Davis. Superintendent of Works to Bath Corporation 1862–1867. Assistant Engineer, Bombay PWD under Fuller. 1876, Government Examiner to Bombay School of Art. 1878, Architectural Executive Engineer for Victoria Terminus. CIE 1889. Principal in practice, Messrs Stevens & Co, *Son*: Charles Frederick Stevens (born 1872). Joined practice from Bristol University 1892, and designed City Improvement Trust Office, Bombay and Edward Memorial Hall, Indore 1906.

Trubshawe, James (fl.1860–1875) Designed Strategic plan for Bombay; plans for Bombay Cathedral; Post Office (with W. Paris), Elphinstone College, Byculla, Bombay; Government House, Poona. Member of Staffordshire family of builders/architects/engineers. Architect to Ramparts Removal Committee, Bombay.

Waddington, Major-General Charles (1796–1858) Completed Town Hall, Bombay on death of Colonel Thomas Cowper. Born St Andrew, Wardrobe, London. CB 1843, Major-General 1843. Died Cox's Hotel, Jermyn Street.

Watson, Lieutenant-Colonel Henry (1737–1786) Designed Defences of Fort William, docks at Kidderpore. Born Holbeach, Lincs. Son of grazier. Ensign 1755, Woolwich RMA 1759, Mauritius 1761, Havana 1762, Field Engineer 1764, Chief Engineer, Bengal 1765. Died Dover.

White, William (1838–1896) Designed Small Cause Court and Presidency College, Calcutta. Served PWD, Calcutta for 13 months. Later examiner at Royal Indian Engineering College, Coopers Hill and Secretary to RIBA.

Wilkins, General Sir Henry St Clair (1828–1896) Designed Secretariat, Public Works Office, Bombay; Deccan College, Sassoon Buildings, Garden Reach, Poona; Waterworks at Aden; palace at Bhuj; restoration of ancient buildings at Bijapur. Son of Ven. George Wilkins of Beelsby, Lincolnshire, Archdeacon of Nottingham. Educated privately and Addiscombe College 1845–1847. Captain 1860; Chief Engineer, Abyssinia 1869. ADC to Queen, mentioned in despatches. Lieutenant-General 1878. Died 77 Queens Gate, Kensington.

Wilks, Colonel (fl.1790–1831) Designed Government House, Mysore. Resident of Mysore 1803–1808.

Winscom, Colonel George Vivian (1826–1868) Designed Mutiny Memorial Hall, Madras.

Wittet, George (1880–1926) Designed Gateway of India, Prince of Wales Museum, College of Science, Custom House, Small Causes Court, Bombay; Agricultural College and Central Government Offices, Poona; Gujarat College, Ahmedabad; Small Causes Court, Karachi. Born Perth, Scotland. Associated in Edinburgh with Sir G. Washington Browne. Assistant to John Begg, 1904. Consulting Architect to Government of Bombay. 1908–1926.

Wyatt, Captain Charles (1758–1819) Designed Government House, Calcutta and uncompleted shell of projected Government House, Barrackpore. Born in Stafford. Nephew of James Wyatt, architect. Arrived India 1782. Captain and Commissioner of Police 1800. Superintendent of Public Works 1803. Retired 1806. MP for Sudbury 1812–1816. Died Kentish Town, London.

Yule, Sir Henry (1820–1889) Designed Mutiny Memorial Screen at Cawnpore.

SOURCES

Prologue

p. 11 Rudyard Kipling: 'The Pro-Consuls'
p. 12 Court of Directors of the East India Company to Calcutta, 9th March 1763
p. 14 Jan Morris: *Stones of Empire*, p. 29
p. 14 James Fergusson: *History of the Modern Styles of Architecture*, p. 412
p. 15 *The Builder*, 27th September 1912: 'Imperialism and Architecture', p. 346
p. 15 Jan Morris: *Stones of Empire*, p. 32
p. 16 Gavin Stamp, *Journal of the Royal Society of Arts*, May 1981: 'British Architecture in India, 1857–1947', p. 372
p. 16 Robert Byron: *Country Life*, June 1931

Chapter 1

p. 18 John Fryer: *A New Account of East India & Persia*. Quoted in Foster, W: *The English Factories in India*
p. 20 Alexander Hamilton: *A New Account of the East Indies*

Chapter 2

p. 23 Charles Lockyer: *An Account of the Trade in India*
p. 23 *Letters from Madras during the years 1836–1839*, by a Lady
p. 30 William Hodges: *Travels in India during the years 1780, 1781, 1782 and 1783*
p. 31 Quoted in G W Forrest: *The Cities of India—Madras*
p. 40 MS Letters of Lady Gwillim from Madras, 29th January 1802
p. 46 Rudyard Kipling: 'Song of the Cities – Madras'

Chapter 3

p. 47 Price: Quoted in *Newman's Handbook to Calcutta*
p. 48 Alexander Hamilton: *A New Account of the East Indies*

p. 51 Kindersley J: *Letters from the Island of Tenerife, Brazil, the Cape of Good Hope and the East Indies*
pp. 52 & 55 Bishop R Heber: *Narrative of a Journey From Calcutta to the Upper Provinces of India*
p. 60 Maria Graham: *Journals of a Residence in India*; 1st November 1810
p. 61 Quoted in Sir H E A Cotton: *Old & New Calcutta*
p. 63 Bishop R Heber: *Narrative of a Journey from Calcutta to the Upper Provinces of India*
p. 67 Viscount Valentia: *Voyages and Travels to India, Ceylon . . . in the year 1802, 1803, 1804, 1805 and 1806*
p. 68 Emma Roberts: *Scenes and Characteristics of Hindostan*
p. 69 James Fergusson: *History of the Modern Styles of Architecture*
p. 69 Maria Graham: *Journals of a Residence in India*
p. 76 Rudyard Kipling: 'Song of the Cities – Calcutta'

Chapter 4

p. 80 Lady Charlotte Canning, quoted by Lord Curzon in *British Government in India*
p. 82 Emily & Fanny Eden: *Letters from India*
p. 84 Grantland Rice: 'Alumnus Football'
p. 88 *Murray's Handbook for Bengal*; 1882
p. 90 Thomas Twining: *Travels in India a Hundred Years Ago*
p. 91 Viscount Valentia: *Voyages and Travels to India, Ceylon . . . in the years 1802, 1803, 1804, 1805 and 1806*
p. 96 *Some Notes on the Hyderabad Residency collected from original records in the Residency Office*
p. 97 Mountstuart Elphinstone: *Diary*, September 1801

p. 97 Quoted in *Some Notes on the Hyderabad Residency* . . .
p. 98 Thomas Carlyle: *Reminiscences*

Chapter 5
p. 103 'Aliph Cheem', Quoted in H A Newell: *Two Famous Madras Memorials*
p. 104 Henry Roberdeau, 1801, Quoted in Sten Nilsson: *European Architecture in India*
p. 104 Bishop R Heber: *Narrative of a Journey from Calcutta to the Upper Provinces of India*
p. 111 Rudyard Kipling: 'Possibilities'
p. 114 Quoted in E J Buck: *Simla Past & Present*
p. 114 *ibid*
p. 115 Emily & Fanny Eden: *Letters from India*
p. 115 Quoted in E J Buck: *Simla Past & Present*
p. 116 Rudyard Kipling: 'A Tale of Two Cities'
p. 117 Oscar Wilde: 'Ave Imperatrix'
p. 120 Rudyard Kipling: *Kim*
p. 128 Lady Betty Balfour, Quoted in Sir Frederick Price: *Ootacamund: A History*
p. 128 Sir Richard Burton: *Goa and the Blue Mountains*
p. 128 Rudyard Kipling: 'The Return (All Arms)'

Chapter 6
p. 135 Sir John Kaye: *History of the Sepoy War*
p. 135 Amy Horne: *Account of the Twenty-One Days in Sir Hugh Wheeler's Garrison*
p. 136 Sir Henry Havelock: *Memoirs*
p. 137 Surgeon-General Munro: *Reminiscences of Military Service*
p. 142 Lord Alfred Tennyson: 'The Siege of Lucknow'
p. 142 Quoted in E H Hutton: *Guide to Lucknow*
p. 143 Lady Clive Bayley: *The Golden Calm*

Chapter 7
p. 147 Samuel Pechel: *Historical Account of Bombay*
p. 148 Bishop R Heber: *Narrative of a Journey from Calcutta to the Upper Provinces of India*
p. 148 *Asiatic Journal*: May to August 1838
p. 153 T Roger Smith in *The Builder*: 1868, p. 350
p. 155 Quoted in S M Edwardes: *The Rise of Bombay*
p. 171 *The Bombay Builder*: Volume 3, July 1867–June 1868
p. 171 *The Builder*: 1880
p. 172 *The Builder*: 1869, p. 857

p. 172 John Begg: 'Architecture in India', *Journal of the Royal Institute of British Architects* 1920
p. 176 Robert Byron: *Architectural Review* January 1931
p. 176 Aldous Huxley: Quoted in S T Sheppard: *Bombay*
p. 182 *The Times of India*: 29th February 1948

Chapter 8
p. 183 Mark Bence-Jones: *Palaces of the Raj*
p. 185 James Fergusson: *A History of the Modern Styles of Architecture*
pp. 186–187 Quoted in J M Crook: *William Burges & The High Victorian Dream*
p. 191 Rudyard Kipling: 'Arithmetic on the Frontier'
p. 192 Jan Morris: *Stones of Empire*, p. 118
p. 194 E B Havell: *Indian Architecture*
pp. 196 and 197 Lord Napier in *The Builder*: 1870, p. 682, p. 1047
p. 200 Quoted in *Hyderabad: A Guide to Art & Architecture*
p. 200 Rudyard Kipling: 'A Legend of the Foreign Office'
p. 202 F Gaekwad, Maharajah of Baroda: *The Palaces of India*
p. 207 John Begg: 'Architecture in India', *Journal of the Royal Institute of British Architects* May 1920
pp. 211 and 212 Lord Curzon: *British Government in India*

Chapter 9
p. 215 *The Builder*: 27th September 1912. 'Imperialism & Architecture'
p. 216 Rudyard Kipling: 'Arithmetic on the Frontier'
p. 217 James Ransome: *Government of India Building Designs*
p. 219 F O Oertel: 'Indian Architecture: Its Suitability for Modern Requirements', *Journal of the East India Association* 1913
p. 224 Lord Hardinge: *My Indian Years*
p. 226 S D Adshead: *Architect and Builder's Journal* 11th December 1912
p. 226 E B Havell: *Indian Architecture*
p. 226 Sir Herbert Baker: *The Times* 3rd October 1912

p. 227 Robert Byron: 'New Delhi I', *Country Life* 6th June 1931

p. 227 Quoted in Robert Grant Irving: *Indian Summer: Lutyens, Baker & New Delhi*

p. 229 Robert Byron: 'New Delhi III', *Country Life* 6th June 1931

p. 231 Mary Lutyens: *Edwin Lutyens*

p. 232 Sir Herbert Baker: Quoted by Robert Byron in *Country Life* 6th June 1931

pp. 234 and 235 Rudyard Kipling: 'Cities and Thrones and Powers'

p. 240 Gavin Stamp: *Journal of the Royal Society of Arts*, May 1981

p. 240 Robert Grant Irving: *Indian Summer: Lutyens, Baker & New Delhi*

Chapter 10

p. 244 Lord Curzon: Quoted in 'Monument Conservation and Policy in India' by F R Allchin, *Journal of Royal Society of Arts*, November 1978

p. 244 Sir John Marshall: *Conservation Manual*

SELECT BIBLIOGRAPHY

The principal journals and articles consulted:

The Architect
Architectural Review
Bengal Past and Present
Blackwoods Magazine
Bombay Builder
Bombay Civic Journal
The Builder
Building News
Country Life
Illustrated London News
Indian Art and Letters
Indian Engineering
Journal of the East India Association
Journal of the Royal Institute of British Architects
The Times
The Times of India
Transactions of the Royal Institute of British Architects

PRINTED AND MS WORKS

Adam, R. & J., *The Works in Architecture of Robert and James Adam*, London, 1778–1822
Allen, Charles, *Plain Tales from the Raj*, London, 1975; *Raj: A Scrapbook of British India 1877–1947*, London, 1977
Anon, *Old and New Bombay: A Historical and Descriptive Account of Bombay and its Environs*, Bombay, 1911
Anon, *Calcutta Illustrated*, Calcutta, 1901
Anon, *Tablets in the Memorial Church, Cawnpore 1857*, Calcutta, n.d.
Anon, *Hyderabad – A Guide to Art and Architecture*, Hyderabad, n.d.
Anon, *Some Notes on the Hyderabad Residency, Collected from Original Records in the Residency Office*, London, 1881
Anon, *Madras City and Civic Guide*, Madras, n.d.
Anon, *Fifty Views of Madras*, Bombay, 1908
Anon, *Plans of the New Viceregal Lodge at Simla*, Calcutta, 1890
Archer, M., *British Drawings in the India Office Library*, London, 1969
——, *Company Drawings in the India Office Library*, London, 1972
——, *India and British Portraiture*, London, 1979
——, 'A Georgian Palace in India: Government House, Calcutta', *Country Life*, 9th April 1959
——, 'Company Architects and Their Influences in India', *RIBA Journal*, August 1963
——, 'Georgian Splendour in Southern India', *Country Life*, 26th March 1964
——, 'Aspects of Classicism in India: Georgian Buildings of Calcutta', *Country Life*, 3rd November 1966
——, 'Benares and the British', *History Today*, June 1969
——, 'Madras's Debt to a Father and Son', *Country Life*, 17th December 1970
Archer, M. & W. C., *Indian Painting for the British 1770–1880*, Oxford, 1955
Baillie, W., *Twelve Views of Calcutta*, London, 1794
Ballhatchet, Kenneth, *Race, Sex and Class Under the Raj*, London, 1980
Barlow, Glyn, *The Story of Madras*, London, 1921
Barr, P., & Desmond, R., *Simla: A Hill Station in British India*, London, 1978
Bence-Jones, Mark, *Palaces of the Raj*, London, 1973; 'Building Dreams of a Viceroy', *Country Life*, 1st and 8th October 1970
Birdwood, George, *Report on the Government Central Museum*, Bombay, 1864
Buck, E., *Simla, Past and Present*, Calcutta, 1904
Burton, Sir Richard, *Goa and the Blue Mountains*,

London, 1851

Busteed, H. E., *Echoes of Old Calcutta*, London, 1908

Butler, A. S. G., & others, *The Architecture of Sir Edwin Lutyens*, London, 1950

Byron, Robert, 'New Delhi', *Architectural Review*, January, 1931

Callahan, Raymond A., 'Servants of the Raj: the Jacob family in India 1817–1926', *Society for Army Historical Research Journal*, Vol 56, 1978

Cameron, R., *Shadows of India*, London, 1958

Carey, William, *A Guide to Simla*, Calcutta, 1870

Chambers, W., *A Treatise on Civil Architecture*, London, 1759

Churchill, W. S., *My Early Life*, London, 1930

Claridge, G., *Old and New Bombay*, Bombay, 1911

Clarke, Basil, *Anglican Cathedrals Outside the British Isles*, London, 1958

Cole, David, *The Work of Sir Gilbert Scott*, London, 1980

Collins, L. & Lapierre, D., *Freedom at Midnight*, London, 1975

Colvin, H., *Biographical Dictionary of British Architects, 1600–1840*, London, 1978

Conner, Patrick, *Oriental Architecture in the West*, London, 1979

Cotton, Sir H. E. A., *Calcutta Old and New*, Calcutta, 1907

Cox, H. E., *The Story of St Thomas Cathedral*, Bombay, 1947

Crook, J. M., *The Greek Revival*, London, 1972; *William Burges and The High Victorian Dream*, London, 1981

Curl, J. S., *A Celebration of Death*, London, 1980

Curzon, G. N., *British Government in India*, London, 1925

Daniell, T., *Views of Calcutta*, Calcutta, 1786–1788

Daniell, T. & W., *Oriental Scenery, Twenty-Four Views in Hindoostan*, London, 1797; *A Picturesque Voyage to India*, London, 1810

Danvers, F. C., *An Account of the Origin of the East India Company's Civil Service and Their College in Hertfordshire*, London, 1894

Darley, Gillian, 'Ooty', *Country Life*, 12th January 1978; 'Sanctuary of the Memsahibs: Ootacamund', *Country Life*, 6th April 1978

Davies, P. H., *Civil Disorder and Military Rebellion in Jhansi, Jalaun and Hamirpur Districts 1857–1860*, Unpublished B.A. thesis, Cambridge, 1972

De Havilland, T. F., *Public Edifices of Madras*, Madras, 1827

Doyle, K., *Bombay: A Historical Review and Travel Guide*, Bombay, 1952

D'Oyly, C. & Williamson, J., *The European in India*, London, 1813

D'Oyly, C., *Tom Raw the Griffin*, London, 1828

Eden, Hon. Emily & Hon. Fanny, *Letters from India*, London, 1872

Edwardes, M., *Asia in the European Age, 1498–1955*, London, 1961; *History of India*, London, 1961; *Battles of the Indian Mutiny*, London, 1963; *A Season in Hell: The Defence of the Lucknow Residency*, 1973

Edwardes, S. M., *The Rise of Bombay*, Bombay, 1902

Fay, E., *Original Letters from India 1779–1815*, London, 1819

Fergusson, J., *History of the Modern Styles of Architecture*, London, 1862

Fido, Martin, *Rudyard Kipling*, London, 1974

Fieldhouse, D. K., *The Theory of Capitalist Imperialism*, London, 1967

Firminger, W. K., *Thacker's Guide to Calcutta*, Calcutta, 1906

Forbes, J., *Oriental Memoirs*, London, 1813

Forrest, G. W., *Job Charnock*, London, 1902; *Cities of India*, London, 1903

Foster, W., *The Founding of Fort St George, Madras*, London, 1902; *The English Factories in India 1618–23*, London, 1931

Fraser, J. B., *Views of Calcutta and Its Environs*, London, 1824–28; *Military Memoirs of Colonel James Skinner*, London, 1851

Gaekwad, Fatesinghrao, Maharajah of Baroda, *The Palaces of India*, London, 1980

Garrett, H. L. O., & Hamid Abdul, *History of Government College, Lahore*, Lahore, 1914

Gibbs, J., *A Book of Architecture*, London, 1728

Gopal, Ram, *How The British Occupied Bengal*, London, 1906

Gopalratnam, V. C., *A Century Completed; History of Madras High Court*, Madras, 1962

Graham, M., *Journals of a Residence in India*, Edinburgh, 1812; *Letters on India*, London, 1814

Grant, Colesworthy, *Lithographic Sketches of the*

Public Characters of Calcutta, Calcutta, 1850

Grindlay, R. M., *Scenery, Costumes and Architecture*, London, 1826–30

Growse, F. S., *Indian Architecture of Today, as exemplified by New Buildings in the Bulandshahar District*, London, 1886

Gwillim, Lady Elizabeth, Manuscript Letters, April 1801–January 1809, Symonds Collection, India Office Library

Hamilton, A., *A New Account of the East Indies*, Edinburgh, 1727

Hardinge, Charles, 1st Baron of Penshurst, *My Indian Years 1910–1916*, London, 1948

Harris, John, *The Indian Mutiny*, London, 1973

Havell, E. B., *Indian Architecture*, London, 1913

Hay, S., *Historic Lucknow*, Lucknow, 1939

Heber, Bishop R., *Narrative of a Journey from Calcutta to the Upper Provinces of India; from Calcutta to Bombay 1824–25*, London, 1828

Herbert, Gilbert, *Pioneers of Prefabrication: The British Contribution to the 19th Century*, Baltimore, 1978

Hersey, George L., *High Victorian Gothic*, Baltimore, 1972

Hibbert, Christopher, *The Great Mutiny*, London, 1978

Hickey, W., *Memoirs of William Hickey*, London, 1925

Higginbotham's, *Guide to the City of Madras*, Madras, 1875

Hill, S. C., *The Life of Claud Martin*, Calcutta, 1901

Hilton, E. H., *Guide to Lucknow*, Lucknow, 1902

Hitchcock, Henry Russell, *Architecture: Nineteenth and Twentieth Centuries*, Harmondsworth, 1971

Hodges, W., *Travels in India during the Years 1780, 1781, 1782 and 1783*, London, 1793

Hodson, V. C. P., *List of the Officers of the Bengal Army, 1758–1834*, London, 1927–47

Hughes, Q., *Military Architecture*, London, 1974

Hussey, Christopher, *Life of Sir Edwin Lutyens*, London, 1950

Irving, Robert Grant, *Indian Summer; Lutyens, Baker and Imperial Delhi*, Yale, 1981

Jha, J. A., *A History of the Muir Central College 1872–1922*, Allahabad, 1938

Kay, M. M., (ed.) *The Golden Calm: An English Lady's Life in Moghul Delhi*, London, 1980

Kaye, John, & Malleson, Col. H., *The Indian Mutiny*, London, 1888

Keay, J., *When Men and Mountains Meet*, London, 1977

Keene, H. G., *A Handbook for Visitors to Allahabad, Cawnpore and Lucknow*, London, 1875

Kindersley, J., *Letters from the Island of Teneriffe, Brazil, The Cape of Good Hope and The East Indies*, London, 1777

King, Anthony, *Colonial Urban Development: Culture, Social Power and Environment*, London, 1976

Kipling, R., *The City of Dreadful Night*, Allahabad, 1890; *The Five Nations*, London, 1903; *Departmental Ditties*, London, 1886; *Selected Poems*, London, 1941

Knox, Collie, *Forever England*, London, 1943

Langley, B., *The City and Country Builder's and Workman's Treasury of Design*, London, 1745

Latif, S. M., *Lahore: Its History, Architectural Remains and Antiquities*, Lahore, 1892

Leighton, D., *Vicissitudes of Fort St George*, Madras, 1902

Lindsay, C. T., *Job Charnock*, London, 1960

Llewellyn, Alexander, *The Siege of Delhi*, London, 1977

Long, J., *Calcutta and Its Neighbourhood*, Calcutta, 1874

Lord, John, *The Maharajahs*, London, 1972

Love, H. D., *A Short Historical Notice of the Madras Club*, Madras, 1902; *Descriptive List of Pictures in Government House and the Banqueting Hall, Madras*, Madras, 1903; *Vestiges of Old Madras*, London, 1913

Lutyens, Mary, *Edwin Lutyens*, London, 1980

Maitland, Mrs J. C., (anon.) *Letters from Madras, by a Lady*, London, 1843

Malden, C. H., *Handbook to St Mary's Church*, Madras, 1905

Mansergh, Nicholas, (ed) *The Transfer of Power 1942–47*, London, 1970–1983

Marshall, Sir John, *Conservation Manual*, Calcutta, 1923

Martyn, M., 'Georgian Architecture in Calcutta', *Country Life*, 3rd December 1948

Moorhouse, Geoffrey, *Calcutta*, London, 1971; *India Britannica*, London, 1983

Morris, J., *Pax Britannica: The Climax of an Empire*, London, 1968; *Heaven's Command*, London, 1973; *Farewell the Trumpets*,

London, 1978; *Stones of Empire*, Oxford, 1983

Morton, B. M., & Cotton, J. J., *A Short Account of the more important monuments in St George's Cathedral*, Madras, 1918

Mosley, Leonard, *Curzon*, London, 1960

Murray, John, *Handbook for Madras*, London, 1879; *Handbook for Bombay*, London, 1881; *Handbook for Bengal*, London, 1882; *Handbook for Punjab*, London, 1883; *Handbook for India*, London, 1880:1887; *The Imperial Guide to India*, London, 1904

Muthiah, S., *Madras Discovered*, Madras, 1981

Newell, H. A., *Two Famous Madras Memorials*, Madras, 1919; *Guides to Bombay, Calcutta, Lahore, Madras etc*, Calcutta, 1920

Newman, *Handbook to Calcutta*, Calcutta, 1905

Nightingale, P., *Trade and Empire in Western India*, Cambridge, 1970

Nilsson, Sten, *European Architecture in India 1750–1850*, London, 1968

Orlich, Leopold von, *Travels in India*, London, 1845

Ovington, Rev. T., *A Voyage to Surat in the Year 1689*, Oxford, 1929

Paine, J., *Plans, Elevations and Sections of Noblemen's and Gentlemen's Houses*, London, 1783

Panter-Downes, Mollie, *Ooty Preserved: A Victorian Hill Station in India*, London, 1967

Parasnis, D. B., *Mahabaleshwar*, Bombay, 1916

Pearson, R., 'A Calcutta Cemetery', *Architectural Review*, July 1957

Penny, F., *Fort St George, Madras*, London, 1900

Pott, Janet, *Old Bungalows in Bangalore*, London, 1977

Price, Sir J. F., *Ootacamund: A History*, Madras, 1908

Pugin, A. W., *True Principles of Christian Architecture*, London, 1841

Ransome, James, *Government of India Building Designs by James Ransome*, London, 1909

Rawlinson, H. G., *British Beginnings in Western India*, Oxford, 1920

Reid, D. M., *The Story of Fort St George*, Madras, 1945; *Report on St Paul's Cathedral, Calcutta 1847*, Calcutta, 1847

Roberts, Emma, *Scenes and Characteristics of Hindostan*, London, 1837

Robertson, E. G., & J., *Cast Iron Decoration: A World Survey*, London, 1977

Robinson, John M., *The Wyatts: An Architectural Dynasty*, Oxford, 1979

Rohatgi, Pauline, *The India Office Library's Calcutta Collection of Pictures*, Calcutta, 1977; *Portraits in the India Office Library*, London, 1983; 'Colonial Architecture in India: St John's Church', *Roopa-Lekha*, Vol 44

Rushbrook-Williams, L. F., (ed) *A Handbook for Travellers in India, Pakistan, Nepal, Bangladesh and Sri Lanka*, London, 1978

Sandes, E. W., *The Military Engineer in India*, Chatham, 1933–35

Satow, Michael, & Desmond, Ray, *Railways of the Raj*, London, 1980

Sen, S. N., *Eighteen Fifty-Seven*, New Delhi, 1957

Sheppard, Samuel T., *Bombay*, Bombay, 1932

Spear, P., *The Nabobs*, London, 1963; *Penguin History of India*, Vol. 2, Harmondsworth, 1970; *Master of Bengal*, London, 1975

Srinivasachari, C. S., *History of the City of Madras*, Madras, 1939

Staley, Elizabeth, *Monkey Tops: Old Buildings in Bangalore Cantonment*, London, 1981

Stamp, Gavin, 'Indian Summer', *Architectural Review*, June 1976; 'British Architecture In India 1857–1947', *Journal of the Royal Society of Arts*, May 1981; 'Urbs Prima in Indis', *Architectural Association Research Paper No 11*, June 1977

Stewart, Charles, *History of Bengal*, London, 1813

Stokes, Eric, *The English Utilitarians in India*, London, 1959

Stuart, J., & Revett, N., *The Antiquities of Athens*, London, 1762–87

Tarapor Mahrukh, 'Growse in Bulandshahr', *Architectural Review*, September 1982

Taylor Braid, Lady, 'The Ghost of Hastings House', *Country Life*, 3rd January 1947

Thapar, Romila, *Penguin History of India Vol. I*, Harmondsworth, 1970

Tindall, Gillian, *City of Gold: The Biography of Bombay*, London, 1982

Trevelyan, G. O., *Cawnpore*, London, 1865

Trevelyan, Humphrey, *The India We Left*, London, 1972

Twining, T., *Travels in India a Hundred Years Ago*, London, 1983

Valentia, Viscount, *Voyages and Travels to India, Ceylon . . . in the years 1802, 1803, 1804, 1805 and 1806*, London, 1809

Vibart, H. M., *The Military History of the Madras Engineers and Pioneers*, London, 1881–1883; *Addiscombe: Its Heroes and Men of Note*, London, 1894

Watkin, David, *Thomas Hope 1769–1831 and The Neo-Classical Idea*, London, 1968

Weeks, Stephen, *Decaying Splendours*, London, 1979

Whiffen, M., *Stuart and Georgian Churches*, London, 1948

Wilkins, H. St Clair, *Reconnoitring in Abyssinia*, London, 1870; *A Treatise on Mountain Roads, Live Loads and Bridges*, Bombay, 1879

Wilkinson, Theon, *Two Monsoons*, London, 1976

Williamson, T., *The East India Vade-Mecum*, London, 1810

Wilson, C. R., *Old Fort William in Bengal*, London, 1906

Woodford, Peggy, *Rise of the Raj*, London, 1978

Woodruff, Philip, *The Men Who Ruled India*, London, 1953, 1954

Yule, H., & Burnell A. C., *Hobson-Jobson, a glossary of Anglo-Indian colloquial words and phrases*, London, 1903

INDEX

Compiled by Jill Ford

Page numbers in *italics* refer to illustrations